UNORTHODOX
VIEWS

Recent Titles in
Contributions to the Study of World Literature

UNORTHODOX VIEWS

Reflections on Reality, Truth, and
Meaning in Current Social, Cultural,
and Critical Discourse

JAMES L. BATTERSBY

Contributions to the Study of World Literature,
Number 111

GREENWOOD PRESS
Westport, Connecticut • London

Library of Congress Cataloging-in-Publication Data

Battersby, James L.
    Unorthodox views : reflections on reality, truth, and meaning in current social, cultural,
and critical discourse / James L. Battersby.
        p.   cm.—(Contributions to the study of world literature, ISSN 0738–9345 ; no. 111)
    Includes bibliographical references and index.
    ISBN 0–313–32166–3 (alk. paper)
    1. Criticism—History—20th century.   2. Relativity.   3. Deconstruction.   I. Title.
    II. Series.
    PN94.B37   2002
    801'.95—dc21   2001050138

British Library Cataloguing in Publication Data is available.

Library of Congress Catalog Card Number: 2001050138
ISBN: 0–313–32166–3
ISSN: 0738–9345

First published in 2002

Greenwood Press, 88 Post Road West, Westport, CT 06881
An imprint of Greenwood Publishing Group, Inc.
www.greenwood.com

Printed in the United States of America

The paper used in this book complies with the
Permanent Paper Standard issued by the National
Information Standards Organization (Z39.48–1984).

10 9 8 7 6 5 4 3 2 1

for

LISA and JULIE

Contents

Preface

As the friends of litotes might say, there is not a little irony in the main title of this book. The unorthodox views it champions are heretical only from what I take to be the heretical perspective of the current orthodoxy. In the transvalued world we find ourselves in, the orthodox is heretical and the heretical, orthodox. Less cryptically, this book subjects to scrutiny the commonsense–violating beliefs and assumptions about meaning, language, thought, truth, and reality underlying and informing current intellectual discourse not only in literary studies, but also in the broader academic culture, especially in the humanities and social sciences (and, increasingly, in the popular media, as the arcane terms and categories in use on the exchange market of theory become common coin in the general marketplace of ideas). Briefly, inscribed on the rock upon which the orthodox faith is founded are these, among other, foundational precepts: words refer only to other words; there is no way to get beyond texts to some extratextual reality that is the source and guarantor of what's what; functional reality—that is, the world we live and function in—is the shape-shifting creature of the contingent forces of history, assuming various temporary forms in response to the dictates of changing power relations in the sociopolitical realm; objective truth and determinate meaning are chimeras, spectral evocations occasioned by the ambient linguistic and cultural climate; and authors, consequently, are themselves by-products (or effects) of language and culture, not independent agents determining the meaning and value of their verbal productions. In briefest digest, the church holds these truths to be self-evident: there is nothing outside of language; whatever can be said or known depends upon a conceptual scheme (and no conceptual scheme is given the ultimate seal of approval by the ways things are, by the facts of the matter), and all conceptual schemes are socially constructed, are contingently formed by history, by, that is, historical/political forces and ideological formations.

The topical and argumentative structure of my "heretical" enterprise in this book is presented in detailed outline in the introduction, but here I would point out that the first five chapters take up the foundational issues, arguing against or exposing the limitations of the most common forms of social constructionism and relativism and then defending vigorously alternatives to the prevailing orthodox dogmas, providing, for example, intellectually robust justifications of determinate meaning, objective truth, ontological realism, and a correspondence theory of truth, a theory consistent with conceptual relativity but, I hasten to add, not compatible with relativism. These initial chapters, which focus on bedrock theoretical issues, prepare the way for the subsequent discussions of more practical but no less controversial and contested matters, such as the determination of artistic effects by human agents (by, yes, authors), the possibility of correct interpretation of authorial meaning, the complex relations of fictional facts and factual fictions, the bases of our emotional and evaluative responses to representations of human life, the justifications supporting our decisions about intrinsic merit, and other matters crucial to our understanding of the meanings and values implicit in human expression.

The approach adopted in this study is deeply influenced by recent work in the philosophy of mind and the philosophy of language, and my large indebtedness to those many philosophers on whose broad shoulders I stand will, I certainly hope, be glaringly apparent to every reader of the text and notes. Two others to whom I am also hugely grateful make their only appearance in this Preface, but they are the inadvertent and unwitting progenitors or instigators of the book as a whole. George Kliger and David Kopf brought together a cluster of commonplaces enjoying currency in the world of poststructural/postmodern critical and theoretical discourse (commonplaces recognizable to anyone with even the slightest familiarity with what passes for "theory" today) and organized them into the list of "Current Orthodoxies" that I have regularly used as a launching pad or a starting point for discussion, as a base from which to enter the thickets of controversy. In a sense, this book is for me a piacular token, an expiatory gesture, offered in compensation for my inability to contribute to the lecture series on "The Humanities: Alternative Visions to Current Orthodoxies" that they planned.

In all the various stages of the writing of this work, I have been the (usually) grateful beneficiary—as well as the occasional pained recipient—of wise counsel, sound advice, friendly but tough criticism, and helpful (and, alas, dismayingly plentiful) suggestions on how to smooth the wrinkles in my prose and to tighten the fibers of my arguments. If I have not always

heeded the good advice or submitted gladly to the correction of my bene-
factors (and every reader will discern where I have not), I have always prof-
ited by it, and I shall continue to make it my study to deserve their care
and concern. Of those many students, friends, and colleagues whose conversation and comments did much to sharpen my thought, gladden my
heart, improve my style, and save me from at least some embarrassment, I
absolutely must mention, whether they like it or not, Ralph Rader, James
Phelan, and Lisa Kiser.

Finally, I must acknowledge my special gratitude to the two women on
whom my human flourishing depends and to whom this book is dedicated—
Lisa Kiser, friend, colleague, and wife, and Julie Hines, friend and daughter,
without either of whom chaos is come again. During the preparation of this
book I found the means to put the extent and quality of their interest in
me to the test. They passed; indeed, one could justly say they surpassed,
and I will hereafter not let a day, an hour pass in forgetfulness of their aid
and comfort or without some effort to make answerable returns.

Introduction: Heresy in an Orthodox World: The Affirmation of Truth, Reality, and Meaning

It is undoubtedly going too far to say that for these last twenty-five years or so literary studies (along with studies in many branches of the humanities and social sciences) have been living under the rule of a kakistocracy (that is, government by the worst citizens), but it is fair to say, I think, that some very weak or limited ideas about language, mind, thought, truth, and reality have exerted hegemonic and largely deleterious influence over the range of inquiry and the manner in which business is conducted in these studies. Of course, the fairness of my saying so would be immediately denied (what is more likely is that the comment would be derided, laughed out of court, or—most likely—ignored), since the prevailing view among the postmodern cognoscenti is that current theory has finally broken through the illusions and pseudo-problems that have bedeviled western thought, enabling us to gain access at last to how it really is with language, mind, reality, and so forth. In a nutshell, this is how it is: everything is linguistic or mediated through language; language is unstable and self-referential; mind, truth, thought, reality are the contingent, historical (political, ideological) products of era- or culture-specific conceptual schemes; authors are by-products of language and culture; meanings, consequently, are fixed (temporarily, for the nonce) by cultures or readers and, hence, are open-ended (necessarily so, given the nature of language-as-such and the paradigm-shifting propensities of different cultures and readers).

The foundational truths upon which the entire edifice of current theory is erected are grounded in the facts (or the nature) of language and history. Idealism, the view that reality is a construct of the mind (or of mentality), takes a linguistic turn, and mind itself, along with its products, comes to be seen as an effect of language. Language, in turn, is buffeted about by the contingent forces of history, with effective expression being governed by shifting power relations. Wherever literary critics fix their gaze—whether on race, gender, ethnicity, class, on patterns of colonial oppression, on mirror stages, on the circulation of social energies in particular eras, or whatever— they see through the glasses supplied by the foundation. To see differently is to see what is not the case, for what is certainly and absolutely true is that there can be no objective truth because there is no way that things are independent of our shifting, culturally determined representations of them. In a review of *Truth and Progress*, a collection of Richard Rorty's philo- sophical papers, Thomas Nagel provides a condensed account of Rorty's version of the bedrock articles of faith: It is unquestionably true "that all experience is shaped by language, that language is contingently formed by history, and that therefore everything we think should be accompanied by a large dose of historicist self-consciousness or irony." Consequently, "the idea that our beliefs, about mathematics or chemistry or psychology or mo- rality or anything else, could be in any strong sense objectively true or false should simply be abandoned."[1]

A further consequence of giving primacy to language and history, of course, is that the notion of the author as the principal agent of artistic production is abandoned. Authors, if not lost entirely, are reduced to "author-effects" or "author-functions" within systems of signification that are themselves functionally operative only within systems of power. To the faithful, the loss (or diminishment) of the author is more than compensated for in the freedom such loss opens up to explore the many linguistic and social conditions upon which the subsistence of literary works (now invari- ably called texts) really depends. In what amounts to a veritable Cook's tour of the history of critical theory from the late 1960s to the present day (in- stead of forty-eight countries in three days, we have nine or ten theoretical approaches in two pages), in which we are first shown how linguistics made the author the "consequence" rather than the "creator" of the text and how historical/ideological study revealed that the "literary text could only de- velop as it did within the context of specific historical ideas," Anthony Eas- thope traces a progress from Marxism to feminism, to psychoanalysis (Lacan style), to race, ethnicity, and colonial studies, to new historicism and cultural materialism, illuminating how each new approach in this progress narrative improved on its predecessor by supplying something missing from its "con- ceptualizations," thereby extending the foundational beliefs to more and more areas of interest. The aim of this narrative is to show how "theory"—a designation that encloses within its embrace all those approaches to litera- ture that have emerged over the last twenty-five years or so—"has produced a *better* understanding of literature" than was possible when criticism was dominated by author- and text-centered approaches. We are further assured that "the study of literature is much more *interesting* than it used to be" under the *ancien régime*, when critics were enchanted by notions of will and agency, of writer-produced works of art, of works as unique products of artistic agency. We are indeed fortunate to live in *interesting* times, for now "the study of literary texts is . . . open to all kinds of questions about class, gender, race; it is in touch with linguistics, semiotics . . . , with theories of ideology, subjectivity and the unconscious, of culture and post-colonialism."[2]

Thus, it is clear that far from believing that they are in the grip of some rather erroneous or crippling ideas about mind, language, reality, meaning, and truth, current theorists believe that they are in possession of ideas that revolutionize Western thought, that, in short, release us from views that have crippled Western thought from its inception, such as the mind- or conceptual scheme–independence of the external world, the determinacy of meaning, the dependence of meaning on the deliberate mental states of agents, and so on. Still, what emboldens the nonrevolutionaries to persist in believing in the ultimately disabling weaknesses and limitations of the foundational beliefs of current theory is that incumbent upon their adoption is the abandonment of much that seems absolutely essential to our getting on in the world, to our voluntary and obligatory practices in the day-to-day world of reading, writing, thinking, understanding, and doing. I have in mind, of course, that world (or worlds) in which we say what we mean (and not some other thing) and mean what we say (and not some other thing), in which what is true depends very immediately (in most cases) on the ways things are at a distance from us and independently of our statements (i.e., a statement is true if things are as we say they are and false if they are not), in which the specific content of what is said is determined by some agent's mental states (since such states determine how something is represented or what it is represented as), and in which actions are made intelligible by reference to the contents of the mental states that cause them (i.e., action of any kind, including linguistic action, is both determined by and explained in terms of the reasons for it, and those reasons are intentional states of conscious agents). In other words, to the nonrevolutionaries, admission to current theory comes at too high a price—the sacrifice of too many loved ones, of so much that is necessary and useful to actual living, on the altar of linguistic idealism and the political unconscious.

When I was in the process of preparing and planning this book, I, like all other witnesses to the current scene, recognized that there were many sects within the church of current theory. (Of course, over the years one sect after another, without losing its standing altogether, has yielded pride of place or preeminence—as measured by acolytes, numbers of books and articles published, conference papers delivered, and so on—to some other sect, as in quick succession the microphone was passed from Derrideans to Bakhtinians to Lacanians to Foucauldians to new historicists or cultural materialists to postcolonial theorists to queer theorists and others waiting in line.) Current theory, in short, is not monolithic, but pluralistic, if only in the sense that it acknowledges many "truths"—though not truth in any objective sense of the term—in the process of relativizing them all to interpretive communities, conceptual schemes, and social formations. I also recognized that some schismatics were willing to endow authors with some limited control over literary effects (enough control, at any rate, to earn for themselves praise or blame for subverting or supporting the dominant culture) and that others were willing to concentrate attention on specific formal properties of literary works (if only to show how they too participated in the larger cultural poetics of the era). Nevertheless, within the recognition of all observers, I think, is the fact that despite the manifold diversity of critical emphases and practices, the various denominations belong, finally, to a single church, or, perhaps more accurately, that even though the sects are divided in their interests, they are united in their subscription to the foundational beliefs in the instability and self-referentiality of signs and the social construction of meaning. And that, I submit, is the problem.

The more I thought about this unity within diversity in current theory, however, and especially about the many genuine achievements realized by those critics who gave prominence to the social and political analysis of cultural products, the more apparent it became that the strength and argumentative power of the criticism were being etiolated, vitiated, or hamstrung by the theoretical commitments in the service of which the criticism was undertaken. Of course, the relationship between theoretical commitments, on one side, and critical projects and pronouncements, on the other, is very intimate, in that the latter are defined and formulated within the former. That is, the statements one makes are relative to the kinds of questions one asks; these, in turn, are relative to the theoretical framework (to the principles, assumptions, terms, distinctions) within which one works, and, finally, one's framework is relative to one's aims, purposes, ends.[3] All statements have theoretical underpinnings and allegiances. Nevertheless, it seemed to me that many of the genuine insights into, for example, the dynamics of power relations, into the gender, racial, class biases of particular eras and cultural products that the criticism diligently exposed were needlessly aligned with theoretical principles and assumptions that were fatally flawed. Briefly, the insights are more durable and valuable than the theoretical wagon they are hauled in on and are, further, in no way dependent for their value on their means of conveyance.

The conviction among current theorists that the insights depend upon and are products of the theoretical commitments stems, I think, from some fundamental confusions at the deep philosophical level, and it was my aim in the book in prospect (this book) to address these confusions and, incidentally, to show that the insights could be accommodated by a radically different set of theoretical principles, a set more nearly consonant with our highly serviceable workaday knowledge and our actual productive and interpretive practices. In what immediately follows, I shall highlight some few of the confusions and misunderstandings that, in my view, needed to be addressed and that I had largely neglected in my earlier work, focusing there primarily on the intellectual shortcomings of particular critical arguments and theoretical positions.[4] In general, current theorists tend to confuse semantic and ontological issues, believing, for example, that any concept of objective truth (a semantic/intentional matter) requires belief in naive realism (an ontological matter), in a preexisting system of entities, properties, and relations. In other words, the prevailing assumption is that the correspondence theory of truth and naive realism are joined at the hip. Of course, in a world in which truth is "truth," in which whatever truth there is, is relative to a conceptual scheme, the notion of an absolute or objective truth is nonsense. But it is important to understand that a correspondence theory of truth entails no particular ontology; such a theory is compatible not only with realism, but with idealism, instrumentalism, and many other isms. In short, one can be a correspondence theorist without being a realist (even though, admittedly, most such theorists are realists).

As a semantic, not an ontological matter, truth is a condition obtaining between (or among) content-bearing inner states (such intentional states, for example, as belief, desire, and so on) *and* external facts (correspondence theories of truth), other representational states (coherence theories of truth), practical ends (pragmatic theories of truth), and so forth. The burden of truth is not to establish the nature of modes of existence; this is the task of ontology. Semantics determines content, but not modes of existence. Briefly, to say that something has content is to affirm that it has semantic properties, such as meaning, reference, and truth conditions, and only things with content—for example, beliefs, sentences, and propositions—can be truth bearers. The separation of truth from ontology can be clearly seen in our ability to speak the truth—to say what is true—about existence-independent things: Othello does not have a faithful friend in Iago; at least one of Santa's reindeer has a nose that glows; there are no elves employed by the National Basketball Association, and so on, ad infinitum. Further, current theorists need to understand that if for correspondentists (those subscribing to the correspondence theory of truth) propositions or beliefs must correspond to the facts to be true, the facts to which they correspond may be mental facts, linguistic facts, cultural facts, or ideological facts, as well as, of course, what might be called "natural" or "brute" facts.

Moreover, contrary to popular belief and to the ingrained assumptions of most current theorists, there is no antagonism between the correspondence theory of truth and conceptual relativity. The realist, for instance, does not believe that nature, the world, or reality has semantic preferences, has a preferred vocabulary for describing the way things just are in the world; for the realist, "reality" is not in the referring or meaning business; it has no semantic franchise. Simply, it is entirely possible to believe, one, that there is a way that things are independently of our schemes and representations *and*, two, that there are indefinitely many ways to describe how things are, including some ways that employ different, incommensurable, and even conflicting vocabularies (terms and concepts). As one distinguished realist puts it, conceptual relativity "leaves us able to affirm that the one real world is such as to accommodate all the conceptualizations that we can successfully work with, and is such as to ground discriminations between true and false statements inside each conceptual scheme."[5] In the end, then, it would be helpful for current theorists to recognize that one can believe in the correspondence theory of truth without being an ontological realist and that one can be a realist even as one endorses conceptual relativity.

And, while we are on the subject of conceptual relativity, another confusion requires attention, the one that seems to entangle current theorists in this apparently inescapable network or sequence of intra-implication: conceptual relativity implies relativism, which in turn implies that anything goes. The train of reasoning that produces this system of mutual implication can be briefly sketched. Since, it is assumed, there is no Transcendental Signified to anchor and secure our sayings in the truth or in the way things just are, our sayings find their only warrant within the language system from which they are generated. And since there is no way to stand outside our culture or language game to see how our terms line up with how things really are, we are stuck with our various particular ways of seeing, with a multitude of equally valid but incommensurable frameworks. Thus, if truth (or what is right, fit, meaningful, etc.) is always contingent, conceptual-scheme-dependent, always relative to the language game in play, to a given culture, class, era, or interpretive community, then it would naturally seem to follow that anything goes. There is nothing in this network of entailments that could serve as defeasibility criteria, as normative standards to which appeal could be made to determine the rightness or preferential status of this or that position, to establish its truth or falsity, or to settle disputes between contending views or interpretations (with the laurel being awarded to the superior, better, or best litigant).

Of course, the "anything goes" charge is strenuously rejected (if not ignored completely) by the theorists against whom it is leveled, but even so, the charge has never been successfully overcome. Nor could the charge be overcome, given the theoretical principles and assumptions from which the radical relativists operate. For example, Barbara Herrnstein Smith adamantly insists that "a rejection of the idea of objectively determinate meaning [does not imply] that anything goes in the domain of verbal practices; . . . that all literary interpretations are equally valid." Nevertheless, after positing the notion of "reciprocal effectivity"—which boils down to the view that speaking and responding in some ways rather than others works out best for us or is locally more effective—as a curb or constraint on expression, Smith is compelled to make the startling admission (albeit in a subordinate clause) that in principle, if not in practice, anything could go: "Indeed, the idea of reciprocal effectivity suggests why, although perhaps anything always *could* go in principle, not everything ever *does* go in fact, either in language or in any other domain of social practice."[6]

In order to transcend or simply avoid the radical relativism, along with its faithful companion, radical skepticism about truth, that is everywhere apparent in current theory, it would first be necessary, it seemed to me, to reexamine such fundamental concepts as truth, meaning, reference, and interpretation, with the aim of showing how it is possible to acknowledge the inescapability of conceptual relativity without succumbing to relativism. A large part of the prospective project, then, would be concerned with showing that some schemes are demonstrably truer, more right, and better than others and that some statements within a given scheme are right, fit, and true and others are wrong, unfit, and false—even while acknowledging that it is impossible to describe anything without relying on descriptions, on some terms and concepts and not others, or to provide an account of anything without employing some conceptual scheme, and while also acknowledging that the same thing could be described in many, sometimes conflicting, ways and that the terms and concepts of a particular conceptual scheme could be used in support of incompatible views. Thus, considerable attention would be focused on demonstrating that there are both external and internal constraints on the expression and interpretation of meanings (more generally, on all that we say or do)—external, worldly constraints and internal, that is, psychological and intentional, constraints. Indeed, such constraints would be shown to be necessary prior conditions of any saying or writing whatsoever and, additionally, independent of any specific conceptual scheme or interpretive community.

Along the way, it would be necessary to argue, among other things, that content of any kind is impossible apart from mental states and that where there is content there is determinate meaning. And it would be necessary to separate the tasks of interpretation and criticism, reserving the former term for efforts of understanding that have as their goal the recovery of those meanings that derive from the conscious intentional states of agents with ends in view and the latter term for all those enterprises in which works are examined in relation to larger artistic, social, political, ideological concerns or as subsumed by or incorporated within one or another extratextual domain of interest (for example, the psychoanalytic, linguistic, anthropological, cultural, rhetorical, or other domain). In the end, then, it seemed to me that the theoretical ground on which the insights of most current critical practices rested was intellectually unstable (at best), that the relativism, skepticism, linguistic idealism, and social constructivism to which the practices were wedded would not withstand much scrutiny, and that, consequently, renovative work would have to begin at the foundational level. To me, a return to foundational issues would involve a consideration of the prevailing principles and assumptions of current theory in light of their competition, in relation to their viable alternatives. Hence, inquiry would explore, among other things, such matters as the defensibility of a kind of realism that is satisfying to our sensibilities and earned knowledge, the number and variety of truths we cannot avoid accepting, the persistent reliance on a correspondence notion of truth in our everyday lives and the intellectual warrant for such a reliance, the nature and bases of linguistic meaning, the sources of content of any kind (what determines it and why it must be determinate or fixed in nature), the possibility of objectivity in a world in which meaning has gone immanent (has gone into conceptual schemes), and so on.

It is clearly time to stop talking about the book in prospective terms, about what *would* be required or *would* be undertaken in such a book and to start describing in a brief overview what the book before you actually contains and why it presents the material as it does. The organizational structure of the book, as distinct from its argumentative structure, is the only begotten child of fortuity. While I was preparing a working chart of topics and the order of their presentation, I received in the mail an invitation to deliver two lectures in a series of several proposed lectures with the general title "The Humanities: Alternative Visions to Current Orthodoxies." Accompanying the invitation was a list of "Current Orthodoxies," to which the speakers were encouraged to refer when discussing prevailing doctrinal winds and suggesting alternatives to them. Because of prior professional commitments and some compelling personal obligations that made fixing lecture dates impossible, I was unable to participate in the series. Nevertheless, I saw in the list of current orthodoxies a device I could use to organize my discussion of the fundamental conceptual and theoretical issues that were central to my book project.

Before supplying an overview of the contents of the book, I need to make a few preliminary remarks. It will be immediately evident to every reader that the doctrines and claims on the list (which I have appended to this introduction) are not constituent elements of a single coherent theory—some belong to different orders of discourse and some are potentially inconsistent with others. Moreover, from the preceding it follows that not every practitioner of theory or every theory-informed producer of critical/material studies would endorse each and every tenet on the list. Nevertheless, it is fair to say, I think, that the list accurately reflects that array of ideas and values that in one or another mix-and-match assemblage informs the thinking and writing of most critics and theorists today. Further, every reader will notice that the six categories of the list are presented topically, not hierarchically (from least to most important, say) or logically (according to some regular system of concatenation, for example). In my handling of the topics, however, I have attempted to address the most fundamental issues first, taking the occasion of the first category (or, more exactly, creating opportunities within the category) to explore alternatives to prevailing conceptions of "reality," "truth," and "meaning," with the aim of showing how we can talk of such things without relying on scare quotes. In dealing with the subsequent categories, I have not limited discussion to the immediate concerns of the topics listed (though I have certainly addressed them) but have considered a variety of issues implicitly contained within or suggested by them, such as, for example, the vexed relations of fact and fiction in literary works, the dependence of our emotional response to art on belief, the contradictions inherent in the incommensurability thesis, the bases of value judgments in the arts, and so on. Also, because the items listed under the various categories are often (usually) presented with maximum concision, in the boldest, baldest, least subtle or moderated form, I have regularly tried to track down the larger conceptual context within which an item has a function before examining its practical and theoretical implications. Finally, throughout the book, my aim is to keep the focus on central conceptual issues and problems without deviating into local skirmishes with particular theorists or arguments, though occasionally, as when I take up certain aspects of relativism and new historicism, I am obliged to call upon specific witnesses to prosecute my case.[7]

In the remainder of this introduction, I shall present a relatively brief preview of the *argumentative* divisions of the book, followed by a complete list of the "Current Orthodoxies," which is included to help the reader find the precise language of the item under discussion, when that item, after its initial quotation, is cited subsequently only by letter and number. The list will rarely need to be consulted, but it is included for the convenience of the reader. The list contains six categories, whereas the book is divided into three sections and contains ten chapters, with five chapters in section one, two in section two, and three in the final section. The first five chapters, which are given over to an examination of the most basic, most fundamental conceptual issues, are occasioned by the items presented in the first category of the list. The second section, containing two chapters, is devoted to category two. The remaining four categories are taken up in chapters eight and nine, and the last chapter, in addition to functioning as a capstone or concluding chapter, makes good on an earlier promise to deal with the antihumanism of current theory and extends and refines an earlier discussion of human universals. Such, then, are the division markers of the book.

The argumentative units are impossible to summarize neatly, but they can be broadly suggested. Against the grain of current theory, chapters one and two differentiate semantic from ontological issues and argue that conceptual relativity is compatible with realism, that the correspondence theory of truth is consistent with conceptual relativity, that genuine objective truth is, despite claims to the contrary, possible, and that there are many varieties of truth, including innumerable transcultural, transparadigmatic, transconceptual-scheme truths. Moreover, in chapter two, I mount a case for both realism and the correspondence theory of truth, arguing, among other things, that realism is the *formal* or *logical* condition of the possibility of any representation's having representational content; without external reality as an operational assumption (i.e., without the assumption of a reality external to our representations or conceptual schemes), there is nothing that the representations can be representations *of.* Without the assumption of such a reality (or external state of affairs), there are no potential contents that can serve as truth conditions of our representations. On the other hand, each particular representational scheme establishes the truth conditions against which the statements and beliefs formulated within that scheme are tested for truth or falsity. Simply, reality has no semantic interests or preferences. We, of course, do have such interests, such content-involving states, but without the assumption of a way things are independently of our representations of them, the truth or falsity of none of the things identified by our interest-relative schemes could be determined. That is, we decide what cats are, what will count as a cat, but whether the creature before us is a cat or not depends on whether certain conditions independent of our scheme obtain.

Chapter three subjects one of the defining traits of current theory—its adherence to relativism—to close scrutiny, showing how in all its various manifestations—from Plato's *Theaetetus*, in which Protagoras makes the relativistic claim that each person is the measure of all things, to Barbara Herrnstein Smith's recent efforts to endow relativism with intellectual respectability—it is deeply entangled in incoherence and self-refutation. In the process of arguing against the central tenet of the relativist's faith, namely, that—because everything is scheme-dependent and the same thing can be described in many different ways—there is no such thing as objective truth, I also make a case for rationality and logic as necessary conditions of the possibility of thought of any kind whatsoever, insisting, moreover, that it is universally (and not conditionally or contingently, as the relativists suppose) the case that there is no thought apart from rationality.

Building on previous arguments and further developing the case against the prevailing belief that literary (or any) texts are incapable of coherence or determinate meaning, I make the case in chapter four that there is no content of any kind apart from the intentional states or linguistic acts of agents. Nature, reality, physics, syntax, 1's and 0's know nothing of content, have no semantic preferences, and are incapable of achieving meaningfulness without intentional states, without the imposition of representational (i.e., informational) functions on things, conditions, states of affairs, and so on. Moreover, because it is impossible to have a thought without thinking about something in some way (under some aspect, from some particular perspective—all seeing is perspectival, is a "seeing as" this or that), having a thought (i.e., being in an intentional state) is having a certain attitude (belief, say) toward a *particular* content. And thought begets thoughts of companionable stripe or kidney; thought, in short, has a vested interest in determination and coherence. At the end of this chapter, I show how this understanding of the dependence of content on the determinate intentional states of agents enables us to distinguish the task of interpretation from that of criticism.

The fifth and final chapter of the first section is in some senses the most important, inasmuch as it seeks to illuminate fatal flaws in the conception of language and meaning upon which the entire edifice of current criticism and theory is largely built (i.e., post-Saussurean or Derridean, deconstructive linguistics), the view that language is that upon which everything depends and that language, because of its relational and differential nature, is unstable, incapable of staying fixed or determinate. Although perhaps few today openly declare themselves to be deconstructionists, virtually all of our emerging social and cultural critics rely in their work on the "deconstructive" conception of language, and consequently on the epistemological assumptions about knowledge and truth and the ontological assumptions about reality that that conception entails. The influence of this linguistics on subsequent theory is exemplified in the cases of new historicism and cultural materialism, and I conclude the discussion of the difficulties involved in conducting social criticism while operating under such an influence with a brief look at a phenomenon collateral to and compatible with new historicism, the emerging field of memetics, which studies the transmission of units of cultural significance (memes) from brain to brain, culture to culture, era to era.[8] In the end, this chapter is concerned to show that although eras, cultures, and periods exhibit trends and fashions, they do not and cannot have contentful states or ends in view (as particular works generated by human agents do); we cannot transfer agency to language, history, culture, memes, or anything else incapable of forming and manipulating representational content.

Chapters six and seven constitute the second section of the book and are concerned, broadly speaking, with matters relating to how we can distinguish fiction from nonfiction, choose between conflicting accounts of things or interpretations of texts, and overcome the "anything goes" implications of conceptual relativism, when, it is generally assumed, all texts are "made up" and no conceptual scheme has more rational warrant than any other. In the broadest terms, these two chapters have as their subjects the skepticism and antirationality of current theory. Conceding that both history and fiction are "made up" and are, thus, in some not entirely irrelevant sense, "fictional," I explore in chapter six some of the similarities and differences between "real" and "fictional" accounts of things and between our responses to these accounts, examining in the process the appropriateness of applying "true" or "truth" to aspects of each kind of text. Additionally, I try to explain why we are moved emotionally by works that are not "true," especially given the fact, as I believe, that emotion is a consequence of belief and the further fact that belief is determined by what is true. In the end, if I am obliged to acknowledge that there is a real but inessential difference between a historical text and a work of fiction, I do so because I have come to see that the sameness derives not from some comprehensive fictionality (from the "fictionality" of all writing and speaking), but, on the contrary, from the durability of a way that things are independently of our descriptions, from a reality that we can be right or wrong about. Works of art, I argue, are "thought-experimentally true"; that is, they would not move if they did not bring realities to mind. In all, the argument is designed to prove that without an anchorage in reality, in what is true, in what is the case, fictions would not move because they would not exist.

The burden of chapter seven is to counter two pervasive beliefs of current theory: (1) because we are locked into the prison house of our own language game, our own conceptual scheme, our own interpretive community, we cannot transcend the conditions of our means of knowing, cannot take up an unbiased position; and (2) because we are so limited, it follows that we cannot compare competing views to determine which is superior to or better (truer, more right) than its rival. At bottom, we have here, I argue, the incoherence of the incommensurability thesis, the view that one language game is incommensurable with another and thus not on speaking terms with it. But to say that the views are incommensurable is to say something that is true about them from outside the views. Moreover, I show that we can always talk *about* what we talk *with*; of any scheme I can say what it is interested in and how it goes about expressing that interest. From outside your scheme, I can state what you are trying to explain and how you go about the business of explanation. On the matter of whether one view has more rational warrant than another, I demonstrate that what is crucial to adjudicating the claims of rival theories, in addition to their having a subject matter in common (having something that they disagree about), is that the outcome of the issue to be decided is not intrinsic to what is shared. For example, competing theories of evolution in terms of "punctuated equilibrium," on one hand, and "continuity," on the other, agree in their view that adaptation is necessary to evolution, but neither theory is presupposed by that view.[9] The rest of the chapter is given over to exposing the weaknesses of the arguments mounted by theorists against the possibility of appealing to rational methods in the adjudication of cases.

As I noted earlier, the last four categories on the list are discussed in chapters eight and nine, categories three and four in chapter eight and categories five and six in chapter nine. Because many of the major conceptual problems recur in several categories and because they have been the focus of attention in the earlier chapters, I have concentrated in these last two chapters primarily on items that raise new issues or complicate old ones, that provide opportunities to show how previous arguments apply to special cases, or that otherwise demand attention. Chapter eight, then, examines the ways in which reader-response and reception theory transfer the source of meaning from authors to readers, from whose interpretive acts textual meanings emerge and in whose evaluations texts achieve their aesthetic merit or social/political significance. Reception theories are by theoretical imperative committed to multiple interpretations. More broadly, the chapter considers the general problem of diversity of interpretation, which involves many readers construing the same text differently, along with its mirror twin, the uniformity of interpretation, which involves many readers construing many texts in essentially the same way. The upshot of the argument here is that although the same texts may come to mean different things to many readers and different texts may assume the same meaning for many readers, and although any interpretation or construed meaning may be used in the service of an extraordinary range of issues of importance to the reader, the fact remains that as systems of intentionality texts cannot mean many different things, though they may certainly express richly complex meanings, in which doubt, ambiguity, irony, uncertainty, and so on may figure prominently. Meaning arises only in particular contexts of use and, hence, only within a particular structure of intentionality; in other words what literary works specifically express depends very immediately on the intentional states of authors, not readers. (And, of course, my saying so in no way limits or impairs every reader's unalienable, constitutionally protected right to read any text in any way he or she pleases—so long as that reading is not confused with an interpretation; authors have rights too.)

Chapter nine initially considers an aspect of social constructionism that was slighted in the earlier discussion (in chapter five) of cultural materialism and new historicism and then makes a case for two things rejected by all social constructivist positions, namely, linguistic and moral universals, on the one hand, and value judgments based on the intrinsic merits of literary works, on the other. At the outset, readers are first asked to consider the two phrases "the social construction of reality" and "the construction of social reality" and then to note that the former phrase—the one adopted by current theorists—subordinates human beings to a congeries of social/political/linguistic/cultural/ideological forces that determine not only who we are but what there is to think about and how to go about our thinking of it, whereas the latter phrase—the one endorsed by this book and by a goodly number of people outside literature and sociology departments—endows conscious human beings with capacities to talk about real and imagined things in a variety of true and creative ways and to do so quite often with the cooperation of the ways things are independently of mind, language, culture, and power relations. Underlying both phrases are strong arguments, but in the end it is clear, I argue, that no matter how heavily freighted with accumulated cultural or ideological significance the terms and locutions of particular eras or cultures may be, the actual meaning of those terms and locutions on specific occasions of use, in the service of particular aims or interests, cannot be predicted from or determined by their meanings in other contexts, however automatic or conventional those meanings may have seemed to become.

The burden of the next section of chapter nine is to make the case that just as there are linguistic universals underlying an immense range of strikingly different languages, so there are moral universals underpinning a richly diverse range of cultures and societies. The argument obliges me to show that like geometric and linguistic knowledge, knowledge of ethical value is a species of a priori knowledge. In making this case, I draw support from a considerable number of writers on linguistics and moral philosophy, including Bertrand Russell, John Rawls, and Noam Chomsky, and end up endorsing the position advocated by Colin McGinn: "the same kind of reasoning that leads to the postulation of an innate language faculty suggests the postulation of an innate moral faculty: poverty of stimulus, richness of result, and uniformity of basic principles."[10] In the final section of this chapter, I scrutinize the nature of value judgments generally, noting, among other things, that value is a relative thing and that nothing has value in and of itself; the specific features of something have value only as these features relate to something else (for example, a tree has a certain size, but it is great or small only relative to other trees, though it is one or the other in terms of its actual physical size). Moreover, any trait or whole work can have multiple values or be multiply valuable (a particular work may be both shorter and more patriotic than others; a given trait, a word, say, may be valued for its sound or its function, or both). This multiplicity of value potential leads to a discussion of the internal and external goods of a literary work, to a discussion of those goods—those traits or features—that contribute to the functioning of the work as a whole, that serve the interests of the overall intentionality (internal goods) and those that are valuable relative to extratextual interests such as holding open a window, serving as a doorstop, achieving fame and fortune (external goods). The argument, along with the chapter, concludes with a brief in support of the legitimacy of examining literary works in terms of their intrinsic merit.

As I indicated earlier, the last chapter (chapter ten) not only serves as a capstone to the argument of the book as a whole, but also enables me to make good on an earlier promise to confront the antihumanism of current theory and, in the process of defending what I call a pragmatic pluralist humanism, to take what has become throughout the text an ongoing, though somewhat incidental and by-the-by discussion of human universals into new areas of concern, thereby establishing a wider evidentiary base. Adoption of the kind of humanism outlined in this chapter makes possible the evaluation of one culture from within another on the basis of intercultural standards. And in concluding the book as a whole, I insist that the humanism championed in this book is, in any case, inescapable, because we are unavoidably content-involved creatures, and content is inseparable from thought and thought from intentionality and intentionality from agency; to have a thought or a world to talk about or be aware of, we must of necessity participate in systems of intentionality and rationality, determining which ones are good and right and true ones for us by appealing to, among other things, our enduring and transcultural conceptions of human flourishing, of right thinking and acting.

Such then is a view of the argumentative structure of the book from the balcony. The reader should perhaps notice that though the categories and items on the list of "Current Orthodoxies" have peer standing within their rank (i.e., categories are not arranged in order of importance, nor are items within categories) and though I by and large discuss both categories and items in the order in which they appear on the list, I have structured the argument so that the most basic and fundamental conceptual issues and problems are addressed first (in the first five chapters). The conceptual issues and problems addressed in the last five chapters, especially in chapters eight and nine, depend for their analysis and resolution upon what has been established in the earlier chapters about realism, truth, content, meaning, and so forth. To facilitate quick and easy reference to specific categories and items within categories, I here append the list to which I repeatedly refer in the text.

Current Orthodoxies

1. Deconstruction
   a. There is no direct access to truth; nothing is immediately given in experience; all knowledge is conceptually/linguistically mediated; all knowledge involves interpretation (antifoundationalism).
   b. A text is incapable of conveying a determinate, stable meaning.
   c. A text is incapable of communicating a coherent message.
   d. Reflexivity of language and texts—language and texts do not represent or refer to extralinguistic or extratextual reality. Language/texts are self-referential— "signifiers chasing signifiers." A text refers to itself and to other texts—"textuality and intertextuality."

2. Skepticism and Irrationalism
   a. There is no direct *or* indirect access to truth.
      i. One implication of (a) is that there is no essential difference between a historical text and a work of fiction ("new historicism").
   b. It is impossible to be objective, impartial, to transcend one's biases in taking up a position—there are no innocent, disinterested positions.
   c. There is no such thing as a rational method or procedure for arriving at knowledge.
   d. Since no position (theory, assertion, knowledge claim, perspective) has more rational warrant than any other, "anything goes."

3. Reception Theory

   a. A text has no intrinsic meaning but means what a given reader/audience takes it to mean.

      i. One implication of (a) is that the same text may be construed to have different meanings and different texts may be construed to have the same meaning.

4. Death of the Author, Subject

   a. Personal agency is denied (antihumanism).

      i. "Language speaks man"—denial that the author generates the text. Somehow the text generates itself, or is generated by language itself, using the individual as its vehicle.

      ii. The subject is "decentered"—unity of the subject, capable of making free, informed, rationally based choices is denied.

5. Relativism and Social Constructivism

   a. There is no absolute or universal truth—every truth is relative to a conceptual/ linguistic framework ("language game," "discursive practice"), the scientific community, race, gender, class, or culture, that somehow "constitutes" or "constructs" it (creates it?).

   b. Similar considerations apply to moral, ethical, aesthetic values.

   c. Reality, nature, the subject are "socially constructed."

6. Politicization of Texts

   a. All texts (including works of art and music) are treated as essentially political.

   b. All texts are treated from a radical leftist perspective, i.e., as instances of "hegemonic discourse" or "counter-hegemonic discourse."

   c. Levels of meaning and issues other than political in a text are disregarded.

   d. All levels of meaning other than political in a text are treated as having political implications or as somehow symbolizing political doctrines.

   e. Different levels of merit in texts are disregarded. Texts are evaluated exclusively on the basis of political content.

   f. There is a tendency to equate the value of a text with the level of its popular appeal, regardless of whether or not it has any intrinsic merit. Standards of intrinsic merit are attacked as "elitist."

LANGUAGE, TRUTH, AND REALITY

Chapter 1

The Truth Is, There Is No Truth

It is a truth universally acknowledged that a person possessed by theory or in the grip of poststructuralism must know with absolute certainty that it is universally true that there can be no truth (or objectivity, or determinate meaning, or correspondence of words or thoughts with facts, with the way things are independent of our conceptual schemes). For the time being, let's allow that sentence to luxuriate in its own majestic incoherence, its own self-unravelment, its aporian splendor; we shall shortly have opportunities to look into the face of the god in whose image that sentence is created—self-refutation. Aside from seeming to hoist itself on its own petard, the claim that we have no access to truth appears to be in clear and indisputable violation of our earned knowledge. Moreover, as you quickly scan the list of orthodox views, you cannot help but be struck by how many of them are counterintuitive or, to appropriate a favorite term, "transgressive" of our ordinary, workaday, stop-on-red, go-on-green sense of things, and, hence, cannot be surprised at the alacrity with which they have won adherents, inasmuch as nothing pleases some among us more than the discovery that things are other than we had thought them to be, indeed, are different from or—the best bested—just the opposite of what we, in our ignorant and illusioned condition, had taken them to be. Of course, no one wants to be taken in by appearances, to keep the scales upon the eyes, to see the world through the veil of illusion, but some of us seem to have a positive lust for any view or thesis that would offend the common understanding or working assumptions of, say, a Rotarian or a Presbyterian or, in short, anyone who, in her personal and private capacity, had a more or less commonsense view of meaning, agency, objectivity, and so on. Among these iconoclasts we would have to number those of our colleagues who are nothing if not *contrari-tropic* (i.e., predisposed or programmed to credit whatever runs counter to common wisdom) and for whom life is frisson-less without the heresies of paradox (i.e., without the advocacy of views contrary to those of received opinion or common belief). Then, of course, there are the wise, the happy, and, alas, the few colleagues among us who are inclined to believe (despite the unintended but unavoidable consequence of aligning themselves in some not insignificant ways with Rotarians and Presbyterians) that views and beliefs indispensable to the conduct of life cannot be either intellectually trivial or wholly false and for whom a life rich in many truths and promise-crammed with others is not frisson-challenged.

Nevertheless, before succumbing too quickly to the alluring charms of moral/intellectual bifurcation, whereby we pit the benighted them against the enlightened us, we should perhaps also note as we scan the list that there is much in it with which we can agree, which in some instances, from a certain angle, under certain circumstances, or from one perspective makes sense, is true or useful. In the argument to follow, my tasks will be to show what might be said in opposition to or in qualification of the current orthodoxies, to explain why what might be true or useful in some sense or for some purposes cannot be invested with plenary authority, and, yes, to shoot folly as it flies. It is crucial to keep in mind, however, that my focus throughout is on the conceptual issues and problems that are stated or implied in the orthodox views. All this can be done, I hope, without rancor and without making the supporters of those orthodoxies out to be somewhat lower on the felony scale than child molesters or chicken violators. The first category, Deconstruction, contains the following four items, to which I shall respond in the next few chapters.

1. Deconstruction
   a. There is no direct access to truth; nothing is immediately given in experience; all knowledge is conceptually/linguistically mediated; all knowledge involves interpretation (antifoundationalism).
   b. A text is incapable of conveying a determinate, stable meaning.
   c. A text is incapable of communicating a coherent message.
   d. Reflexivity of language and texts—language and texts do not represent or refer to extralinguistic or extratextual reality. Language/texts are self-referential—"signifiers chasing signifiers." A text refers to itself and to other texts—"textuality and intertextuality."[1]

Although there are undoubtedly few self-proclaimed deconstructionists on the job today, the tenets listed under this category are widely accepted by most theorists, with the possible exception of those registered under (d), which are either openly rejected by cultural materialists, Marxists, and other socio-politico-cultural critics or quietly tucked away in the inactive file, if only because naming names and assigning blame (or praise) are impossible if language cannot refer beyond itself; certainly race, class, and gender studies would never get under way or ever have any social relevance if signifiers chased only other signifiers.[2] The four main clauses of (a) are perhaps best seen as a system of dependencies, a family cluster of ideas in intimate relationship: nothing is immediately given in experience and access to truth is not direct, *because*, it is assumed, all knowledge is conceptually/linguistically mediated, and, hence, all knowledge is a form of interpretation, a species of viewing through one or another mediating lens.

No thoughts here are beyond the reaches of our souls, and no ghost needs to come from the grave to tell us this. Few today would maintain that from some standpoint outside of thought and language we can directly apprehend how things just are, that we can position ourselves in some middle distance between language and the world to see how one aligns or matches up with the other. Long before Kant, Alexander Pope knew—from hints dropped by Locke and others—that the reason Man has not a microscopic eye is that Man is not a fly, knew, that is, that between the out there and the in here our sensory machinery intervened.[3] Over the noumenal is draped the veil of experience, designed and shaped by *our* peculiar sensory equipment, not by that of, say, the fly or the bat. Of course, at this point in late empiricism or in the post-empiricist world, after idealism and other isms have taken the linguistic turn, we are more than inclined to suspect that our concepts and language itself are not so much our ambassadors to the world as, odd as it may seem, the worlds themselves—the only worlds that we can know or know about, at any rate. The litany has these, among other familiar elements: all observation is theory-laden; all that we know—indeed, all that we can know—is simply an implication or consequence of the terminology in terms of which we do our observing; all knowledge is (historically, culturally, politically, racially, interpretive-community, etc.) contingent, that is, scheme-dependent; or, more radically, language is simply a system of signs and relations among signs with no positive (extralinguistic) elements, and, consequently, signs refer only to other signs, texts to other texts, and so on; there is no way to hook our signifiers onto a world external to our system of signs, since signs only hook onto other signs; and because all such things as the preceding are so, not only is there no direct access to truth, but there is no real truth to access: truth is like Bottom's dream—there is no bottom (i.e., no foundation) to it.

Unquestionably, item (a) is a full suitcase of ideas and conceptual entailments, one that cannot be completely unpacked item by item and implication by implication in the space available here. Nevertheless, a few useful reminders can be offered and a confusion or two untangled. For example, it is perhaps worth noting that truth is a semantic matter, not an ontological one; basically, truth is a condition obtaining between (or among) content-bearing inner states (e.g., such thoughts, propositional attitudes, or intentional states as belief, desire, and so on) and external facts (correspondence theories of truth), other representational states (coherence theories of truth), practical ends (pragmatic theories of truth), and so forth. The task of truth is not to determine the nature or status of modes of existence (this is the task of ontology). To say that something has content is to say that it has semantic properties, for instance, meaning, reference, and truth conditions, and only things with content, such as beliefs, sentences, and propositions, can be truth bearers. The separation of truth from ontology can be neatly illustrated in our ability to speak the truth about existence-independent things: Cordelia is a loyal daughter; there are no unicorns in the San Diego zoo; I feel a sharp pain in my (amputated) leg; leprechauns are not very tall, and so on, ad infinitum.

Interestingly, with the exception of the pain-in-the-leg truth, these truths, like countless others, are not locally, psychologically, historically, or culturally contingent truths (though, of course, they are all language-dependent, scheme-dependent, are all, in some sense, theory-laden). Despite persistent assurances from some quarters that cross-cultural, transhistorical truth claims are impossible, these truths are true absolutely, positively, for now and for the time to come, come what may in the sociopolitical realm, however revolutionary or paradigm-shifting. Indeed, in the great cosmos of actual, potential, and possible truths, countless galaxies are made up of broad, general, universal, era-, person-, culture-, race-, gender-transcending truths, for instance, all truths by definition (so-called analytic truths: bachelors are unmarried men, wives are female, etc.), by stipulation (let the breaking of this plane by this spheroid be called a touchdown), as well as the truths of logic, geometry, and so on and so on.

Well, even if we grant that there are many truths and many kinds of truth (including many kinds of culture-transcending truths), the fundamental issue of the mind-, language-, or scheme-dependence of our truths remains, the issue of the break of truth from reality (ontology), from the way things really are. If the only contact we have with reality is by means of our terms, categories, and interests; if, further, the same event can accommodate an indefinite number of descriptions, or if different, even conflicting, conceptual schemes can characterize the same state of affairs, then truth becomes, it seems, an internal matter (a matter of coherence within schemes of interpretation or expression), not a correspondence between our assertions and assertion-independent things or states of affairs. Truth, such as it is, is immanent, is, apparently, term-, mind-, scheme-, language-bound. Reference doesn't hook up with anything external to the system of relations internal to the linguistic scheme in play. Consequently, truth is relative, and objective knowledge (i.e., scheme-independent knowledge) is a myth. Moreover, what is also clear to virtually all the theorists who subscribe to item (a) is that there is a necessary logical connection between (naive) realism and the correspondence theory of truth (true statements are true if and only if they correspond exactly with the way things really are) and that belief in such a strict connection is simply, flat-out wrong. Further, even though bona fide, card-carrying, paid-up members of this particular truth/realism cult are rarer than tan lines at a nudist colony, to current theorists of the orthodox persuasion true believers are everywhere, and anyone who registers a demurrer to any form of relativism, skepticism, or constructivism or mounts a defense of determinate meaning, objective knowledge, and so on is either a realist dupe or a realist sympathizer.

In the interests of clarity, it is perhaps worth noting at this point that adoption of a correspondence theory of truth—a view that avers, for instance, that a proposition is true only if it directly coincides with existent states of affairs or the way the world really and truly is—does not carry with it by logical or any other necessity a commitment to any particular *ontological* theory, to a particular stand on the nature of facts or the world (though it is true that most correspondence theorists are also realists). To be sure, for the correspondence theorist propositions must correspond to facts, but those facts may be mental facts, linguistic facts, cultural facts, and institutional facts, as well as what some are inclined to call brute or natural facts. For example, "The police officer gave me a speeding ticket," "I waited angrily in the dean's office," and "She was married on the eighth of June," are statements rich in institutional facts (i.e., facts created entirely by human beings and depending for their existence and intelligibility on collective agreements among members of a speech community) and are absolutely, unquestionably true if and only if I was indeed given a ticket, if I so waited in such a place, and if she was actually married on that date. Moreover, nothing prevents a correspondence theorist from endorsing conceptual relativity, from acknowledging—even championing—the view that the same state of affairs can be accurately and truly described in many ways. The chair in front of such a theorist can be seen as a piece of furniture, as a source of fuel, as a solid object, as a gappy bundle of subatomic particles, and so on. In short, correspondence theorists can identify themselves not only as realists, but as idealists, as instrumentalists, as constructivists, as new historicists, as this-ists and that-ists, and they can accept many descriptions of the same state of affairs, however they identify themselves.

Still, most correspondence theorists are also realists. Even so, most realists are not naive advocates of the view that nature or reality prescribes that one and only one language be given the description franchise, be assigned the rights to describe how things really are, so that language, truth, knowledge, and reality form a perfect union and a closed circle, outside of which is mere noise or nonsense. Notwithstanding the apparently unshakeable conviction among most current theorists that realism and conceptual relativity have taken up residence at the antipodes, there is nothing inconsistent or inco-

herent in embracing both realism and conceptual relativity. It is quite possible, in other words, to believe that there is a way that things are
independently of all our schemes and representations *and* that there are
indefinitely many ways to describe how things are, including some ways that
rely on incommensurable or conflicting vocabularies (terms and concepts).
What there are not for realists (and some other "ists" as well) are limitlessly
many good, right, and true ways of describing things; some descriptions are
right, good, or true, whereas others are certainly, absolutely, positively, unquestionably not good, right, or true. For example, within the substance/
property ontology—the intellectual framework or conceptual scheme val-
orizing people and medium-size objects—the absolute, objective truth of
the statement that the cup just to the left of the keyboard on my desk is
full of coffee depends very directly on whether the cup to the left of the
keyboard on my desk is indeed full of coffee. From another realist perspective—one sponsored by chemistry or molecular physics (by a micro-object
ontology), say—a true description of the same cup, desk, keyboard, and
coffee would rely on a radically different vocabulary to designate the facts
of the "same" situation.

   The point of the immediately preceding, of course, is to counter the widespread—and, in literary studies today, the virtually universal—assumption
that realism (usually denominated "naive realism" or the "classical" or "traditional" view and attributed to anyone who betrays any signs of deviating
from the orthodoxies under review) can make no allowances for conceptual
relativity without sacrificing the bedrock faith upon which it is founded,
for—so the line of reasoning runs—to allow one thing to be now this and
now that depending upon which conceptual lens is in place is in effect to
place quotation marks around "reality," making it immanent to and dependent upon languages or conceptual schemes. The complaisance and af-
fability (as well as the intolerance) of realism is cogently put by William
Alston:

[Conceptual or] Ontological relativity leaves us able to affirm that the one real world
is such as to accommodate all the conceptualizations that we can *successfully* work
with, and is such as to ground discriminations between true and false statements
inside each conceptual scheme. Nor is this a wholly trivial claim. Not all conceivable
conceptual schemes will work—will fit the world as it is. Constructing the world as
wholly consisting of real numbers, . . . rodents, or caloric fluid will not enable us to
get around efficiently in our environment. . . . Moreover, it is by no means insignificant that within a given *useful* conceptual scheme, the world permits us to make
distinctions between true and false statements using the concepts of that scheme.[4]

We can all add to Alston's list of conceptual schemes that do not or cannot
work, that do not "fit the world as it is" (phlogiston schemes, astral influ-

ence schemes, witch schemes, and countless other schemes easily generated on the spot from the safety and comfort of the nearest armchair), and we have mentioned above several instances in which we can distinguish truth from falsehood once we have a scheme in operation. If, to take a new example, the cowtalk scheme is in place, then we can quickly determine whether it is true or false that there are cows in a given pasture. As Alston says, these are not trivial or insignificant matters. To bring the last few paragraphs to summation, it is fair to say—despite prevailing opinions to the contrary—that one can be a correspondence theorist without being an ontological realist (realism, like every other ontology, is not intrinsic to the correspondence theory of truth) and that one can be a realist while endorsing conceptual relativity (conceptual relativity is not antithetical to realism).

By now, it should also be clear that one can recognize the inescapability of conceptual relativity without subscribing to relativism. That is, one can acknowledge that any object can belong to an indefinite number of classes or kinds, can be categorized or classified in countless ways (every object is like any other object in some respects—both are on the same table, are round, belong to the state of Rhode Island, are hairless, are shorter than a martini glass, heavier than air, and so on ad infinitum), and that any event can be described in an indefinite number of ways, from a vast array of viewpoints (e.g., from the engineer's, chemist's, physicist's, doctor's, husband's, economist's, et cetera's point of view). One can grant the ubiquity of conceptual relativism and still reject what every supporter of the current orthodoxies seems to accept: relativism, the view that since all knowledge is relative to some scheme, some culture, some ideology, or whatever, there can be no such thing as objective knowledge, as an objective and true fit between statement and fact. Unquestionably, whatever there is to know is filtered through some mesh or other of our biology (our sensations or neuron firings) or of our manufacture (our concepts, language, culture, etc.). Nevertheless, it does not follow from the fact that our access to reality, things, nature—to whatever we know and discuss—is mediated that there is nothing but systems of mediation. Because we cannot represent how things are without relying on some system of representation or describe anything at all without resorting to descriptions, we ought not to conclude that there are only systems of representation and descriptions. Even in our ordinary ways of talking in the everyday world we distinguish between the word "water" or "balloon" and the water or balloon we have in sight; it is always incumbent upon us to distinguish between what is represented and what does the representing (between the painting and the paint, the character revealed by the words of the speaker and the words spoken by the character). And whether our representation is true or accurate or fitting depends on whether things are as we represent them to be, whatever conceptual resources we employ to do the work of representation. Where representations are concerned, truth or fittingness is regularly or in a vast number of cases decided by matters external to the system of representation, by things at a remove from the speaker or representer.

In any adequate consideration, conceptual relativism is, as John Searle has noted,

an account of how we fix the application of our terms: What counts as a correct application of the term "cat" or "kilogram" or "canyon" . . . is up to us to decide and is to that extent arbitrary. *But once we have fixed the meanings of such terms in our vocabulary by arbitrary definitions, it is no longer a matter of any kind of relativism or arbitrariness whether representation-independent features of the world that satisfy or fail to satisfy the definitions exist independently of those or any other definitions.*[5]

In brief, we provide the conditions of reference (we say what counts as a dog or a banana split), but we do not determine whether in the case of this or that object the conditions obtain. A rose by any other name is still a rose, but only so long as it has those properties by which we identify roses; we may call a rose "joe" if we wish, but "joe" will be a rose (a joe) only if it has what we have decided to be the differentiating features of a rose (a joe). By any other definition or description a joe is not a rose. In other words, we do not make roses; we supply the terms and conditions that only the mind- and language-independent objects we call roses can satisfy.

As should be clear from earlier comments, nature or reality has no semantic preferences, no preferred vocabulary or language, no point of view to push, no intrinsic propensity to label this as cause and that as effect. Neither syntax nor semantics is native to nature or the things out there. Nature is not in the naming or referring business; it knows nothing of *content*, of objects, categories, and so on. Yet it remains the case that what is out there is truly distinguishable by means of the linguistic or terminological conditions we set, but only if those conditions truly *apply* to the objects they are applied to. Language determines the reference conditions to be met by objects in the world, but objects-in-the-world determine the truth conditions of the identifying terms, determine, that is, whether the terms of reference are correctly applied to the objects, just in the way that the daffodil says no to the conditions of reference for the rose, determines the inapplicability to it of the rose's conditions of reference. As Michael Devitt has wisely noted, "naming a property does not make an object have it; ignoring the property does not prevent the object's having it."[6] Furthermore, just as there is no limit to the *number of categories* to which any object may belong, so there is, consequently, no apparent limit to the *number of true properties* any object may have. In his rejection of the view that we make the world with our language and minds, Devitt supports the preceding point and bolsters his rejection by affirming truly that he did not make echidnas (those rather small, odd-looking, egg-laying, toothless, Australasian mammals) "peorincreds" (that is, incredible to tourists from Peoria, extending beyond the reach of Peorian credibility), but they do indeed have that property. Moreover, not only do they have it now, along with many other creatures, but they also have always had it, and certainly had it long before there was a town in Illinois called Peoria.

Of course, to know whether anything does or does not have the property, it must be named and applied to specific objects; but, crucially, the naming does not endow the object with the property.[7] And what is true of this and countless other named and unnamed properties is also true of such currently named but formerly unnamed objects or states of affairs as oxygen, cancer, trade deficits, mean molecular energy, attention-deficit disorder, microbes, and so on. Oxygen, for example, is not a late-eighteenth-century creation, appearing suddenly on a scene where there had been no oxygen before. And as it is with oxygen, so it is with a vast plenitude of the terms, categories, properties, and objects that emerge in the course of time, indeed, at specific points in cultural, political, and intellectual history. If it makes no sense to say that there was no oxygen until late in the eighteenth century, it also makes no sense to say, as some modern theorists with Foucauldian or historicist proclivities have, that there were no cases of homosexuality or subjectivity until the nineteenth century or of attention-deficit disorder until the twentieth century. Once the categories or concepts are established and rigidly defined, they can apply across time periods and cross-culturally, if the conditions to which they are applied obtain, so that, for example, if there were such a thing as the Oedipal complex or the law of supply and demand, nothing would prevent us from discussing *Hamlet* in terms of the one or a feudal economy in terms of the other, even though nobody in Elizabethan England or in a feudal economy could or would conceive of matters in such terms.[8]

From the preceding, however, it would be foolish to conclude that many (perhaps most) truths and facts are *not* the products of specific times and places and particular cultural and personal interests and exigencies or do *not* reflect the social milieu or even the ideological culture of their origin. A touchdown is inconceivable apart from football, a Dow Jones Average apart from capitalism and stock trading. Moreover, many of our most interesting and important facts and truths are solely the product of our minds and language systems, are, as we say, mind-dependent or language-dependent. Trees and oxygen are mind- and language-independent in ways that trade deficits, supply and demand, shortstops, marriages, contracts, banana splits, money, and the office of the dean are not. To be sure, we couldn't talk about trees or rocks or mountains without "tree," "rock," and "mountain" language, but we don't make trees, and so on with our language (as we have seen); on the contrary, trees make our language just, true, appropriate (statements about trees are truth bearers just in case the facts about trees are truth makers). But we do make our arti-facts, our social facts, and our ad-hoc facts with the resources of our minds and language—there are no such things apart from our makings and doings; they are all very directly mind-dependent.

To impose in some way some meaning, form, value, or function upon some material not natively inclined to exhibit or express any form, value, or function on its own for some purpose or for the sake of some interest is to set in motion the great human enterprise of referring and making. From such activity springs language itself and all the products and facts of artistic and sociopolitico-institutional life. It is by such imposition that in English, the collection of letters (or, more exactly, *marks*) "t" "r" "e" "e" takes on the information function of meaning tree and a certain sound pattern takes on the same function. By such means, doing and saying such and such under certain circumstances constitutes a marriage. From this time forth, these and only these metal disks will function as coins, will be coins of the realm; only the breaking of this plane by this object will be considered a touchdown; only such and such will be a law, a contract, a zoo, and so on and so on ad infinitum. All artifacts and social facts come about by this human, mind-dependent process, as do, of course, those nonce-collectives, those ad-hoc categories that are most frequently created on the spot in response to some local interest or exigency—for example, things to remove from a burning building, foods a supermodel is likely to avoid, peeves that so-and-so will adopt as pets, things that pass my understanding, stores in which the Sultan of Brunei is unlikely to do his shopping, books banned in Boston, and all the multitudinous rest. Mind-dependent as all these artifacts, social facts, and ad-hoc facts are, they are as real, in a very nontrivial sense of real, as any mind-independent facts. Upon them we can perform the same operations of determining their sense and reference and their objective status that we can perform upon mind-independent facts.

Although interest-relative and context-dependent, although deriving their status from our impositions and purposes, these facts are as factual as facts can be, as determinate and objective as any other facts. We can run bump into poles or chairs as readily as trees, can establish whether the office of the dean has been filled (i.e., whether a given individual has been selected to serve as dean) as certainly as whether there are any elephants in my yard, can know whether the items packed are suitable for a camping trip in as objectively determinate a way as we can know whether the items before us are all minerals. The rather modest point of all this is that both mind-dependent and mind-independent facts can serve as truth conditions of our factual assertions. Whether the statement that "there is a wolf in front of me" or the statement that "there is a banana split in front of me" is (absolutely, definitely, make no mistake about it) true or not depends very immediately upon which one of the two is in front of me. As Lynne Rudder Baker observes, although "rocks and dinosaurs are mind-independent in an obvious sense [the sense in which they would have existed whether there

were minds or not] . . . , the mind-independent/mind-dependent distinction has next to no metaphysical significance [at least so far as it concerns
'successful human practices']. In particular, it marks no important boundary
between what is real (or genuinely real) and what is not."⁹

In bringing the immediately preceding section to conclusion, I would
make three points. First, a real distinction can be made between mind-
independent and mind-dependent things. When we refer to rocks, stones,
and trees on the one hand and sandals, epic poems, and boards of trade on
the other, we are referring to different kinds of things; different kinds of
things are the objects of reference. Not all objects of reference are mind- or
language-dependent, though, as I stated earlier, nothing can be described
without recourse to descriptions.¹⁰ Second, we can make objectively, determinately true or false statements about either kind. That is, we can establish
with absolute certainty whether the following statements, "The dean is in
his office" and "Our pet duck is sitting on the pond," are true beyond any
shadow of a doubt by checking to see if the appropriate making-true conditions obtain—that is, by simply looking into the office or toward the pond
to see if the dean's in his office or the duck's on the pond. Finally, in
practical terms and relative to immediate *practical* contexts of meaning and
action, the distinction between mind-dependent and mind-independent
things has no very important ontological significance. Both kinds are real
and both are truth makers of assertions, propositions, beliefs, and so on.
And, interestingly, in terms of practical action or behavior, the status of the
object of reference (whether mind-dependent or mind-independent) is not
crucial to the beliefs and desires that rationalize (make intelligible) one's
actions relative to the object. Simply, whether the object in front of you is
a real gold nugget or an ersatz, handcrafted replica of one, the belief that
it is a gold nugget and the desire to have it for one's own will explain one's
reaching for it. In such practical contexts, beliefs and meanings (i.e., the
informational contents upon which one acts) are more important than references (i.e., the specific nature or physical constitution of the objects), since
actions are determined by the actual mental states that are the reasons for
them. Akeel Bilgrami makes the point by declaring that in local, practical
contexts of interpretation, he has "given up reference for beliefs and descriptions [because] there is no way to think of concepts being individuated
by external objects, except as constrained by an agent's beliefs."¹¹

Before moving to the next stage of these reflections, an excursus on realism and the correspondence theory of truth (the focus of the next chapter),
I need to remind the reader quickly of the overarching sense informing item
(1.a). What fuels or drives the cluster of claims in item (a) is the conviction
that things are dependent upon words and thoughts, not the belief that
thoughts and words are dependent upon things or the belief that our
thoughts have a source and guarantee in the way things are independently
of our contributions, of our various and contingent representations of them.

This is what antifoundationalism amounts to—the loss of any secure grounding for our claims. Since every act of seeing is a form of interpretation (a seeing in the light of what our categories and concepts disclose, not a seeing directly on), since a theory-neutral view of the world is impossible, and since, even when the same body of data is at issue (the same state of affairs, the same text, or whatever is concerned), an indefinite number of distinctly different and sometimes ostensibly conflicting hypotheses can accommodate and account for all the data—since all this is so, it has come to seem to the vast majority of current theorists that reality, such as it is, is various, something locally and contingently determined, and that truth, such as it is, is also contingent, defined in terms of local efficacy and established by various mechanisms of power and persuasion. To register a demurrer of any kind to any aspect—indeed, to any implication—of this congeries of claims and assumptions is to identify oneself as a (naive) realist and an advocate of a (naive) correspondence theory of truth.

I have already shown, I think, that although many truths are made true by local and contingent conditions, many others are not tied to particular times, places, or cultures. Some are logical, conceptual, analytic, or stipulated truths: husbands are male, a touchdown occurs under such and such conditions, and so on; and, once defined, "brinkmanship," along with countless other late-emerging and culture-specific categories or social constructions, can be applied cross-culturally and transtemporally to social and political conditions long past, as well as, prospectively, to those yet to come. Further, I have shown that in a vast number of cases whether we are talking about trees or touchdowns (bananas or bicycles, mountains or money, etc.) how things are at a distance from our representations determines the rightness or truth of the application of our terms and representations. I have shown, in other words, that what is represented is distinct from what does the representing and that, consequently (to supply a homely example), only my having waffles for breakfast (what is represented) can make true my truth claim about my breakfast, "I had waffles for breakfast" (what does the representing). If this is obvious, it is not trite or trivial. Without these conditions at a remove from our conceptual and linguistic resources, we would have nothing to apply (rightly or wrongly, correctly or incorrectly) our resources to and have, finally, no beliefs at all, since beliefs, to be beliefs, must be true or false, with the result depending on whether what the beliefs are about obtains or not, and nothing within the system of resources—considered apart from referentiality and the right application of terms of reference—is about or directed toward anything outside the system. Of course, many theorists positively embrace the view that language is self-reflexive and, hence, does not refer to extralinguistic facts, but because this view is the subject of item (d), I shall defer any further discussion of it here, noting only that once we let the nose of truth into the tent (once we make room for any kind of truth at all, as many of our theorists do by insisting that all *knowledge* is mediated—a truth claim if I ever saw one), we are well on our way to sharing our quarters with the whole camel—to having to deal with what is implicated in any truth claims.

Let me bring this brief overview of the terrain that we have so far traversed to a conclusion by recalling the principal points made about realism and the correspondence theory of truth earlier, as a prelude to the next chapter in which specific versions of both will be defended. First, I noted that realism is an ontological issue concerning modes of existence, whereas truth is a semantic one concerning meaning, reference, truth conditions, the relations between language and what it is directed to. Further, I demonstrated that conceptual relativity is not incompatible with belief in realism, that being a realist does not preclude the recognition and acceptance of various and divergent accounts of the same state of affairs. Finally, I argued that although most correspondence theorists are realists, the correspondence theory of truth does not logically or necessarily entail realism, since idealism, instrumentalism, and many other isms can produce correspondence theories of truth; a fortiori, the correspondence theory of truth is also consistent with conceptual relativity.

Chapter 2
Realism and Truth, Together Again

In the following discussion of the correspondence theory and realism, as they impinge on the concerns of item (1.a), I shall be working with a body of concepts exogenous to poststructuralism (and, hence, to most contemporary theorizing in literary studies) but indigenous to a broad segment of current philosophical writing—that is, concepts relating to people with attitudes about contents, to intentional states, to the thoughts and actions of agents, and so on. If we wish to talk about possible relations between our statements and the world or, more generally, relations among words, thoughts, and things, then we must initially find a way to get people and contents into play, because, given the reluctance of the world to supply ready-made categories or to express categorical preferences, the only way to the world as we know it is through the thoughts and words of the person, through the mental states and linguistic acts of agents.

The world or nature has no semantic preferences, no preferred descriptions, in the sense that it picks out only one among the indefinitely many possible descriptions as its very own (though of course it applies its imprimatur only to each and every true description). Every event can be described in infinitely many (true and false) ways, every object can belong to infinitely many classes of things, and no object or event can be completely described or classified—and all this is so because the world or nature is not in the defining, classifying, referring, representing business. Nature or the world doesn't know a thing about things, but it does know what it likes—it likes what, under the specified circumstances, is true, real, good, fitting, and beautiful (or so it seems). Its mercury molecules, even when housed in a thermometer, know nothing of temperature, know nothing, for that matter, either of mercury or molecules. Its hydrogen and oxygen atoms know nothing of water or of the various other things in which they participate. As real and as richly individuated as it is, nature is neither object-focused nor content-directed, and, sad to say, it knows nothing and means nothing.

In these respects, it is similar to such personally and humanly near and dear features of our existence as language and sensation, which, considered apart from intentional states, also have neither content nor meaning. As a system of formal relations, as, in short, a syntactical entity, language is a set of rules governing the ways in which strings of elements can be put together, with the nature of the elements—whether 1's and 0's or variously colored beads or large and small tin cans—being largely a matter of indifference. At the syntactic level, language is a formal system of allowable or appropriate moves with and among meaningless counters; it is only at the semantic level that language points beyond itself and has directedness to the world, has, as we say, intentionality.[1]

And as it is with linguistic units in their formal, syntactic relations, so it is with sensations or nerve stimulations, in that they likewise are without content or meaning. As Donald Davidson has noted, "although sensation plays a crucial role in the causal process that connects beliefs with the world, it is a mistake to think it plays an *epistemological* role in determining the *contents* of those beliefs," since contents are individuated by concepts—by mental states—not sensations; sensation is uniform, but content is various.[2] Briefly, the sensations or nerve stimulations will be the same regardless of how we construe or conceive of things. Whether I see what is before me as a water glass or a hollow cylinder with one closed end, as a tree or the largest object in the yard, as a piece of furniture or a source of fuel, as a stockbroker or a fellow commuter, the nerve stimulations—the physical sensations and electrochemical activity—will be the same. Without the sensations or stimulation I undoubtedly would not see any of the objects *as* anything, but the stimulations do not and cannot dictate what the objects will be seen *as*. For example, when my pet monkey, Murray, and I play catch with a red ball, we both have a red experience, but only I have an experience *of* red; in other words, we have what for the purposes of this argument we can call the same sensory stimulation, the same experience, but not the experience of the same thing, redness. Murray has, by my lights at least, no conception of red or, more exactly, no color qualia of any kind, since a creature must have color concepts to have color qualia. And, of course, what the monkey catches is a "ball" only to me.

If the preceding example smacks too much of speciesism, we can bring any human neonate to the witness stand: the newborn and I both hear the teakettle whistling—we hear exactly the same sounds, and they engage our nervous systems in the same activity—but only I hear the sound as "whistling" and as emanating from the "teakettle"; the infant is short, not on experience, but on representational skill. Or, if this example has the least odor of child bashing about it, take my situation before and after I learn that what is before me is a can opener. When I learn that the object is a can opener I undergo a change in my information state or representational repertoire (I will hereafter see it *as* a can opener) but not in my experience state, since on the neuronal or sensational level I see exactly what I saw before. Similarly, when *"La neige est blanche"* is spoken in my presence before and after I learn French, I do not hear different sounds at these different times (the neural, electrochemical activity remains essentially the same), but I do hear the sounds differently (after instruction, I hear them as elements of a meaningful assertion that an English speaker would be inclined to translate as "the snow is white." In other words, the learning process changes my epistemological condition, not my sensational condition, changes what I know, not the mechanism by which I came to know it.[3]

The aim of the immediately preceding discussion is to put legs under the not particularly revolutionary—indeed, in some circles, rather commonplace—idea that sensations or nerve stimulations, taken as biological or electrochemical phenomena, do not have content, in that they do not function informationally by representing something as something else, representing that over there, say, as a tree or tie rack, as something distant and distinct from whatever does the representing. For purposes of illustration, I have simplified matters, but in so doing I may have inadvertently obscured an important distinction by using the term "sensation" restrictively to refer exclusively to stimulations at nerve endings and the subsequent series of afferent and efferent nerve firings. Sensations as mental states—as distinct from brain or neuronal states—are representational or contentful in the sense that as perceptions and experiences they are directed to things and conditions apart from the mind or brain or nerve system in which they are registered. The can opener is not initially seen *as* a can opener, to be sure, but it is seen as a distinct bounded entity; the red ball is not seen as "red" and as a "ball," but it is seen as "redly" (rather than "bluely" or "greenly") and as suffusing a "round object"; and the pain I experience I experience, if not as "pain" (i.e., not conceptualized as pain), at least as unpleasant in an unidentified sense and as having a location (in my hand, in my leg, etc.—I have the pain at the periphery, at the site of the injury, not at the nerve center in the brain or in the electrochemicals).

As creatures, we seem to be prewired, predisposed, or precalibrated to have a certain range of sensations (with delimited amplitudes and intensities—natively disendowed of lynx's eye and dog's ear), a particular range of perceptions (with a tendency to privilege faces, people, and objects, especially medium-sized objects, rather than microscopic or macroscopic objects), and undoubtedly a specific range of cognitive resources for dealing with and manipulating what we feel and perceive (deduction, induction, analogy, extension, substitution, metaphor, synecdoche, irony, etc.).[4] At any rate, perceptual experience seems to be in some sense already concept-infused, already directed outward, already in a world- or content-directed orientation. Indeed, because we seem to be constitutionally equipped to make the cuts in the same places, to appeal, that is, to the same quality spacings (I see red as you see red) and to the same partitioning principles (I mark the boundary between this and that just as you do), we are in the epistemologically happy condition of being able to share the same world, to direct our attention to the same perceptual and conceptual features of the same world. This intersubjectivity—this sharing of references across subjec-tivities—provides the necessary framework, of course, for objectivity, for achieving objective knowledge of this and that, since it creates the condition for two and more people to agree on what's what by appealing to the same evidence, the same states of affairs, and the same worldly facts, or, on the linguistic side, by appealing to publicly shared meanings. But I get ahead of myself. Further commentary on shared objective knowledge will be deferred until later.

If sensations as mental states (as distinct from sensations as neurological or brain states) are inner states with what we might call a sense of direction, with, that is, a directedness to the world, then they are contentful, in the minimalist sense at least of having a relation to outward or extramental conditions. Nevertheless, full-fledged, bona fide, card-carrying content is the only begotten child and heir of intentionality—that "capacity of the mind to represent objects and states of affairs in the world other than itself . . . that feature of representations by which they are *about* something or *directed at* something."[5] What is more to the point of *particular* content, I suppose, is that not only do intentional states represent things and states of affairs in the world, but they also represent them *as* something, represent them under some aspect or another, so that whatever is taken by us is taken as given in a particular way or under a certain aspect. Our representations are concep-tual and aspectual, and all seeing is perspectival, a seeing-as. If at the per-ceptual or mere sensation level quality spacings and partitioning principles are honored (i.e., we distinguish among hues and cut our bounded entities in certain ways, cut them at what are for us the joints), it is at the intentional level that our concepts (and our conceptions of things) emerge, that we see red *as* red, blue *as* blue, and so on and identify that over there *as* a table, carburetor, fork, shoe, horse, martini, friend, tree, or grandmother. Inten-tional states are object-discriminating, content-involving states. In the ear-liest stages and at the most basic level our concepts and contents are undoubtedly fixed ostensively as a result of someone's pointing to or show-ing an object and pronouncing a name or quality in its presence; thus, words and things arise together, are coeval. Moreover, their co-emergence pre-cludes any skepticism about what corresponds to what, since it is clear, for example, that "dog" corresponds to dog, "tree" to tree, "red ball" to red ball. For all of us, our worlds begin with Helen Keller moments, with, that is, the recognition of the confraternity of word (sign) and thing (water), as one says to the other "*mon frère, mon semblable.*"

In the course of time it may, and invariably does, happen that the same thing or the same state of affairs is multiply described or identified; or because of differences in the circumstances at the originating scene of identification, it happens that what is individuated as this for me is individuated as that for you: in either case, what is water may also be H_2O, dog may also be *chien*, Uncle Bob may also be the cat burglar, the object in the corner may also be a chair, a piece of furniture, a source of fuel, and so on through a limitless list of variants. Consequently, for purposes of understanding or interpretation it is crucial to determine what particular intentional state is informing the linguistic or other behavior in use, inasmuch as specific content is a function of a person's local intentionality, a person's current attitude toward a presently individuated state of affairs. Content is always local. At the locality of use, meaning is fixed, not deferred. As has been frequently noted by many contemporary philosophers, to have a particular thought is to have a certain attitude—hoping, fearing, believing, suspecting—toward a certain content. To have a thought is to be in an intentional state, and to be in an intentional state is to have a particular attitude toward a propositional content (a belief, say, "that it is raining," "that it is a red ball," a desire, say, "that the Red Sox win the pennant," "that the car will start"). From all this it follows that the only local habitations of contents are intentional states and linguistic acts (at least such acts as have reference and meaning, for these are coterminous with content).

Thoughts (or propositional attitudes, or intentional states) are, then, inner states (beliefs, desires, wishes, fears, understandings, and so on) with an aboutness or directedness about them. And in our dealings with one another and the world we find them to be indispensable on two counts. In the first place, they are indispensable because, as we have seen, they are representational (i.e., they are inner representations of the external world, both the mind-dependent and mind-independent external world—indeed, any world that can be represented, any world to which reference can be made), and because nothing else is representational, not physics, not language—at least not as a system of sequence and substitution rules—not history, not neurons, not brain states, not anything else). To talk about anything at all is to presuppose such states. And they are indispensable, in the second place, because there's no accounting for action or behavior (as distinct from motion or movement), without them, in that they supply the necessary reasons for the actions, reasons that are also, most crucially, the causes of the action. I not only had my reasons for going to the bar for a martini, but those very reasons were the *cause* of my going to the bar. I *wanted* a martini, I *believed* I could get one at the bar, and, thus, I *went* across the room to the bar, doing so precisely *because* I had that desire and that belief. In Davidson's formulation, "actions are events which are intentional under some description, the description under which they are rationalized by the contents of the mental states which are the reasons for them."[6] If it's action (including linguistic action) or behavior (all the various doings of our livelong days) that has our interest (and how could it be otherwise when deciding, judging, making, and doing are inescapable and pervasive), then it's to intentional states that we must turn for our explanations, our reasons and causes.

Unquestionably, we are explaining creatures, as well as creatures in need of and in quest of explanations, and one would hardly be charged with presumption or courageous intrepidity for suggesting that notwithstanding our rage for all sorts of "scientific" and "technological" explanations, we are positive zealots for explanations of behavior and action, for explanations of action, rather than motion. In highlighting the difference between explanations of motion and explanations of action, Fred Dretske makes a telling and useful point when he observes that what "thoughts, feelings, and desires explain is not why your arm moves (when you move it intentionally), but why you move your arm."[7] The first sort of explanation—that is, of why your arm moves—is the province of neurophysiological psychology, of chemistry, physiology, brain studies, and so on, whereas the second sort— that is, of why you move your arm—belongs to philosophy and to foreign and domestic affairs, the affairs, that is, of everyday living, belongs to the world in which we are interested in understanding what people do and mean when they do and mean something.

Michael Dummett makes an analogous point about language and meaning, when he notes that "philosophy is not concerned with what enables us to speak as we do, but what it is for our utterances to have the meanings that they have, and nothing that happens in the brain can explain that."[8] To understand what enables us to speak, we can, at one level, call upon anatomy and physiology to elucidate the roles and functions of larynx, tongue, teeth, uvula, and so on and, at another level, upon brain studies to illuminate the workings of synapses, neurotransmitters, parallel distributed processing, modularity, connectionism, and more. But if our aim is to grasp what our sentences mean, then we must have recourse to the sorts of intentional states that motivate and endow with content all our actions, including our linguistic or verbal acts. Incidentally, the point that Dummett makes about brain states and the explanation of meaning applies as well to language, as we have seen above: nothing that happens in language as a formal system of combination and substitution rules can explain why our sentences mean what they mean.

Before returning to the issue of our concepts being fixed, at least initially or at the most basic level, by correlating utterances with external objects or events, I want to call attention to an important point that Dretske draws from discriminating between explanations of why your arm moves and explanations of why you move your arm: "Mental content can explain behavior without supervening on the neurophysiological events and processes that cause bodily movement. The mental is not robbed of its explanatory relevance by being extrinsic."⁹ Basically, then, movement and action require different kinds of explanations. And although I do not pretend to know what the percentages are, I can safely suppose, I think, that by a considerable percentage margin we are more interested day by day, week by week, lifetime by lifetime in action than in movement explanations. Also, although I believe it would be impossible to be in a mental state without being at the same time in a brain state, a brain state account of, say, arm activity would never be sufficient or satisfying to our interest in the activity as an action, if only because both our interest and the action belong outside the range of brain state explanations—because interest and action are terms belonging to systems of intentionality, not systems of physical states. As physical conditions within and among nerve cells, brain states do not represent external things, certainly not *as* external things, and they certainly do not represent them under specific aspects (as water, as H₂O, as trees, as rectangular, as red, as a frigate, etc.); they are not object-fixing or content-defining states, and, consequently, they cannot have any attitudes toward such objects that can function as reasons for the activity.

Moreover, because brain states are neither representational nor action-controlling, it seems evident that the same brain state (the one you're in when you're angry, say) could underlie many different actions (slamming the door, clenching your fist, muttering to yourself, grinning menacingly, kicking the dog, etc.), even as the same action (closing the door) could be correlated with many different brain states, the ones you're in when, say, you're cold or angry or in a blue funk or a brown study or disturbed by the noise from the street. Further, it is highly unlikely that everyone who wishes that it will rain tomorrow or believes that Grandma is old or fears that Venice is sinking or whatever is in the same brain state. Brain states can be appealed to in accounts of movement but not in accounts of action, because actions, unlike movements, belong to systems of rationality; that is, actions are rationalized by the contents of the mental states that are the reasons for them. Mere motions or movements have (physical) causes but no such rationalizations. The point here is that brain and mental states do not form (token-token or type-type) identity relations. But again, even if we assume— as I think we must—that for every particular propositional-attitude condition there is, necessarily, a brain-state condition that corresponds to it, the fact remains that the brain-state explanation cannot account for a good deal of what has our interest, cannot explain why you move your arm, why you avoid the dean, why Othello kills Desdemona, and so on. The mental state explanation cannot be reduced to the brain state explanation, and the former cannot be eliminated by the other. They explain different things, even as they both provide genuine explanations.

At this point, we can conveniently return to the issue of the correspondence of words and thoughts to things, to the simultaneous emergence of all three. At the simplest or most basic level, words and thoughts are about the things that cause them, regardless of whether those things are socially or artifactually constructed mind-dependent things such as touchdowns or tortillas or whether they are mind-independent things such as tornadoes or tomatoes. Crudely, you point to something that you call a tomato, and I make an identification of the word "tomato" and the concept and thing *tomato*; after pointing to another thing that I call "tomato," you say "yes," and I go home with a relatively, or at least temporarily secure tomato concept.

What causes our words and thoughts to have the contents they have is the result of this sort of direct confrontation with things external to the two participants, the pointer and the learner, and the condition of the possibility of thought and language is the *causal* and *conceptual* sharing of objects, things, and states of affairs in encountered worlds, for it is by such means that we establish things to refer to and talk about, establish, in short, content. And clearly, it is upon the condition of such sharing—such intersubjectivity relative to contents—that truth and objectivity are based, in that objective truth is a matter of things being as we represent them to be. So, whether there is a tomato in my basket depends—and depends only—on whether, in a world of tomatoes and baskets, there is a tomato in my basket. Thus, contrary to one of the principal tenets of item (a)—"there is no direct access to truth"—it seems that a kind of sense can be made of the view that we have "direct access to truth."

And item (a)'s companion view that "nothing is immediately given in experience" also seems somewhat less than self-evidently true, in that, at least according to one very influential position in contemporary philosophy, the contents "of our words and thoughts are *directly fixed* by our causal relations with whatever . . . things we interact with."[10] In short, the contents of many (perhaps the vast majority) of our words and thoughts are fixed by their actual causes, not by some linguistic or internal mediator (such as sensation or nerve stimulation). Exploring an interesting consequence of this view, Colin McGinn writes that "where the empiricists took meaning to be possible only if it stems from experience [i.e., all knowledge is mediated by our sensory mechanisms], Davidson takes the theory of meaning to be possible only if experience plays *no* role in fixing meaning [content]. Meaning, for him, results from a direct collision, or collusion, between belief and fact."[11] Of course, sensation and experience play a causal role in linking the world to people, but they do not play a role in fixing the content or meaning of a belief, in determining what we "know" or believe.[12]

A strikingly significant further consequence of this view is that it leaves no room for skepticism about our knowledge of the world, certainly not for the sort of radical Cartesian skepticism that suggests the possibility that for all we know all our thoughts and "experiences" are phantasms created by the illusionary tricks of a mad genius or that we are all brains in a vat. It may still be possible to have doubts about the truth of our beliefs in some circumstances (we may be deceived from time to time), and we may occasionally get some things wrong, but given the way we acquire our knowledge of the world, it is inconceivable that we could get most things wrong most of the time. On this point, Davidson speaks quite persuasively:

What a person's words mean depends in the most basic cases on the kinds of objects and events that have caused the person to hold the words to be applicable; similarly for what the person's thoughts are about. An interpreter of another's words and thoughts must depend on scattered information, fortunate training, and imaginative surmise in coming to understand the other. The agent herself, however, is not in a position to wonder whether she is generally using her own words to apply to the right objects and events, since whatever she regularly does apply them to gives her words the meanings they have. Of course, in any particular case, she may be wrong in what she believes about the world; what is impossible is that she should be wrong most of the time. The reason is apparent: unless there is a presumption that the speaker knows what she means, i.e., is getting her own language right, there would be nothing to interpret. To put the matter another way, nothing could count as someone regularly misapplying her own words.[13]

Moreover, because it is impossible to have a thought without thinking *about* something in some way (i.e., under some aspect, from some perspective), to have a thought is to have a certain attitude about a *particular* content—for example, to believe that Bob is the shortest person in the class; in this case, the attitude is a belief about Bob. Bob is the intentional object of the intensional content—the belief—that he is the shortest person in the class. As with all intentional states (or propositional attitudes), this belief has satisfaction conditions, which in this case, since we are talking about a belief, are truth conditions. This belief is true if and only if Bob is the shortest person in this particular class, if and only if the condition of Bob's being "shorter than" is satisfied relative to each and every other member of the class. With regard to this belief (and countless others) we can have absolute, unequivocal, objective knowledge of its truth or falsity. And since we believe only what is true (what we believe to be true), the content of a belief is the particular condition under which it is true. The content of a desire, on the other hand, is the condition under which it is satisfied—a desire is satisfied or not by the realization of certain, very specific conditions, those answerable to the specific content of the desire. In other words, since the content of an intentional state (desire, belief, or whatever) is aspectual, the conditions under which the state is satisfied must be those under which the state does its representing. That is, the desire for a glass of water is satisfied by a glass of water, not a glass of H_2O, since it is *as* water that the substance is desired; similarly, my wish to have a drink with your favorite cousin will not be satisfied if the person who elbows up to me at the bar is the notorious night stalker (who is also, unhappily, your favorite cousin), since the night stalker does not answer to the content of my wish, my intentional state. I have no desire to have a nightcap with the night stalker.

As should be abundantly clear by now, we need intentional states to gain access to content. In the line of philosophical thought that I am following, there is no content apart from intentional states. Furthermore, content at the most basic level (and in the vast majority of cases) is a function of two or more individuals sharing a *causal* and *conceptual* relation to objects or events in the external world. And because the acquisition of our concepts (and hence, of content) occurs in a specific, usually ostensive, context, our concepts of the external world are always aspectual (we have no access to things themselves, to things in their essential nature—as several philosophical wags have noted, there is no essence to reference). Now, all this matters to us for the simple reason that it is because intentional states have specific, publicly sharable aspectual content that we can come to understand and explain human action, including linguistic action, since it is clear that our actions are determined by how we size things up, by how we understand things to be. The importance of intentional states as *representational states* (i.e., as inner representations of the external world) *and* as *inner states* (such as belief, desire, hope, fear, etc.) that are causally responsible for behavior should now be evident. We act the way we do because we believe things to be a certain way, the way we represent them to be; our belief in the representation is determined by the truth of our representation, by whether the external situation is as we represent it to be (whether the external situation *corresponds* to our representation of it); and our representation has the content it has as a result of the contextual conditions of its acquisition. Akeel Bilgrami makes the point quite economically: "Intentional states such as beliefs and desires get their point and rationale from the role they play in the commonsense psychological explanation of behavior. . . . What makes it possible for intentional states to have a role in the . . . explanation of behavior . . . is the very fact of their possessing content which is externally constituted."[14]

We are now in a position to understand clearly why a correspondence theory of truth is perfectly compatible with the notion of conceptual relativity. Because the same state of affairs can be truly represented in many different ways, it can supply truth conditions for many different beliefs and function in many different conceptual schemes. And since we act upon things according to our conception of them, the same state of affairs can be responsible for a diverse range of behaviors.[15] As I noted much earlier, in the system of ideas that I have been outlining, words, thoughts, and things emerge together, and, thus, there can be no question of what corresponds to what. But ultimately, whatever emerges is externally constituted (unless, of course, our concern is with formal or a priori truths, those of logic, arithmetic, verbal definition, or terminological relation, for example). The success of our various conceptual schemes—at least all those with content—

rests finally on the conformity of the statements we make within each scheme to the way things are. Success here is another name for truth, and conformity another name for correspondence.

Of course, there is perhaps nothing of which a current theorist is more certain than that the correspondence theory of truth is hokum, bunk, nonsense—the assumptions underlying item (a) are quite vociferous on the point—yet it is precisely this theory on which we rely every day of our lives in our dealings with one another and the world, whenever we attempt to explain or to understand the behavior of the people with whom we interact or try to justify to ourselves and others the actions we perform or the meanings we express. Whenever in our efforts to understand one another we relate actions or behavior to mental states we necessarily appeal to our commonsense principles of psychology, which presuppose people with attitudes about contents, i.e., intentional states directed to external objects or states of affairs. Our commonsense psychology goes along with a commonsense view of external objects, in that, except when we are operating under special circumstances (when, say, we are in the lab or on the heights of Mount Afflatus), our attention is generally directed to people whose contentful focus is not on microscopic (a human is not a fly) or on macroscopic (a human is not an angel taking in the all in all) but on medium-sized objects. Our commonsense psychology and folk metaphysics would seem to be better than true, useful, and beautiful; they are apparently indispensable, at least so long as we continue to have our cakes and eat them, too, to grant and deny tenure, to purchase Swedish automobiles, to colonize native populations, to Disneyize or otherwise Americanize France, to evaluate, grade, pass, fail students, to tickle the ivories, to fetishize our commodities, and so on.

A correspondence theory of truth that allows for multiple true descriptions of the same state of affairs would seem to elude all the objections raised by theorists against that bogeyman correspondence theory, which is the only begotten son and heir of naive realism or foundationalism, but to which, as far as I can tell, no one today has declared a profession of faith, even though we are regularly assured that there are countless extant specimens of true believers in such a naive theory. At any rate, it is clear that, as Frederick Schmitt notes, "when we explain human behavior, including our linguistic behavior (our writings, our texts, for example) by ascribing beliefs and desires, we implicitly use a correspondence notion of truth." Furthermore, as we have seen (and as Schmitt goes on to observe), "ascribing beliefs and desires to others for purposes of explaining their behavior requires ascribing propositional contents to these beliefs and desires. That is, it requires treating the beliefs and desires as having propositions as contents." Now, "to ascribe contents to beliefs and desires is to ascribe truth-conditions to these beliefs and desires, since propositions necessarily carry with them truth-conditions."[16] From all this, we easily conclude that the correspondence theory of truth can be appropriately invoked as the theory of record for an immense variety of claims, indeed, all those that have content and, hence, truth conditions, all those informed directly or indirectly by intentional states.

Moving now to the issue of realism, it seems clear to me that for the contents of our propositions to serve as truth conditions, there must be a way that things are that our intentional states can correctly or incorrectly represent; that is, our representations are true or false, depending on the way things are, on the nature of the external facts of the matter. If the facts of the matter were facts internal to the representations or the representational devices (sounds, markings, or, more generally, language), there would be nothing outside the system of language relative to which the representations would be correct or incorrect, right or wrong; there would be no correct representations and no misrepresentations. Indeed, there would be no genuine representations, only formal relations between and among symbols, markings. It seems, then, that along with an enriched, though quite commonplace, correspondence theory of truth, we are stuck with a rather plebeian, ordinary, blonde-wood, peas and carrots conception of external reality. Stuck at least with the view that there is a realm of things and states of affairs that is independent of any of our representations, a realm against which any of our representations, however mundane or arcane, can be checked for rightness, accuracy, correctness, truth.

In the affairs of quotidian life we manage quite nicely with our rather homely but quite serviceable conception of reality that gives prominence to people with attitudes toward mostly medium-sized things, who because of such attitudes function as agents of actions. I walk to the fridge to get a beer, and I do so because I want a beer and believe that one can be found in the fridge and that one can be had by walking over to the fridge and opening the door; this combination of belief and desire *causes* me to walk to the fridge and to open its door. In many of our more specialized lives we are concerned with greater or lesser objects, sometimes even with general or abstract "objects," and concerned with them not relative to the mental states and behavior of some agent, but relative to physical forces of movement or motion (or perhaps relative to hidden psychological or astral forces or influences). Of course, to be concerned with anything at all—even an existence-independent thing such as a tooth fairy or leprechaun—is to be in a contentful mental state, is to have an attitude toward a particular content. Nevertheless, abroad in the land are those who are determined to put aside agents and actions, along with their attitudinal auxiliaries, and to replace them with or subordinate them to physical, linguistic, or social forces and motions, to chemical or subatomic particles in motion, to electrochemical brain states, to one or another kind of genetic determinism, to the nature of language as such—to its structural and formal obligations and proclivities, to the discursive moves allowable within dominant or prevailing social vocabularies, and so on. It is difficult to understand how these folks could believe that these views are true, since to do so is to betray an allegiance to the country from which you defect.

Undoubtedly, much is to be learned by studying things in terms of atomic particles and behavior in terms of brain states, neurons, and neurotransmitters, but despite what certain cognitive scientists or students of artificial intelligence claim or what certain physicalists or eliminativists (all those who would reduce everything to matter in motion, to the closed world of physics—closed, that is, to mental states and consciousness) assert, the ordinary, everyday world of people and familiar objects stubbornly refuses to go away and unashamedly continues to provide the material for necessary and useful explanations. That world is not and cannot be supplanted by, eliminated in favor of, or reduced to the world of physics. Lynne Rudder Baker wisely observes that a "psychology that did not employ concepts (like belief) from the framework of commonsense psychology would threaten the conception of persons neither more nor less than a physics that employed no concepts of medium-sized objects would threaten mundane truths like 'upholstered chairs are more comfortable than church pews.' "[17] From our durable and enduring need for certain kinds of objects and certain kinds of explanations of engagements with objects, we can conclude, with Baker, that "the commonsense conception of reality . . . is not wholesale replaceable by a theory or by anything else that lacks categories for medium-sized objects or for persons with attitudes with propositional content." Her position "is not that the commonsense conception is knowable a priori but, rather, that it is required to serve our (nonoptional) interests in getting along in the world."[18] Also, although we have plenty of examples of theory revision in commonsense psychology (we always stand ready to revise our explanations of behavior in the light of new information or subsequent behavior), we have no instances of jettisoning the commonsense theory altogether. "In contrast to the cases of theory change [in, say, physics, chemistry, molecular biology, astronomy, genetics, optics, or alchemy], we have no historical examples," Baker insists, "of any society's ever having abandoned the commonsense conception of persons with intentional states."[19] It is not very clear how a society could consent to do so. And whatever an eliminativist may be in the lab, she is a person with attitudes about contents when she stands before a lectern at a conference, drives home, feeds the dog, gets a beer from the fridge, swings a racquet, offers uncomplicated congratulations to a colleaque who has been awarded the grant for which she also competed, and so on.

As I turn now to a brief consideration of realism before concluding my reflections on item (a), it is important to recall what was said earlier about realism, truth, and the correspondence theory. What postmodernist theorists have invariably assumed is that to be opposed to their views is to be committed to a simple correspondence theory of truth and a naive realism, and committed to both because, it is assumed, one entails the other. As we have repeatedly seen, however, one can support the correspondence theory and realism without endorsing views that are either simple or naive. With regard to the correspondence theory, I have shown, I think, that it has no necessary commitment to any particular ontology, and, further, that it is entirely compatible with conceptual relativity—with, that is, multiple descriptions of the same objects, events, or states of affairs. Truth, as we have seen, is a semantic, not an ontological, matter, one dealing with such things as meaning, reference, and truth conditions and, thus, inseparable from intentionality, the representational capacity of the mind. It is the case, of course, that according to the correspondence theory of truth, a claim, assertion, or proposition is true only if it corresponds to the way things are, corresponds to the facts, but nothing in this conception of relations compels the conclusion that the facts are "realistic" facts, rather than, say, "idealistic" facts (or language- or culture-derived facts).

Realism is undoubtedly the concept that produces the most difficulty for us, since in the common understanding it seems to presuppose a rich amalgam of more or less well defined or circumscribed objects or things existing antecedently of language, mind, consciousness, or representation, an assortment of somethings that our representations must square with to be true. The difficulty emerges when to this understanding we add the commonly held but apparently incompatible notions that there are, for us, no things, objects, or experiences apart from mind, language, consciousness, or representations, that this object before us is one thing under one description and quite another under a different description, and that every account or representation of reality is interest-relative, context-dependent, and conceptual scheme–determined (is, alternatively, discourse-derived or socially constructed). To say that the difficulty comes about as a consequence of confusing semantic, empirical, or linguistic matters with ontological ones is, although true, perhaps not much help in untangling or cutting the perplexed knot. Nor, I suppose, do the scales fall from the eyes when I affirm that the kind of realism that I am prepared to endorse is simply the ontologically prior *logical* condition of the possibility of any representation whatsoever. But I believe something in the way of plain sense can be relatively quickly extracted from these cryptic remarks.

From the beginning we should understand that realism is an ontological matter (one relating to modes of existence or to the possibility of modes of existence), and, as such, it neither sponsors nor entails any specific theory of *truth, language,* or *knowledge*; it does not say what objects there are, how they are to be described, or how we come to know them.[20] Moreover, as we have repeatedly seen, realism is consistent with conceptual relativity, with the view that different, even incommensurable, descriptions of the same things or states of affairs are equally faithful to reality. Realism is no more threatened by the prospect that the dining room table is at one and the same time both a solid object and a gappy bundle of fermions than it is by the fact that it is both rectangular and wooden (or, analogously, by the fact that the morning newspaper is both readable and combustible, as well as being solid and porous and a tool of market capitalism). At this point we can take our cue once again from William Alston (whose view I cited earlier, in chapter one): "Ontological [or conceptual] relativity leaves us able to affirm that the *one real world* is such as to accommodate all the conceptualizations that we can *successfully* work with, and is such as to *ground* discriminations between true and false statements inside each conceptual scheme."[21] Realism doesn't say how things are in the world (such saying is the job of a conceptual scheme, a point of view, an interest-relative description), but it does grant operating permits to some and not other conceptual schemes. It also allows us to differentiate true from false claims within systems of representation, to determine in a manner that is as objective as objective gets whether such and such is the case or not—whether, for example, the dog is on the prowl, the pie on the table, the wound on the mend, or the refrigerator on the fritz (because such things will be so or not only if the *conditions* upon which their truth depends actually obtain); relative to the medium-sized object ontological scheme, it is possible to determine absolutely, once and for all, and beyond a shadow of a doubt whether the pie is on the table—if the *truth conditions* of the claim obtain (if, that is, the pie is on the table), then the *statement* that the pie is on the table is, make no mistake about it, true.

Characteristic of virtually every form of poststructuralist theorizing are *radical skepticism* about the possibility of objective knowledge and *radical relativism* with regard to conceptual schemes. On the other hand, the kind of realism that we are endorsing puts severe restrictions on conceptual schemes, admitting only those that we can successfully work with, and establishes criteria by means of which we can determine the truth or falsity of statements made within any work-with-able conceptual scheme. The sad truth is that realism has room for both conceptual relativity and objective truth, but the radical relativism and skepticism of poststructuralist thought have no room for realism.

Still, we need to remember that reality itself has no point of view; it is, rather, what makes *true* and *good* and *valid* points of view (and true and good and valid claims within each point of view) possible. It is a logico-formal realm rather than a realm of entities, properties, features, or qualities. Speaking of the function of language, Raymond Tallis makes a point about reality that is useful to our interests here. For Tallis, reality is not "already ordered into facts, waiting to be reflected in the mirror of language." Quite the contrary, "it is language that orders reality into factual reality; it transforms reality into truth conditions of factual assertions."[22] We can broaden the point to cover conceptual schemes and, even more broadly, intentional states generally, as well as language, since both meaning and content subserve intentionality, and meaning and content determine the truth conditions of our truth claims. So, if language—or, more extensively, intentional states—transforms reality into the truth conditions of factual assertions, then reality is the condition of the possibility of such transformation. And this is so for the good and simple reason stated much earlier in this piece: if representations are to be representations of anything at all, then there must, of necessity, be something of which they are the representations. Representations are not equivalent to what they are representations of; they cannot be without losing their function as representations. To take the simplest of cases, I represent the tall leafy object over there as "tree," the round piece of metal as "money," the thing on my foot as "shoe," and so on even to the limits of abstraction. (Abstractions or general categorical terms are as real as rocks and stones and trees; for example, the "office of the dean"— i.e., the academic post of dean—is ascertainably real, in that we can determine that the office may really be empty—i.e., there is no incumbent—even when the dean's office is really full—of furniture, painters, electricians, etc., and vice versa.) In John Searle's words, "The claim [being made here] is that reality is not *logically constituted* by representations. [Quite the reverse is the case, in that reality is the logically prior condition of all representations.] Representations are one thing, the reality represented another, and the point is true *even if it should turn out that the only actual reality is mental states.*"[23]

Perhaps the clearest expression of the position I am attempting to articulate here has been given by Searle:

Realism is the view that there is a way that things are that is *logically* independent of all human representations. Realism does not say how things are but only that there is a way that they are. And "things" in the previous two sentences does not mean material objects [i.e., objects in space and time] or even objects [realism does not mean the existence of matter]. It is, like the "it" in "It is raining," not a referring expression.[24]

By way of analogy, we can think of realism as we think of, say, rationality. On the one hand, rationality is the condition of the possibility of meaningful utterance; without rationality, the utterance has no sense or content of any kind. It is only in relation to a set of justification conditions, a structure, a "form of life" (as Wittgenstein says)—in short, a system of rationality—that the words make sense, have meaning. On the other hand, each utterance has its own particular rationality or set of justification conditions. So, rationality can be discussed as a condition of the possibility of any meaning whatsoever and as the particular system of rationality that informs the local utterance with its determinate meaning. (Determinate meaning, I know, is one of the concepts most vigorously contested by theorists—about which I shall say much more below, when we move to other items.) Similarly, realism is the formal and contentless condition of the possibility of any representation's having representational content; without external reality as an operational assumption (i.e., without the assumption of a reality external to our representations or conceptual schemes), there is nothing that the representations can be representations *of*; there are no potential contents that can serve as truth conditions of our representations. On the other hand, each particular representational system or scheme of representation has its own set of truth conditions to which it must conform if it aspires to truth in any real sense. So, realism can be discussed as the logical condition of the possibility of content *or* in terms of the set of local conditions conferring truth (or falsity) upon our beliefs in particular contexts of representation.

That there is a way that things are independently of our representations, then, is not itself a truth condition but a condition of the possibility of contentful expressions with truth conditions. Reality is not interest-relative, but without its presupposition the truth or falsity of none of the things distinguished by our interest-relative schemes could be established. Simply, we decide to call a certain creature a cat and a certain object a mat, but whether what is on the mat is a cat or whether what the cat is on is a mat is not up to us, since our claim that a cat is on the mat is true only if certain conditions independent of our representation obtain, only if the claim squares with the "facts" of the matter. But, of course, there is no transcendental realm, a reality, where cats always already sit on mats, a realm to which the contingent world can come into a relation of correspondence. As Searle explains,

The point is not that in understanding the utterance we have to presuppose the existence of specific objects of reference, such as Mt. Everest, hydrogen atoms, or dogs [or cats and mats in my example]. No, the conditions of intelligibility are still preserved even if it should turn out that none of these ever existed. The existence of Mt. Everest is one of the truth conditions of the statement; but the existence of a way that things are in the world independently of our representations of them is not a truth condition but rather a condition of the form of intelligibility that such statements have. The point is not epistemic. It is about conditions of intelligibility and not conditions of knowledge. . . . The point is simply that when we understand an utterance of the sort we have been considering, we understand it as presupposing a publicly accessible reality.[25]

Throughout most of the immediately preceding discussion the focus has been on mind-independent things such as cats, dogs, hydrogen atoms, Mount Everest, and so on, but the case for the kind of realism we are advocating applies equally well to artifacts and such socially constructed, mind-dependent things as marriages, touchdowns, stock markets, money, and so on. As Searle notes, "any truth claim presupposes that there is a way that things are regarding the content of that claim," whether we are dealing with "mathematical statements such as $2+2=4$ . . . statements about personal experiences such as 'I am in pain,' " or social statements such as "the wedding will be at two o'clock."[26]

In a much earlier discussion, we established that specific content depends on intentional states; such states are representational states, and, according to Dretske, "all representational facts are facts about information functions."[27] That is, representational facts represent something *as* something, represent this as that, for example, this piece of metal as a coin, the *as-relation* constituting the information function. The functional states of things depend on our intentional states, since functions are not intrinsic to the physical nature of things but are assigned to things by creatures with mental states, by namers and users. What has been assigned the informational function of metal (metal knows nothing of metal, knows not its own name) is then given the additional informational function of money. Thus, a mind-independent thing such as a piece of copper takes on the mind-dependent, socially constructed function of money. With the notation of this reliance of the mind-dependent (the socially constructed) on the mind-independent we can bring this excursus on realism to conclusion, giving Searle the last word on the topic:

Marriage and money, unlike mountains and stars, do not exist independently of all representations [they are socially constructed] . . . [but it is clear that] a socially constructed reality presupposes a nonsocially constructed reality. . . . Because the logical form of the creation of socially constructed reality consists in iterations of the structure X counts as Y in C [i.e., this piece of metal counts as a penny under these socially agreed upon conditions], the iterations must bottom out in an X element that is not itself an institutional [i.e., social] construction.[28]

In the end, much of what is stated and implied in item (a) is open to serious challenge. As we have seen, our access to truth can be direct, if the contents of our thoughts are directly fixed by what causes them, and if we are mostly right about what we believe. And if our thoughts are fixed by such causal encounters, then something is immediately given in experience. Moreover, although what we *know* is mediated by our descriptions, there is no reason why we cannot make discriminations among descriptions, distinguishing better from worse, right from wrong, true from false. And finally, if all knowledge involves interpretation (all seeing, as we have seen, is seeing-as, and seeing-as is, of course, a form of interpretation) and is, thus, antifoundational, the facts remain that some interpretations are better than others and that all things bottom out in noninstitutional facts and depend, finally, on how things are independently of our interpretations.

Chapter 3
Conceptual Relativity and Relativism

In this chapter I shall consider items (1.b) and (1.c) in relation to relativism, reserving for the following chapter a consideration of them in relation to interpretation and stable meaning. Items (b) and (c) can conveniently be considered together, since they are inextricably entangled with each other and, in their expression, are perfectly outfitted to serve together as poster children of the self-immolation that characterizes so many of the commonsense-defying pronouncements by means of which current theorists elicit our startled attention. In open-faced, if not, alas, in shamefaced impudence, they insist that

(b) A text is incapable of conveying a determinate, stable meaning

and that

(c) A text is incapable of communicating a coherent message.

Now, one might observe immediately that one could do no greater violence to (b) and (c) than to affront—indeed, assault—them with understanding, for understanding what they say and mean constitutes an ontological threat to their well-being. To the extent that (b) conveys a determinate, stable meaning and (c) communicates a coherent message, the two statements (these two texts) are false if true; they are, as we say, self-refuting, in that the incapability that they express is violated in the process of its expression. Because the meanings expressed are determinate, stable, and coherent, the sentences realize precisely those conditions that, the sentences affirm, are beyond their achievement.

What needs to be recognized at the outset, I think, is that the problem identified here (i.e., self-refutation) is not a local phenomenon, afflicting only these two sentences, but is endemic to every branch of current theory that subscribes to skepticism or relativism about truth, that denies that our meanings can be determinate, that our knowledge about this or that can transcend class, culture, interpretive community, or whatever, or that our understanding or interpretation can be justified in an absolute, objective sense. The problem with these sentences is of a piece with that internal to such other self-igniting commonplaces of current theory as, for example, "A text has no intrinsic meaning but means what a given reader/audience takes it to mean,"[1] and "There is no absolute or universal truth—every truth is relative to a conceptual/linguistic framework . . . , [to] the [interpretive] . . . community, [the] race, gender, class, or culture that . . . 'constitutes' or 'constructs' it."[2] The unstable rock upon which these and so many other truth claims of current theory are founded is, of course, relativism. Or, perhaps more aptly, relativism is the true bride of self-refutation for whom objectivity and determinacy of meaning are anathema or are the alluring but, finally, impossible shapes by which the Antichrist hopes to lure the naive into simple belief.

It is important to recognize, for example, that (b) and (c), in addition to being internally self-defeating or self-contradictory (by virtue of their coherence and determinacy), are the natural progeny of the kind of relativism that has our immediate interest here and, hence, are implicated, at one remove, in an additional form of self-refutation, as a result of their genetic endowment, their inherited complicity with the originating sin. The network of affiliation works this way: Texts—or claims—are incapable of conveying determinate, coherent meanings or messages *because* their meanings (and thus their truths) are not "intrinsic" but relativized to readers/audiences or to linguistic/conceptual frameworks, interpretive communities, cultures, and so on. All truths and meanings are, then, as a matter of conceptual necessity, "truths-and-meanings-for-me" (or "for-you") or "truths-and-meanings-for-us" (or "for-them"), that is, truths and meanings with their scare quotes on ("truths" and "meanings"), shuddering in fear of being accused of suggesting that even within a particular scheme or culture there could be absolute, objective truth or genuine determinacy of meaning. With such relativizing comes incommensurabilities, for what is true or meaningful for this reader/community/class, and so on is not true or meaningful for that one, since truths are constituents of meanings, and meanings are constituted by readers/communities/classes. Of course, we must always keep in mind that the orthodox, true-believing relativist would, mind-bogglingly, insist that the truth or meaning that is "true" and "meaningful" relative to such and such conceptual scheme or culture or community is itself relative, since, by doxy, there can be no stable, fixed, determinate meaning, and anything suggestive of objective truth, even within a particular conceptual framework, would be tantamount to apostasy. As a result of their implication in this network, (b) and (c) participate in the self-refutation of the encompassing relativism, since (b) and (c), like all the other claims we are considering, appear to articulate absolute and universal truths, to make claims, at any rate, whose meaning and intelligibility are in no way dependent upon the assumptions or directives of any specific community or audience, other than the broad English-speaking audience.

To what community of interest must one belong to determine the intelligibility of the claim that "every truth is relative to a conceptual/linguistic framework," or to enunciate the claim that "a text has no intrinsic meaning but means what a given reader/audience takes it to mean," or that "a text is incapable of conveying a determinate, stable meaning"? Clearly, neither the production nor the reception of these claims depends upon membership in any particular race or class or interpretive community at any specific time or place. On the contrary, the claims appear to be setting forth, in no uncertain terms, what simply and absolutely is the case for me and for you, now and in the time to come, what indeed is, has been, and always will be the case, forever and ever, thereby violating or invalidating the sense of what they expressly state. The conditionality or relativity of meaning, its historical, cultural, or personal contingency, is apparently lost in the absoluteness and universality of its expression. The engineer is hoisted with his own petard; the canker is in the rose; the claims are self-refuting. Unless, of course, the contingency or relativity applies to the claims themselves, but if this is so, then the capacity to mean or think anything at all would seem to be placed in jeopardy, if only because one cannot conceive of a way to make the large, general claims according to the restrictive covenants of a class, gender, interpretive community, or whatever. There simply is no way of saying or thinking the thoughts without violating the conditionality upon which the relativist insists.

In the process of showing how (b) and (c) implicitly participate in the self-refutation inherent in relativism, I may have inadvertently obscured or confused issues that need to be clearly distinguished. So, in the interests of clarity, I offer the following overview of the issues under discussion: The claims of (b) and (c) are self-refuting because, despite what is claimed in them, they determinately and coherently express themselves. They link up with relativism more generally because, as claims, they depend, at least in part, upon prior assumptions about meanings and truths being unstable and indeterminate as a consequence of their relativity to people, cultures, or communities, as a consequence, in my examples, of their relativity to readers ("A text has no intrinsic meaning but means what a given reader/audience takes it to mean") or to the conceptual frameworks of interpretive communities, classes, cultures, and so on. ("There is no absolute or universal truth—every truth is relative to a conceptual/linguistic framework . . . to the [interpretive] community, race, gender, class, or culture that somehow 'constitutes' or 'constructs' it.")

Now, these representative instances of relativism are self-refuting, because, in the first case, what the claim about reader determination means is not differently determined by each reader and because, in the second case, understanding or assenting to the truth of the interpretive-community claim does not hinge on membership in any particular community. Furthermore, both instances are self-refuting because the claims they make are large, general, absolute, universal claims about the way things are, precisely the sorts of nonhistorical, noncontingent claims expressly denied passports to the realm of meaning and truth by relativists. To the extent that (b) and (c) derive their warrant from an underlying assumption about the relativity of meaning and truth, they too participate in this form of self-refutation, for they too are general, universal claims about what is the case for all meanings regardless of subsidizing authority, whether class, race, culture, historical period, or whatever.

The point of this whole discussion is to clear up any lingering confusion about conceptual relativity and relativism so that we can subsequently address the possibility (indeed, as I shall argue, the inevitability) of determinate meanings and coherent messages, the two things denied by (b) and (c). It is certainly true that we cannot talk about anything at all in the absence of some conceptual scheme, some system of rationality, warrant, or justification. It is only by relying on some conceptual scheme that we can identify and discuss things and their relations and values, and there are clearly no meanings apart from conceptual schemes. It is only within conceptual schemes that there are truths and meanings. So, we concede this much to relativism: meaning and truth are relative to conceptual scheme. But from this concession it does not follow, as relativists seem to think, that we are deprived of access to objective truth and determinate meaning.

Among true relativists the prevailing view is that to say that something is true within a given discursive framework is not to say anything about it that is true in any real sense, any truly objective sense, but only something that is "scheme-true" or "true-for-me," not generally true or true for-him/her/them/us, as well as for me. (Fully extended, or tracked to its lair, this view leads to methodological solipsism, where each relativist—or community of relativists—lives in the splendid isolation of monkish "monadicism.") But, as I argued earlier, although the fact that my living-room chair is upholstered is true—and only true—within the substance/property ontology or the medium-sized object conceptual scheme, it is also an absolutely and objectively true fact within that scheme. Moreover, it is as true for me as it is for you, and as true now as it was yesterday and as it will be tomorrow. Additionally, it is a general truth, a truth not *of* the conceptual scheme but *about* it, for, like you and everyone else, I cannot *discuss* the scheme from within it. To say that something is true according to some conceptual scheme or, for that matter, according to this or that cultural or economic model is not to say something from within the scheme or model, but to state an objective fact about the scheme or culture from outside it (though not, of course, outside all conceptual or linguistic schemes altogether—there's no saying what things are like outside all conceptual schemes).

With the relativist, then, we can assent to the tautological claim that it is impossible to describe reality or anything else without relying on descriptions, to provide an account of anything at all without having recourse to some linguistic/conceptual regimen or scheme, but we part company with our fellow "relativist" when it comes to the issue of assigning objectivity to our scheme-dependent knowledge and determinate meaning to our utterances. The denial of any objective truth is a central or cardinal feature of the relativist's faith. As Hilary Putnam observes, "The whole *purpose* of relativism, its very defining characteristic, is . . . to *deny* the existence of any intelligible notion of *objective* 'fit.' Thus the relativist cannot understand talk about truth in terms of *objective* justification conditions."[3]

In the Western tradition, the primal scene of the relativism controversy is found in *Theaetetus*, the dialogue in which Socrates subjects to examination Protagoras's relativistic doctrine that man is the measure of all things, a doctrine precluding objective judgment, since when each man supplies the measure of evaluation, no measure can be taken as authoritative; the situation is as Alexander Pope described it many centuries later in his *Essay on Criticism*: " 'Tis with our judgments as our watches, none/Go just alike, yet each believes his own."[4] Of course, as Socrates goes on to show, the doctrine itself would seem to be exempt from the condition it depicts, in that it describes in no uncertain and quite universal terms how it is with us, with all of us who take the measure of things. Moreover, it offers itself to us, at least implicitly, as superior to its negate or to any alternative doctrine, as, in short, better than the doctrines of Tom, Dick, and Harry. Despite having sustained a death blow in perhaps its first major contest, relativism has enjoyed an enduring spectral existence, troubling the world's peace in every age and finding in every period, it seems, its myrmidons and acolytes.

One of relativism's most recent and most vigorous defenders is Barbara Herrnstein Smith, who, in *Belief and Resistance*, asserts that relativism does not reduce to an "anything goes" policy (to the view that any opinion or judgment is as good as any other, as naive readers of the Protagorean doctrine have suggested); on the contrary, it allows for "better" and "worse" judgments but by relying on something other than "objective" measures. Only those "classical scholars" operating "within the closures of traditional epistemology and philosophy of language"—that is, all those who are not postmodern relativists, but especially those trained in the analytic tradition—stick with the "unshakable conviction that differences of 'better' and 'worse' must be objective or could not otherwise be measured." Smith (linking

herself with the countertradition of relativism, which by her reckoning includes in its ranks, in addition to Protagoras, such luminaries as Friedrich
Nietzsche, Thomas Kuhn, Paul Feyerabend, Michel Foucault, Jacques Derrida, Jean-François Lyotard, Nelson Goodman, and Richard Rorty) goes on
to explain how evaluations could be measured otherwise:

> Not all theories are equal because they . . . can be, and commonly will be, found
> better or worse than others in relation to measures such as *applicability, coherence,*
> *connectability* and so forth. These measures are not objective in the classic sense,
> since they depend on matters of perspective, interpretation, and judgment, and will
> vary under different conditions. Nevertheless, they appear to figure routinely, and
> operate well enough, in scientific, judicial, and critical practice. Thus theories, judg-
> ments, or opinions (and so on) may still be seen as better or worse even though not,
> in a classic sense, as more or less objectively valid.[5]

Clearly, what Smith must resist is any view or judgment that aspires to or
achieves objective validity, for once something is objectively true or valid, it
is true or valid for me and for you (indeed, for anyone who can determine
that something is definitely, absolutely true within this or that conceptual
scheme, or according to the rules of such and such language system or such
and such culture). For Smith, the judgment apparently loses its contingency,
its dependence on such contingent matters as perspective and interpretation,
when it becomes generally, universally true, albeit within a particular conceptual scheme. In any case, it seems that Smith, like all relativists, cannot
provide any accommodations for objective judgment, for any decision, for
example, capable of pronouncing that by the standard, say, of coherence (or
applicability or connectability or whatever) this is absolutely, objectively
speaking, more coherent or fitting than that. Of course, however threatening
absolute, objective truth or judgment may be to *relativism* it is perfectly
compatible with *conceptual relativity*; indeed, truth—absolute, definite, objective, make-no-mistake-about-it truth—is possible *only* relative to some
scheme or system.

There is a sense, of course, in which what Smith says is perfectly reasonable, for we would all agree, I think, that a judgment is right or wrong—
or better or worse than another—depending on whether it is applicable,
coherent, or connectable under these or those specific circumstances or
within a given operative perspective or interpretation. The trouble arises, I
think, as a consequence of Smith's unexpressed but clearly functional belief
that any objective judgment inevitably entails a commitment to a discredited
naive realism, to a language- and concept-free view of things. Whatever the
case may be, however, the fact is that Smith has created a "classic sense" of
objectivity that, as far as I can tell, virtually no one endorses or supports.
No one trained in any nonrelativist tradition assumes that we can have a
nonperspectival take on things; all seeing is "seeing-as," seeing from this

perspective or that, under this aspect or that. We cannot talk about anything except under one aspect or another, and all understanding depends upon interpretation. As we have seen in the first two chapters of this book, where there is any content at all, there are intentional states, and intentional states are representational states, and as representational states they represent their conditions of satisfaction under certain aspects. On all this we are agreed. What distinguishes the nonrelativist from the relativist view is the conviction that perspectivalism does not preclude objective judgment, that it in fact is a condition of objectivity.

Also, it is worth noting that the measures or standards cited by Smith— applicability, coherence, connectability—are not themselves "matters of perspective, interpretation." They are appealed to in scheme-dependent circumstances, but they are not themselves scheme-dependent. Coherence, for example, is a transparadigmatic standard that is called upon to adjudicate an indefinitely large number of cases, though, of course, each case is coherent or not depending on specific local circumstances. It is with coherence as it is, for example, with grammaticality: it is the standard against which we measure an infinite number of sentences, even though in itself it has no allegiance to any particular sentence. But whether a given sentence is grammatical or not is a matter of objective fact; grammaticality is the condition making possible the grammatical well- or ill-being of each and every sentence. The grammaticality of the English sentence "The cat is on the mat" is ascertainable in no uncertain terms; it is, by the standards of English grammar, grammatical, and that is an objective fact of the sentence, in the *only* sense in which objectivity is a fact of the grammaticality of the sentence. There is no "classic sense" of objective to be distinguished from Smith's sense, whatever that might be. To be sure, it is an objective fact relative to the standards of English grammar, but objectivity just can't get any more objective than that, and there ain't any other kind of objectivity that the sentence can have relative to English grammar.

Perhaps the issues at stake here would benefit from an additional example of the interimplication of fact and value and of objectivity and conceptual framework. To determine which are the best seats in the house (in the tent, the amphitheater, the church, the stadium, and so forth), we first consult the transparadigmatic—that is, the non-scheme-dependent—optimality standards for viewing and hearing and then set about identifying what are absolutely the best seats under the various architectural, spatial, and acoustic conditions, indicating "bestness" by charging, where appropriate, the highest prices for the identified seats (fine-tuning the value system in regular gradations of price according to the perceptible distances from the optimal conditions). It is a plain, objective fact of the matter that judged by the transparadigmatic standards of optimal viewing and hearing, these seats in the first row of the loge are definitely better than those in the last row of the third balcony directly under the air-conditioning unit. As always, of course, "bestness" is determined by one's interests; value and fact, optimality and objectivity, follow the line of interest or purpose. If one is interested in going to the theater to be especially close to a special someone, to be unobserved among all observers, then the seats in the last row of the third balcony would be best.

In these cases, as in all conceivable cases where determinations can be made, better and worse are matters of absolute fact; that the evaluation depends upon circumstances (or upon one's perspective or interpretation) does not alter the objectivity of the facts, releasing them from the classic objective sense of fact and transforming them into some unobjective sense of fact, since, as we have seen, there are no knowable or discussable facts or values apart from contentful intentional states, from perspectives, points of view, frames of reference, and so on. In the end, I think it is fair to say that Smith's "classic sense" of objectivity is a red herring, a fish, at any rate, for which no one today, to my knowledge, is actively angling. If Smith's measures (coherence, applicability, etc.) yield "better" and "worse" (or "right" and "wrong," "fit" and "unfit") judgments under varying circumstances, then the results achieved are as objective as objective gets, and there is nothing "nonobjective" about them. Shining the most flattering light on the case, we can say, not without justice, that Smith has inadvertently provided us with a "classic" instance of objectivity. The scoundrel she unceremoniously ushered (or bum-rushed) out the back door, she has unwittingly welcomed as a guest at the front door, it seems.

What Smith appears to find most annoying about the "classical scholars" who "operate within the closures of traditional epistemology and philosophy of language" in their attacks on the self-refuting nature of relativism in all its various forms is the confidence with which they proclaim that "certain concepts, claims, and commitments are deeply connected with ('presupposed by' or 'fundamental to the nature of') our mental and discursive activities."[6] In substantiation of the prevalence of such proclamations, Smith quotes what one commentator borrows from Husserl: "The content of such [relativistic] assertions rejects what is *part of the sense . . . of every assertion*." She then goes on to record other instances:

For another commentator, it is "*the very notion* of rightness" that is undermined by Protagoras and latter-day relativists. He cites in support Hilary Putnam: "it is a *presupposition of thought itself* that some kind of objective 'rightness' exists." A passage in the recent work of Jürgen Habermas is relevant here as well. He writes: "[In the process of] convincing a person who contests reconstructions [of the *inescapable presuppositions* of argument] that he is caught up in performative contradictions[,] . . . I must appeal to the *intuitive preunderstanding* that *every* subject competent in speech and action brings to a process of argumentation."[7]

Some ungenerous readers might be inclined to suspect that Smith has not selected passages with an eye toward maximizing the intelligibility or intellectual force of the points made by those cited. At any rate, what these critics of relativism are saying—and what in their writings they make perfectly clear they are saying—is that such things as rationality, consistency, coherence, and logic are the inescapable conditions of the possibility of any thought or expression, whatever its import, whether relativist or nonrelativist, mystical or commonsensical, or whatever. Thought simply is not possible in their absence, and they owe fealty to no philosophical position, are partisans of no faction. What Habermas means by "performative contradictions" is captured quite nicely in (b), "A text is incapable of conveying a determinate, stable meaning," in that its expression falsifies its expressed content, as it is likewise in all attacks against or denials of rationality, in that in formulating one's challenge and critique one necessarily relies on and presupposes what one would, as they say, put into question. As Hume, speaking of performative contradiction *avant la lettre* in connection with reason, famously noted,

[Reason's] enemy . . . is obliged to take shelter under her protection, and, by making use of rational arguments to prove the fallaciousness and imbecility of reason, produces, in a manner, a patent under her hand and seal.[8]

I shall return to these inescapable conditions of the possibility of thought and expression in a moment, when I consider them in relation to items (b) and (c). For now, it is necessary to consider briefly why the beauty of their demeanor to nonrelativists makes them ugly to relativists. Well, in the first and obvious instance, such inescapable conditions have not contingent but universal applicablility; they are functional in all discourses, however diverse, written then and now and by you and me and this one and that one. And, relatedly, they are instrumental in the fixing and stabilizing of meanings (within frameworks or schemes, of course). Thus, in her final assault, Smith is determined to contain them, to endow them with the contingency that they so shamelessly eschew. She insists that such allegedly "inescapable presuppositions" are "neither universal nor inescapable." "On the contrary, it is possible to believe," as Smith fervently does, "that such concepts and the sense of their inherent meanings and deep interconnectedness are, rather, the products and effects of rigorous instruction and routine participation in a *particular conceptual tradition and its related idiom*." Such things are local, conditional, contingent, relativizable, after all—they are merely the megalomaniacal progeny of a specific intellectual tradition. And if so, it "is also possible to believe, accordingly [for Smith it is more than possible; it is necessary to believe], that instruction (more or less rigorous) in *some other conceptual tradition, and familiarity with its idiom*, would yield other conceptions and descriptions of 'the fundamental nature' of 'thought itself' and of what is 'presupposed' by 'the very act of assertion.' "[9] It may be *possible* to believe some such thing, but, I would insist, not without depending on the very conditions one would deny and, thus, not without falling into what some might call a performative contradiction. One wonders, at least, how this alternative tradition finds means to give expression to its theses without supporting itself on the props it would kick away.

Still, to say, as I do, that it is impossible to use words meaningfully in the absence of logical, rational constraints, in a context free of some "rules" that determine the allowable linguistic moves one can make, is not to put any severe limitations on *what* can be said, inasmuch as there is ample room left within the rationality restriction to say whatever can be intelligibly expressed, however outrageous, bizarre, incendiary, counterintuitive, iconoclastic, however offensive to reason it may be. The nonrelativist is no jackbooted martinet arrogantly limiting our powers of expression. As Imlac in Samuel Johnson's *Rasselas* says, when his interlocutor suggests that his views seem to "limit the Creator's power," "It is no limitation of omnipotence . . . to suppose that one thing is not consistent with another, that the same proposition cannot be at once true and false, that the same number cannot be even and odd."[10] So, it is no limitation of the relativist's (or any other ist's) expressive power to suppose that the conditions of the very possibility of thought cannot be transcended or bypassed by electing to work within what Smith calls an alternative "conceptual tradition." The conditions of possibility are the same for "classicists" and "postmoderns," traditionalists and revolutionaries, conservatives and anarchists, realists and idealists; there is simply no place to stand where one can deliberately and meaningfully oppose or deny the conditions.

Unless you obeyed such constraints, we would not know what you were saying and, perhaps not surprisingly, neither would you. One handy way of seeing how we are necessarily implicated in these conditions when we speak or write is to look at the roles of such humble and commonplace verbal functionaries as "not," "and," "but," "or," "if . . . then," and so on, each and every one of which is a logical operator working in the interest of, for example, conjunction, disjunction, negation, and so forth. Also relevant here is the gist of Wittgenstein's argument against "private languages." Reduced to its bare bones (and condensing what is expressed at various points in the *Philosophical Investigations*), the argument is that

language essentially depends on public rules for the use of expressions, rules that are public in the sense that in principle there are ways available to all the members of a community for determining when the rules are being followed or violated. Without such rules no expression has the kind of *use* that makes it possible to employ it to say something meaningful.[11]

Of course, some individual (or pair or group of individuals) might construct a "private language," one, that is, understood by one or few, but even that language is obliged to have rules for acceptability and unacceptablility, correctness and error, rules that are, in principle, recoverable and knowable by others (rules, at any rate, that the users of the language must follow and obey and that are, thus, recoverable and analyzable in principle). Thus, there can be no truly private language, not even for the originator of the language. These rules are the *formal* rationality and logical constraints, the "inescapable presuppositions" of thought (in that language) that Smith wishes to attach to a particular philosophical tradition and idiom, in opposition to which she would place "some other conceptual tradition." But, of course, there is no—and can be no—conceptual tradition that can free itself from the conditions of its own articulation, from the conditions upon which thought of any kind depends.

In the realms of thought, meaning, interpretation, intelligibility, and so on, there is no way to transcend, bypass, short-circuit, circumvent, subvert, ignore, or otherwise do an end-around logic, rationality, consistency, and coherence, though, as Smith regularly shows, it is certainly possible to write or speak so cryptically, allusively, or suggestively that sense is completely eluded and intelligibility confounded. Nevertheless, complete nonsense is difficult to pull off in any deliberate fashion, for the tidal forces in our gene pool are always rolling toward meaning, it seems. Despite our best efforts to escape the bonds of rationality, we keep deviating into sense; or, we find that we are creating and following "rules" for randomness so as to avoid falling into some pattern or order. In other words, to be faithful to randomness we are obliged to be very attentive to what we can and cannot say or do.

At any rate, at the end of the day, we can say that any and all acts of meaning—and thought generally—presuppose rationality and logic. But saying so imposes no very onerous restrictions on what can be said. Indeed, the indispensability of logic to thought is an idea without any particular metaphysical or epistemological assumptions or predispositions. Moreover, the idea that it is universally—and not conditionally or contingently—the case that there is no thought apart from rationality is no more tied to a particular conceptual tradition than is the claim that to be a property is to be a universal, to be applicable, that is, to a wide variety of objects or conditions—for example, this object is "red," and so is that one and that one, and so on. Further, it is true beyond question (beyond refutation by this or that tradition, this or that culture) that the person who claims that all judgment is relative (or conditional, or contingent) does not express with this claim a relative, conditional, or contingent truth. In short, this claim has universal aspirations; it aspires to say how things just are. Unfortunately, however, its ambition is its undoing, as we have seen. Nothing that Smith offers can rescue this or any such claim from the charge of self-refutation, and nothing can be said in behalf of self-refutation to make it serviceable to the interests of critical or theoretical disquisition or argument.

The desire to build one's case on the foundation of a self-refuting claim is tantamount to a benighted wish to visit Gertrude Stein's Oakland; just as, in the case of Oakland (according to Stein), there's no there there, so, in the case of relativism, there's no it to it. And no matter how wearisome the charge of self-immolation may be to the advocates of one or another newly minted relativism, the charge retains its explosive force. Relativism remains the enduringly fascinating Humpty Dumpty of intellectual debate, of whom a conditional, contingent, and historically marked avatar seems to make an appearance in every period, varying his gestures and intonations in every performance perhaps but always coming to the same tragic conclusion. With doleful regularity, the frequency of his reincarnations is always matched by the inefficacy of the efforts of all the king's horses and men to make him sound in wind and limb, or to prevent him from toppling to destruction under the fatal influence of his own weight.

It would seem that I have allowed the original topics of this chapter—determinate meanings and coherent messages—to languish in benign neglect while I have been busy about, on the one hand, the suicidal urges of relativism and, on the other, the life-enhancing and meaning-informing capacities of reason, logic, and so forth. In fact, of course, the interests of (b)—determinate meanings—and (c)—coherent messages—have been in our sights throughout, if not directly in the foreground of our attention.[12] Both (b) and (c) participate in the sort of self-refutation that is characteristic of relativism, and relativism invites further investigation because, in principle, it rejects any notion of objective fit, objective rightness and denies the legitimacy—indeed, the very possibility—of any transparadigmatic (i.e, noncontingent) values or meanings. Now, objective fit or rightness is, I shall argue, an ineliminable feature of determinate meaning; furthermore, essential to the production and understanding (interpretation) of any meaningful utterance or expression is rationality (or logic), the noncontingent antecedent condition of coherent message or determinate meaning. Thus, our primary topics have remained within the frame, if not at the direct center, of our focus.

With regard to logic (or rationality) as a necessary condition of any thought or meaning whatsoever, I would note that this is a commonplace within much contemporary philosophical thought (though not, of course, within current literary theory), endorsed by a wide variety of people whose views are not otherwise so univocal and harmonious. For example, Hilary Putnam has observed that "logic has *no metaphysical presuppositions* at all"; rather, it "is a doctrine of the form of coherent thought." Indeed, as he says, the laws of logic "are the *formal presuppositions* of thought (or, better, judgment)."[13] And Akeel Bilgrami has similarly remarked that "Logical norms are highly context-free," and that the "norms of logic form an a priori constraint on the very possibility of [meaning] and interpretation."[14] In a companionable vein, Simon Evnine, elucidating aspects of Donald Davidson's views on meaning and interpretation, says that Davidson "has placed in centre stage the crucial insight that rationality, consistency, coherence, and logic are not 'optional extras' for creatures that have content-bearing mental states and use language." Indeed, his "insight that without reason there is no thought is so valuable that I believe it should be bought at almost any price."[15] James Harris makes a related point when, in a Wittgenstein-influenced discussion of the grounds of meaning, he comments, "Any meaningful use of language must take place against the context of a rule-governed situation within which there are recognizable proper and improper 'moves.' "[16] To bring what could be an extremely long list of citations to a point of rest, let me conclude this catalogue with Thomas Nagel's observation that logic is simply "the system of concepts that makes thought possible and to which any language usable by thinking beings must conform."[17]

However much the writers cited in the preceding paragraph may disagree among themselves on no matter how many specific points of difference, the inescapable fact is that they could not express their differences without also silently enforcing or exhibiting the validity of the general view to which they collectively attest in the quoted remarks. And if these writers can in some sense be said to belong, despite their serious and rigorously defended differences, to a single conceptual tradition (what, speaking loosely, we might call an analytic tradition), the authoritative force of their general view on the underlying conditions of thought is not and cannot be restricted to (or characterized as idiosyncratic to) that tradition, and no alternative tradition (what, speaking loosely, we might—with the help of Barbara Herrnstein Smith and others—call a postmodern or Continental tradition) can deny, give the lie to, or put into question the validity of the view without, as Hume says, being "obliged to take shelter under [its] protection," thereby producing, "in a manner, a patent under [its] hand and seal."

Chapter 4

Determinate Meanings and Coherent Messages

Having talked the talk, I would now like to walk the walk by putting some legs under the general view that rationality is a condition of the possibility of meaning. To this end, I will take items (1.b) and (1.c) as my initial exemplary models of rationality-based discourse, broadening the scope of discussion to other examples as the argument progresses. I have argued that what is immediately striking about (b)—"A text is incapable of conveying a determinate, stable meaning"—and (c)—"A text is incapable of communicating a coherent message"—is that they are self-refuting, in that, as texts themselves, they accomplish what they claim is impossible. They take away the flooring they stand on in the process of laying it. Moreover, though they are subcontractors working under the direction of relativism, they bite the hand that feeds them by expressing general, nonrelativistic views, views that speak to and for the world at large and owe no special allegiance to any particular political state or interpretive community. Further, the views expressed are what we cannot avoid calling "truth claims"; they tell us what is so, what is definitely, make no mistake about it, the case about texts. Never mind, for now, that as truth claims they are false (or, as I have elsewhere more paradoxically put it, they are false, if true; that is, if the claims were true, they would be false to the extent that they coherently and determinately conveyed their messages; or, even more weirdly, if the claims were true, they could not be intelligibly expressed, and we could not acquire knowledge of them). Taken merely as claims, they have content; they express the belief that texts cannot have the properties of coherence or determinate meaning. The claims are made because certain beliefs are held about certain things called texts; at least it is certain that if the beliefs were not held, the claims would not be made, and the holding of the beliefs explains why texts are represented as not being capable of meaning or coherence.

Certainly it would be difficult to come up with a more satisfying explanation of why the claims are made, and what such an explanation does, of course, is to *rationalize the behavior* (that is, in this case, the linguistic act of making the claims) by specifying the *reason* for it (in this case, the belief that such and such is the case about texts). Without this sort of rational interrelation of belief and action, the text (the sentence, the linguistic act) would be without meaning or content. One of the principal tasks of semantics is to explain behavior, and, as Michael Devitt notes, "such behavior as does arise from beliefs and desires—actions—must, of course, be rational, given those beliefs and desires. That is what it is for behavior [here, the linguistic act] to be an action."[1]

At this point, it might be useful to recall a few points made in the first chapter. To say that something has content is to assert that it has semantic properties, such as meaning, reference, truth conditions. Now content depends upon intentionality, the capacity of the mind to represent things or states of affairs beyond itself, to be directed at or be about something. Consequently, semantics is intimately connected with intentionality, in that it is concerned with the meaning, reference, and truth conditions of intentional states. We captured such conceptual interdependence by noting, for example, that the content of belief is the condition under which it is true, or the content of desire is the condition under which it is satisfied. Intentional states have satisfaction conditions, and they are satisfied or not under the aspects of their representation (as I shall explain in greater detail below). In the sentences under review here, the conditions of satisfaction are not and cannot be met, and, hence, (b) and (c) are false: to satisfy the beliefs about texts the sentences expressing the attitude toward texts should themselves, at a minimum, avoid determinacy or coherence.

Furthermore, not only are these sentences coherent and determinate in their meaning, but their very intelligibility as thoughts depends upon their being underwritten by reason. Coherence and determinacy are aspects of the rationality informing the sentences. We should notice that we have two levels of satisfaction at work here (as we do in all sentences): first, coherence and determinacy are conditions necessary to the satisfaction of sentence meaningfulness, in that without them we would have no way of knowing what any sentence means (and in that they are requisite to our understanding of what the sentence says); and, second, the conditions necessary to the justification of the belief expressed must be met, if the belief is to be true. (In this case, the conditions are not met, and the belief is false.) Thus, the sentence is justified relative to meaning but is without justification relative to truth. In general, the conditions of *meaning* are satisfied or not depending on whether or not the words are used correctly (in the usual cases this means used in such a way as to fit the context from which the words derive their functionality), but, of course, the satisfaction of meaning does not ensure the satisfaction of the *truth conditions* of what the statement says or means. Sentence meaning is what makes possible the formation of true and false utterances; truth conditions make utterances true or false. We can find a convenient range of examples of this division in satisfaction conditions, in which one set is met while the other is not, in lies or false statements. Nevertheless, the two levels are operative in all expressions, inasmuch as to know whether a statement is true (or whether the attitude exhibited in the remark is justified) or not, we must first know what it means.[2]

Earlier I noted that the only things with content are intentional states (or, as otherwise depicted, propositional attitudes, thoughts) and linguistic acts. Nature, the world, reality, physics, syntax, 1's and 0's, and so on have no semantic preferences and are incapable of achieving meaningfulness in the absence of intentional states, of the imposition of representational (i.e., informational) functions on things, conditions, states of affairs, situations, and so on. Without such intentional states, we would have nothing to talk about and no reason to talk about it or to act in one way or another relative to it. Such states, then, are crucial to interpretation and meaning, for it is only by reference to them that we can explain behavior (including, of course, linguistic behavior) and come to understand how things are represented. Only by consulting these intentional states can we arrive finally at meaning, reference, and truth, can we determine whether what we say and do is meaningful, true, appropriate, right, fitting, justified, warranted—is any of these, that is, under the immediate governing conditions of belief and representation. Understanding (or interpretation), then, depends upon a grasp of how beliefs (and other intentional/representational states) represent things and cause a person to do or to mean this or that (thereby rationalizing by supplying the *reasons* for behavior). At any rate, with Michael Devitt, I assume that "something is a meaning if and only if it plays a 'semantic role,' that is, if and only if it is a property . . . that [can] explain behavior and/or can be used as a guide to reality" (can be seen, for example, as a representation of "aspects of the world of interest to the organism").[3]

And so far from its being the case that texts are incapable of conveying determinate meanings or coherent messages, it would seem to require, if not extraordinary, at least conscientious effort to prevent them from doing so. Well, I suppose it takes no special skill to string together nonsense syllables or to take the meaning and intelligibility out of more and less complex sentences by rearranging their parts (as in, for example, "mat sat cat the on the"), and we can always multiply sentence meanings by deliberate or inadvertent punning (as in, to take a couple of veteran examples, "Flying planes can be dangerous," and "Tex likes exciting sheep") or by dumb carelessness (as in "The stolen painting was found by the tree"). Of course, in the punning and carelessness instances, there is no problem with intelligibility or determinacy; the problem is one of applicability, of deciding which determinate meaning applies in the current situation. The painting was found "beside" or "next to" the tree, *unless* we are in a fictional world—a children's tale, for example—in which trees can be, say, detectives. And the preceding or following sentence would undoubtedly resolve whether the "flying" of the planes *is* dangerous or the "planes that are flying" *are* dangerous. But in the absence of some perverse or retrograde ambition not to be understood, we tend to say and write what we mean, hoping and believing that our drift will be caught, not only because it is in our own best interest to express ourselves in a way that can be understood, but because—and this primarily or essentially—what we mean is a function of *our* beliefs and *our* way of representing things. As Colin McGinn has wisely observed, "There is no such thing as meaning something by a word and it being undetermined what counts as a correct utterance of the word. . . . So any account of what constitutes meaning must respect these norms of correct use; it cannot leave open or indeterminate what is to count as meeting the conditions of correctness of a word's use."[4]

Without correctness conditions, our usages would not be capable of being fitting or proper (or right or true), and they would not be fitting or proper unless they were determinate. Also relevant here is a passage from Davidson's "Knowing One's Own Mind," in which he argues that although an "interpreter of another's words and thoughts must depend on scattered information, fortunate training, and imaginative surmise" in coming to understand the other,

[the] agent herself . . . is not in a position to wonder whether she is generally using her own words to apply to the right objects and events, since whatever she regularly does apply them to gives her words the meanings they have and her thoughts the contents they have. . . . unless there is a presumption that the speaker knows what she means, i.e., is getting her language right, there would be nothing to interpret. To put the matter another way, nothing could count as someone regularly misapplying her own words.[5]

In getting our language right, we say what we mean and not something else, and our saying is the product of our attitudes about some content (a product of what we *want* to say and what we *believe* about *this* or *that*). Saying (or writing) otherwise would be a mistake, an error, would be incorrect and unfitting. Coming at determinacy of meaning from a different, though perfectly companionable angle, Thomas Nagel addresses the challenge of the skeptic by saying that

the thought that I mean something [definite] by my words is a Cartesian thought—a thought that I cannot attempt to doubt without immediately discovering the doubt to be unintelligible. Just as I cannot doubt I exist, I cannot doubt whether any of my words have meaning, because in order for me to doubt that, the words I use in doing so must have meaning.[6]

Intentional states (propositional attitudes or thoughts), such as belief, have specific content as a consequence of the way we represent the objects, events, or conditions that cause them, as a consequence, in short, of the conditions under which we learn or acquire them. This is just another way of saying that we represent things under certain aspects. All our mental states are representational states, and our representations are aspectual; our seeing is *seeing-as*. Over the course of time, we may represent the same things under different aspects and come, consequently, to hold a variety of beliefs, say, about the same things. To want something as water is not the same as wanting it as H_2O, and an interest in the maple tree in the backyard is not equivalent to an interest in the largest object in the yard, even though the maple tree is the largest object in the yard. Thus, as Davidson maintains, it is only "at the sentential level that language connects with the interests and intentions that language serves, and this is also the level at which the evidence for interpretation emerges."[7] Our words, then, have meaning only in the context of a sentence, and our sentences, only in the context of some informing structure or purpose, only within a system of use, a set of justification conditions, a framework of rationality, or, as Wittgenstein insists, a form of life. What counts in the individuation of objects or topics of interest and, hence, meanings is the informational content of belief at the local, functional level, the level, that is, of use.

The upshot of the preceding paragraph is that propositional attitudes (thoughts, intentional states) have specific, definite content (we never focus on things or conditions in all their aspects) and that discussions of any topic are meaningful only relative to some specific justification conditions, to something determining the appropriateness, use, and fit of the constituents of expression. We can talk about only so much of a topic as falls within the logical and semantic range of the terms of our discourse, a range delimited by operative beliefs and functional purposes or intentions. If it is meaning, it is determinate and coherent, of conceptual necessity, it seems. For example, to fix the content of a belief—that it is about water, not H_2O; about our friend Mikey, not the insufferable brat on Elm Street; about the cigarette, not the drug-delivery device or the cancer stick, and so on—is to be already deeply involved in the realm of rationality in the sense that this fixing also puts constraints on what can properly be said about the thing subsequently and what kinds of relations in which it can participate (even as the fixing of belief ties the thing to countless other things and other beliefs).

Let me explain. Any belief (or any other attitude) entails countless other beliefs, belongs to a large network of functional but unexpressed intentionality. Fixed as a fork, say, the object of the attitude loses all connection with atomic structure and any number of other conditions, states, and relations in which it might participate if it were construed differently or seen under different aspects, even as it forms strong family bonds with countless other conditions and beliefs, such as, for instance, knives, spoons, and other utensils, plates, stoves, food, cooking activities, eating, stabbing, table manners, and on and on beyond the reach of my ingenuity and every reader's patience. Making an ancillary or related point, Mark Greenberg suggests that part of "what it is for a thought to have a particular content is for it to have certain connections to other thoughts" that form part of the "background" assumptions integral to the operative world of discourse.[8] Greenberg finds a convenient example in a thought of a triangle, which, he avers, is necessarily embedded in that network of associations that includes such concepts as "three" and "side." And, in the second chapter, I made a similar point when I said that my desire to have a drink with your favorite cousin would not be satisfied by sharing a brew with the notorious night stalker (though the two were one and the same individual), since the night stalker is not a satisfaction condition of my representation of a drinking partner. Content in contexts of use is specific, determinate.

Language in use, then, has some definite, determinate content (it necessarily talks about something in some way for some reason or other), and any meaningful use of language depends upon working faithfully within the imperatives of a system of intentionality, a system establishing the justification conditions of our expressions or utterances, which demarcate the boundaries between right and wrong, proper and improper, fit and unfit moves in the operative intentional system—the specific linguistic practice, language game, "form of life" under way or in use. The operative system of intentionality both implies and is implied by the specific nature of the terms and concepts at work in the text. In the absence of such a controlling and informing system of intentionality, we would have no ability to say what we mean, or, more radically, to say anything meaningful at all. Apart from some system of rationality, there is no thought, no meaning. (And, of course, without rationality there is no action—linguistic or otherwise—only motion, and, further, where there is rationality, there is agency, the necessary condition of content and action, since mental states, upon which content and action depend, are traits of agents.)

At bottom, we are concerned here with meaning holism and what Davidson and others have called semantic opacity. In briefest digest, meaning holism is simply the view that the parts have meaning relative to the extent to which they function in the service of the whole (crudely, words functioning in the service of sentences, and words and sentences in the service of the whole work or the specific practice or task). Semantic opacity, on the other hand, is shorthand for definite, specific, particularized content. When we ascribe belief (or any propositional attitude or intentional state) to an agent, we are indicating that the object of the attitude has specific content, is to be taken under this rather than that aspect. And, as Davidson observes, "One way of telling that we are attributing a propositional attitude is by noting that the sentences we use to do the attributing may change from true to false if, in the words that pick out the object of the attitude, we substitute for some referring expression another expression that refers to the same thing."[9] John Searle expresses the same point in these terms: "Substitution of coreferential terms in function contexts fails to guarantee preservation of truth values."[10] For instance, if we were to describe some behavior as H_2O-seeking behavior, instead of as what it in fact was (water-seeking behavior)—thereby substituting in the process one term for a "coreferential term," or one "referring expression" for "another expression that refers to the same thing"—the *content* of the desire responsible for the behavior would be misrepresented; and it simply is not true that the person under scrutiny is seeking H_2O. In intentional states, as we have seen, conditions of satisfaction are represented under specific aspects, the aspects in terms of which things, conditions, states of affairs are seen, believed, wanted, feared, intended.

At bottom, then, it seems that as content-driven, symbol-using creatures we are unavoidably implicated in a rather tight network of entailments: our intentional states have definite, determinate content; that content is tied to countless other beliefs and to a variety of background assumptions that delimit the range of connections and associations that are possible to the content (tree talk underwritten by the interests of botany or dendrology cannot drift off into tree talk sponsored by the emotional turbulence of young love, without some major mediating work being done to smooth the transition); and the whole shebang of affiliated contents achieves the functionality that we call meaning only when it follows the direction of some system of rationality, some end in view, some principle of construction that provides the justification conditions for all the conceptual contents. In short, without these justification conditions—the conditions in relation to which the intentional states or propositional attitudes have information functions—without some structural principle of coordination, emphasis, value, meaning, without, in short, some system of rationality, there would be no thought, no content at all. With such a system—and only with such a system—there is meaning, and that meaning is definite, specific, particular, determinate.

What is true for me is, I assume, true for you (and all the others like us, of course), and that is that when I speak or write, I speak and write a kind of sense, express something meaningful that is recoverable by others endowed with imagination and content-involving mental states, and that no matter how much I extend my expression (even to the length of an article or a book, a short story or a novel) I tend to stay more or less on course. I tend to fill in or fill out the developing line of argument or plot in sometimes striking, unpredictable, quite original, but always (or at least most of the time) remarkably appropriate, just, or felicitous ways, ways internally pleasing and satisfying to—I hesitate to say but cannot avoid saying—the work itself, to its homeostatic well-being. Finding the right, proper, fitting word and developing the case or the action in the most cogent or effective way possible are not easy tasks, of course, but that we can talk about the rightness or cogency of our verbal choices is itself quite interesting and informative, as is the fact that others can oblige us to recognize that we have gone astray, committed an error, missed the boat, the target, or the opportunity to gild the lily, add frosting to the cake, or, less tropically, satisfy in a maximal rather than a minimal sense the interests of the text's own making. At any rate, what is clear is that definite content and determinate meaning are contingent upon intentional states and systems of intentionality. Further, our contents and meanings are recoverable by others, because we share a public language, and we share a public language—a prerequisite to our capacity for mutual understanding—because, as I argued earlier, we have common conceptual and causal links to the world. If we did not, the transmission of meanings to one another would be impossible.

If in the production of meanings we can sometimes make mistakes and miss the boat by failing to meet the conditions of our own systems of intentionality, we encounter even more problems when we engage in the interpretation of others' meanings, since the justification or assertibility conditions of texts are nowhere to be heard in the sound waves or descried in the ink marks; they are the invisible hands shaping and directing the way things are in the text; they are no more *in* the physical features of the text than the music is in the score or the damsel in distress of the bodice ripper is on the page or within the covers of the book. And we cannot distinguish the incidental from the essential features of any text merely by staring at the words very intently, with due deliberation and dedicated determination. Each new text presents us with a new challenge to our interpretive capacities. To understand the text we must form a hypothesis about the theory of truth, the theory of meaning, the system of rationality informing the text with determinacy, about the justification or assertibility conditions that give intelligibility to the parts. As Hilary Putnam observes, however, the "assertibility conditions of an arbitrary sentence [i.e., any sentence considered in isolation] are not surveyable."[11] Meanings come fairly easily to us because we've all had lots of experience making sense of a wide range and diversity of verbal practices, as well as numberless opportunities to figure out why we and others do what we do, to understand the reasons for our actions. But meanings are not worn openly on their faces, and they just ain't in the words of the text, considered apart from some mental component, apart from the intentionality endowing them with specific content and function.

To get some sense of the variability of the justification conditions of an "arbitrary sentence," that is, a sentence removed from its context and practice, simply repeat "I didn't say he stole it" six times, emphasizing a different word with each repetition and thereby creating six different senses, six different justification conditions for the sentence. Now take each of those readings of the sentence and say it ironically, solemnly, gloomily, excitedly, comically, portentously, affectedly, smarmily, and so on through as many variations as your wit and your talent for vocal mimicry will permit. But if the assertibility conditions of such sentences are not surveyable, how do we learn them, how do we learn which are applicable in this instance of use? Well, as Putnam goes on to observe, "We learn them [as Wittgenstein, Michael Dummett, and others have suggested] by acquiring a practice,"[12] which amounts to making informed guesses about the nature and kind of discourse that one is engaging with, based on one's accumulated stock of information about how people and texts have gone about making sense in the past.

There is, in short, no algorithm for acquiring practices, for learning which system of rationality we are presently confronting. Davidson puts our case as interpreters succinctly: "An interpreter of another's words and thoughts must depend on scattered information, fortunate training, and imaginative surmise in coming to understand the other."[13] In amplification, I would say that we must rely on our imaginative capacities to construct and understand new structures and on our rich experience with making and understanding an enormous variety of systems of rationality, guided by some such assumptions as these: that there is no content at all in the absence of intentional states; that only rational creatures—not cultures, historical epochs, languages, epistemes, or whatever—have intentional states with full-blown (i.e., specific, determinate, and fine-grained) content; that such creatures act in conformity with or in a manner determined by their beliefs and desires, thereby making their behavior an action—something caused by reasons—not a mere happening or motion; that people believe what is true (or, more exactly, act upon what they believe to the case) and want what is answerable to their needs or desires, and that . . . (here supply all those "rules" on which you customarily rely when making sense of all the linguistic and nonlinguistic actions you encounter in any given week).

In going about our business as interpreters, we silently ask such questions or seek to know such things as who (i.e., what kind of person, of what character or disposition) is speaking to whom (i.e., what kind of person), under what circumstances and for what purpose, or to what end? What kind of text am I dealing with? Is it a botany text, an editiorial, an epic poem, a treatise, a nineteenth-century novel, a constitutional amendment, a jeremiad, a Philippic, a fable, an allegory, a sermon? Is it two or more of these at once, in varying dosages at various points in the text? Is it serious, comic, satiric, droll, bitter, accusatory, apologetic, ironic, tragic, dyspeptic? What kind of language is in play (or what kinds, in what combinations, at what points): literal, metaphoric, symbolic, bombastic, flatfooted, jargon-laden, baroque, Rubenesque, grandiloquent, fussy, perspicuous? And so on.

Moreover, as Michael Dummett insists, we understand that it is "essential to our use of language and to any faithful account of the phenomenon of human language that it is a rational activity, and that we ascribe motives and intentions to speakers" and writers. He goes on to note that in "any linguistic interchange, we are concerned to discern such intentions: to understand why a speaker [or writer] said [or wrote] what he did at a particular

stage, why he expressed it in that particular way, whether he meant it ironically or straightforwardly, whether he was changing the subject or, if not,
why he thought it relevant—in general, what his point was or what he was
getting at."[14] At any rate, it is in coming to know the network of beliefs,
motives, and assumptions underlying linguistic action and determining specific content that we come to an understanding of the determinate meaning
of the verbal acts that we encounter.

In all our encounters with language, we are involved in the process of
coming to understand a new practice, a new language game, but we never
have to begin from scratch. We begin with our accumulated competencies
for understanding, that is, our developed and developing capacities for rationalizing behavior, for determining the *reasons* that cause action, impro-
vising as we go, but sustained by the knowledge that where there is specific
content, there is rationality precisely of the sort that we ourselves use in
forming our beliefs, getting what we want, doing what we intend, and so
on. John Heil, expanding on and clarifying one of Davidson's points, notes
that in "delivering an utterance, I produce something that possesses a definite sense, one that I can reasonably expect my audience to recover." "The
recovery of sense, interpretation, is a matter," says Davidson, "of bringing
to bear a 'theory of truth.' " Further, "the production of an utterance is
something in part because it expresses a definite, recoverable, intentional
content. [And] productive capacities go hand in hand with interpretive capacities, we have reason to assume."[15] What Davidson calls a "theory of
truth," and what Michael Dummett calls a "theory of meaning," I, focusing
on the interpretation of literary works and all other writings, would call a
tentative, working hypothesis, a controlling conception of the operative justification conditions, which functions to render the unfolding words and
sentences meaningful, and only in relation to which are the words and sentences intelligible. In essence, I am talking about the conditions of the possibility of a "practice," those conditions that in a holistic network of
intentionality give the work its specific content, its determinate and coherent
meaning. Thought and language are inextricably joined, as are truth (that
is, meaning and reference) and justification conditions.

With a few brief, summary remarks, this chapter can be brought to conclusion, I think. Essentially, what I have sought to establish in this chapter
are the following: there is no content whatsoever in the absence of an agent's
intentional states (propositional attitudes, thoughts); there is no action (linguistic or otherwise) in the absence of the intentional states (belief, desire,
intention, hope, fear, etc.) that are the reasons for (and causes of) them;
content is aspectual and, therefore, definite; meaning has correctness (or
rightness, fitness, satisfaction, appropriateness) conditions built into it—otherwise, there would be no limits on what any utterance or sentence could
mean and, hence, no meaning (nothing could be ruled in or out); meanings
are determinate, in other words, by virtue of what it is to count as a mean-

ing; words derive their reference and meaning from the contexts of use in which they are functional parts; as words serve the interests of sentences, sentences serve the interests of the system of rationality from which all the terminological and conceptual parts acquire their functions; meaning, thus, is holistic as well as determinate. Codicils could be added to this list, wrinkles to this fabric, but in the aggregate the additions would not qualify or undermine but only strengthen the main point—that, contrary to what items (b) and (c) dogmatically, definitely, and, alas, self-refutingly assert, meaning must be determinate, given its origins, its nature, its use, and its functions, given, in short, the kind of thing it is.

Finally, a brief and summary word or two about interpretation, the possibility of which hinges, of course, on the determinacy of meaning. Interpretation is difficult because it is based initially on guesswork and tentative hypotheses and is always open to revision (or rejection) when confronted with new information or a more compellingly satisfying hypothesis about the informing system of rationality. But because the text is informed by a system of rationality, it is available to a correct interpretation, is a possible site, as we might say, of a correct interpretation. The fact that we produce successful interpretations of verbal behavior every day of our lives should provide some grounds of both encouragement and confidence. What makes the notion of a correct interpretation such a fingernails-scraping-the-blackboard sort of thing, I think, is that, in addition to supposing a determinacy of reference and meaning that is denied by most postmodern theorists, it appears to be an open and flagrant violation of what has come to be recognized as the conventional or common wisdom, namely, that just as all objects and events can be described in indefinitely many ways (there being no one correct, true, or best description and, hence, no one thing the object or event just is), so all sentences and texts can be read in many different, even incommensurable ways.

The trouble here involves, I think, a confusion of interpretation and criticism. Interpretation's task is to recover that meaning inherent in an intentional system, the rationality informing the parts and whole of an intentional system produced by an *agent*. Criticism's task, on the other hand, is to discuss the text in terms of or in relation to as many things, categories, states of affairs, concepts, and so on as may happen to interest the *critic*. The same *objects* and *events* can be described in various ways because they are not, prior to our descriptions, semantical/intentional things or objects, whereas *texts* (including our descriptions) are intentional when we encounter (or produce) them. Thus, there is never any question of recovering the meaning of the objects and events in themselves—they have, as I have perhaps grown too fond of saying, no semantic preferences. As readers, we are often least interested in texts as sites of interpretive activity (though to talk about them at all, we must understand them in some sense or other), and most interested in them as they reflect, express, reveal, or impinge on other things;

we are interested in the qualities, values, terms, ideas, and so on that texts share with other things or works by participating in the common causes of human activity—language, mind, gender, politics, race, culture, production, consumption, commodities, dominant ideas, tropes, concepts, and so on through an exceedingly long list of topics of interest to human beings. To read texts in the light of, or in relation to, these interests and values is to engage in criticism, not interpretation. And that this or that work, in whole or in part, can be read through one or more of these lenses and be seen, consequently, as deeply tinted with the hues of one's interest is a potential cause for celebration, since much that is interesting, illuminating, and true (of nature, politics, truth, psyche, etc.) may undoubtedly be learned by trying on what different lens crafters have fashioned. But interpretation is another matter; it involves the recovery of the intentionality inherent in something that is a system of intentionality and rationality to begin with, something that is—and with this we bid farewell to (b) and (c)—both determinate and coherent in meaning.

Chapter 5

Paying Deference to Reference

If the darkness has a heart (that is, a core or nucleus), the beast a belly, or the inspissated gloom an origin or center, it can be found in item (1.d):

Reflexivity of language and texts—language and texts do not represent or refer to extralinguistic or extratextual reality. Language/texts are self-referential—"signifiers chasing signifiers." A text refers to itself and to other texts.

There is very little in contemporary "theory," at any rate, that does not owe fealty to (or at least pay tribute to) what is stated or implied in this set of interrelated and interimplicated doctrines. Of course, not all members of the Church of Linguistic Idealism are acolytes; some are what might be called "occasional conformists," and some others might not inappropriately be styled members of the unitarian wing. Nevertheless, the rock upon which the faith of all is founded is the belief that reality, meaning, truth have no stabilizer bars to hold them steady, that, in other words, there is no rock to which we can tether our sayings and signings (no God, Reason, Reality, Author, Transcendental Signified, or whatever, to authorize, validate, and make good on our promissory notes).[1] Reality, determinate meaning, truth cannot appear in public (or private) without being adorned with "scare quotes," because what some have long suspected turns out to be the truth, the whole and only secure truth: the clothes make the man/woman, or, less cryptically, language is that upon which everything depends, and language, alas, because of its relational and differential nature, is unstable, incapable of staying fixed or determinate. Other relations and, hence, other meanings and uses are always and necessarily implicated in current meanings and uses, so that no matter how hard one may try to say what one means and to mean what one says, the congenital proclivities of language just will not let one get away with saying only this and not something else as well.[2]

THE LANGUAGE OF DECONSTRUCTION

As one slogan has famously put the case, "there is nothing outside the text," outside the system of relations among signs and signifiers. Of course, when the focus shifts to language as the conditioner of all conditions and, more particularly, to the relations of signs to other signs, the role and importance of the author, writer, speaker are diminished if not elided completely. And once signs and relations among signs become the locus of attention, it is difficult not to conclude that everything is intertextual, since interimplication is inevitable in a world where marks and inscriptions are, as Derrida has insisted, iterable in illimitable contexts and, thus, always already other than they locally seem. In other words, the capacity of marks and sounds to be repeated makes it inevitable that our meanings will always already mean something other than what *we* mean. Consequently, any text before us is interesting and indeed intelligible, not as a discrete locus of meaning and value determined by an intentional agent with a purpose or end in view, but as a complex of intertexts, or, in Julia Kristeva's terms, a "mosaic of quotations."[3] Since there is no getting beyond signs and their interrelations to some bedrock fact or truth or meaning or intention, everything is entangled in the always shifting, wavering, tottering world of textuality, where temporary alliances among "semes" (linguistic units), sounds, images, tropes, themes, and "memes" (symbolic units of social or cultural significance—about which, more later) are momentarily realized before dissolving and then reforming in new configurations, and where every text, as another theorist affirms, "emerges as interpretive discourse caught up in a network of other interpretive discourses."[4]

Central to this line of thinking, then, are the relations and connections among terms, images, themes, and so on, with writers/speakers taking a minimal, subordinate, or incidental role (if indeed they have any role at all) in the production of verbal discourse. J. Hillis Miller, for example, has set himself squarely against any efforts to reinstate in critical conversations any "traditional ideas about personal identity, agency, and responsibility."[5] And we have long been familiar with the efforts of Michel Foucault and Roland Barthes to eliminate or to reduce to a minimum the role of human intentions, of individual choice in the making of utterances or writings, regularly seeking to supplant talk of the human agent with such notions as "thinking without a subject" and the emergent, historically contingent nature of authorship or individual agency. The author becomes, at bottom, either an "author-effect" created by the play of language—a product of linguistic relations, rather than the creative agent of production—or a creature of critical economy designed by the critic to set limits on the potential free play of meanings inherent in literary (and all other) texts. Indeed, addressing all those benighted antediluvians who remain in the grip of the metaphysics of presence and an outdated and intellectually bankrupt conception of agency, Foucault, in his own quite distinctive and self-affirming way, has notoriously written, "To all those who still wish to talk about man, about his reign or his liberation, to all those who still ask themselves questions about what man is in his essence, to all those who wish to take him as their starting-point in their attempts to reach the truth . . . to all these warped and twisted forms of reflection we can only answer with a philosophical laugh"; man is "simply a fold in our knowledge," destined to "disappear as soon as that knowledge has found a new form."[6]

By now it is common knowledge, I suppose, that the principal source and origin of the doctrines expressed in item (d) can be found in Saussurean linguistics—especially in its treatment of *langue*, that aspect of language highlighting, not the particular utterances of speakers on particular occasions (the focus of *parole*), but the differential system of sign relationships—as filtered through Derridean philosophy of language. In this view, language at all levels, from the most basic phonemic or graphemic unit to the largest unit of textual significance (up to the level of concept, theme, or thesis), is a system of differences. No element is positively present because whatever seeming "presence" (or fixedness or definitiveness of reference) it has depends on the traces of the system of differences of which it is a part. Presence, in other words, is always caught up in self-deferral, since "positive" elements can never be validated, corroborated, authorized, or authenticated by anything outside the system of differences. Consequently, whatever seeming determinacy of meaning or stability of reference an element (sound, word, image, phrase, sentence) may have is an "effect" of the *nonpresent* meanings of the other elements in the system, which by their difference from the focal element make possible the element's having its current, albeit shaky and ungrounded, significance. The apparent determinacy is an "effect" of the "trace" of the others (the other meanings, in relation to which the element's difference is marked) on the focal element, giving it an aura of determinacy and, not incidentally, providing the critic with something that can then be shown to be unstable. (One hard problem might be in determining where and how to begin discussion, since at bottom there are only differences without significances or "effects," and since differences, like relations of similarity, strike off in all directions, lacking the decency to follow some linear, well-worn path—a problem for the theorists to solve, and one we can, for the time being, leave them to contemplate.) But, to resume, such an "effect" is an absolutely necessary feature of the system, if it is ever going to get down to the business of talking about this or that, about this or that's instability and indeterminacy. The play of signifiers produces "effects" of determinacy, but because there is no warrant for anything expressed in any given text (or utterance) outside of or independent of the system of signs, the stability of meaning or reference is illusory. The "effect" is always open to dispersal or "dissemination" by the play of forces that brought the seeming or transient stability into being in the first place.

Now, this is heady stuff, not easily processed or assimilated by common intelligences (or so it seems to me, at least). Basically, the idea is that no phone or word or concept or larger unit of meaning can break free of the endless chain of referral (which is also, it would seem, as a matter of internal necessity, a chain of endlessly deferred meaning), since it is only relative to this chain that its difference is marked. Differences are marked in a system of differences. Thus the "sl" of "sleep" and the "sh" of "sheep" are in a sense mutually implicative in that the functioning of the one is impossible without the functioning of the other, and both are functional within a class of sound differences. And, as noted above, what is "true" at the level of sound is "true" at the higher levels of signification as well, for as Derrida insists, "no element can function as a sign without referring to another element which itself is not simply present. This interweaving results in each 'element' . . . being constituted on the basis of the trace within it of the other elements of the chain or system." Thus, "nothing, neither among the elements nor within the system, is anywhere ever simply present or absent. There are only, everywhere, differences and traces of traces."[7]

To those not already members of the choir, there is undoubtedly much in this sermon that would cause one to hesitate at the altar and that would give even the credulous occasion to pause before swallowing the wafer whole. Others there are certainly who, like the honorable France in *King Lear*, would find this view of language *incroyable*, belief in which would demand a "faith that reason without miracle [could] never plant in [them]."[8] In the first place, it is difficult to see how any element in the system could ever be constituted as a sign of anything at all, inasmuch as *the elements (at whatever level) as elements have no syntactic or semantic proclivities*; there are no designating or representing functions inherent in a system of differences. There are only differences, differences without significance. For example, "sleep" carries within it as necessary conditions of its "effective" individuation or identification not only "sheep," but also "sleet," "slap," "shape," "slope," "soap," "hope," "hop," "mop," and so on endlessly. Moreover, none of the *elements* in this endlessly proliferating chain of deferrals of "positive meaning" refers to what you and I refer to or describe when we talk about soap, sheep, sleet, slope, hope, and so on, because chains of elements have no intentionality, no powers of representation, no informational content, and, most important, no truth or satisfaction conditions, which all contentful mental states and linguistic acts do have (as the previous chapters have shown). Derrida, then, must undoubtedly be speaking metaphorically or mystically when he claims that "no element can *func-*

tion as a sign without *referring* to another element" (my emphases). (In the a,b,c,d . . . system, for example, a does not *refer* to b, b to a, a to c, c to b, etc.)

Just as nature/reality has no semantic preferences, so the constituents of language have no "referring" capacities; sounds or letters—phones or graphs—do not refer to or represent anything. Functions are not intrinsic to the elements, and they cannot be assigned by the elements to the elements. Moreover, *referring* is not something that goes on apart from mental states, in the absence of intentionality, or so it is the burden of this book to maintain and to demonstrate. Referring and representing are operations at the semantic/intentional level, and it remains unclear how the elements can give themselves functions or, for that matter, how functions can emerge from the material bases of language (sounds and marks). Indeed, it is unclear how the "relation" relation can emerge, since syntax itself (i.e., the branch of semiotics concerned with the relation of signs to other signs) is not an inherent feature of the elements. "Trace," "deferral," "difference," and so on, like "similarity," "sequence," "antecedent," and so on are agent-assigned, conceptual terms. Finally, on this matter, though we determine what in our contexts of use will count as, say, similarity or difference, whether something in that context is similar to or different from something else depends, in most instances, on the way things are at a distance from us, unless the similarity/difference relation is merely verbal or definitional, as in "bachelors and unmarried men are alike or similar"—the identity relation (bachelors/unmarried men) representing the highest form of similarity.

At the higher reaches, analysis in this mode tends to emphasize a binary opposition of conceptual elements, to focus, at any rate, on semantic or ideological units that subsist in antithetical or complementary relation to one another or, at a minimum, that are variously but distinctively in a relation of "otherness" to one another, most often in some socially marked condition of otherness (black/white; capitalist/worker; majority/minority; nature/culture; writing/speech; rulers/subjects, and so on). In practical terms, the dependable, indeed predictable, result of inquiry is that every text is "discovered" to be implicated in self-betrayal, in undermining that which it appears on the surface to be deliberately and sincerely committed to establishing. Regardless of how doggedly and grim-facedly writers (or texts) set about the business of making a specific point, expressing a particular view, articulating a single, coherent, philosophical or political position, or defending a steadfastly held judgment, they will inevitably subvert or undermine the positive "present" meaning they have set out to establish in the very process of establishing it. And this is so because, as a matter of linguistic necessity, the "other" (or the "contrary" or "complementary") that they would suppress—by that "inattention" that is the result of focusing on what one wishes to state clearly in no uncertain terms—is a necessary condition of the something they conscientiously aim to express; it is part of the system of differences upon which their positive claims depend. All this we know because we know that nothing can signify without referring (implicitly but necessarily) to other elements in a system of differences. And what could be more clearly implicated in "yes" than "no," in "up" than "down," or more surely entailed in one's being opposed to oppression of any kind than one's being a covert promoter of oppression, or more deeply revelatory of one's willingness to support restrictive covenants in housing than one's membership in the ACLU. One inescapable consequence of this view of language is that writers (and speakers) are powerless to delimit the range of meaning that they would express, inasmuch as reference and meaning are, ultimately, out of their control, are floating features of systems always on the move and with no place to call home.

The clear and present danger implicated in this conception of linguistic entanglements is that discussion could meander off in any direction at all, since there is no limit to the number of relations in which one thing—one term, image, concept, idea, or whatever—may stand to another, since any thing or event can be described in an indefinite number of ways, since a ground of similarity can be established between any two (or more) things, however disparate and apparently dissimilar, and since any isolable element of a text may have predicates of quality attached to it that may also be attached to a remarkable range of quite different things.[9] A truly amazing number of things may share a capacity to hold open a window or to serve as a paperweight; a comparable number may be alike in their hairlessness (a quark, a Buddhist temple, a college dean, for example), in their being east of the Mississippi, and so on. And by means of double predication, for example, we can first attribute a rage for order in the state of England upon the restoration of Charles II in 1660 and then go on to attribute a "similar" rage in the literary production of the Restoration period, as manifested in the adherence of the writers to the "rules" and "proprieties" of composition, and then suppose that this "relation of ideas" reflects a "matter of fact" relation (to borrow Hume's terms) between the political and the poetical (an implicit causal relation, perhaps). On the other side, the power of the negative is such that everything is different from everything else in some respect; even identical twins are different in countless ways, and *this* is always and ever *not that* and *that* and *that* and so on. In a system of differences, where can the differences end, and how can any "other" be prevented or prohibited from leaving its "trace" on what it is other than? Who or what is empowered to say "no" (i.e., not right, not relevant, not appropriate, not fitting, not just, and so on) to any difference that shows up to play the signifying game?

Once we move beyond simple phonemic or graphemic units, once we enter the realm of larger semantic units (words, images, sentences, and so on), it is virtually impossible to limit or determine what system of *conceptual* differences serves to mark significance or to create the "effect" of apparent stable meaning or reference, since the units can participate in innumerable systems of difference. Simply, as Hilary Putnam has maintained, "the assertability conditions of an arbitrary sentence [i.e., a sentence lifted from its informing context, from the specific intentional states supplying the conditions of its justification] are not surveyable."[10] The "effective" meaning or significance of such a sentence can be marked by an incalculable host of differential conditions. If we say that the *context* in which the sentence appears restricts the "effect" or determines the (temporary, local) meaning, then we cannot claim that the iterability of the sentence in other contexts makes it inevitable that the sentence always already means something other than it means, because that sentence's meaning is never any part of its differently contextualized meanings; that *meaning* is not iterable in the new context, in the new meaning-determining context. If, on the other hand, we insist it is the trace of differences that creates the "effect" of meaning, then we are back to where we started, in the thicket of wildly branching differential possibilities (i.e., a wide range of other beliefs and background assumptions about the elements or contents of the sentence).

Any arbitrary sentence will serve to make the point; for example, such sentences as "The cat sat on the mat," "I didn't say he stole it," "Shut the door," or "There are lots of dogs in South Providence" will serve as well as any others that ingenuity or laziness might supply. The "Providential dogs" sentence, for instance, can be marked as significant in relation to an extremely rich number of background beliefs and semantic assumptions (i.e., a rich number of differential systems), all of which are entailed by the conception of language underlying item (d) and endorsed by a vast number of theorists. Not only will the many different people who utter or write the sentence about dogs in South Providence realize the thought that the sentence expresses in different brain states (that is, it is neither necessary nor likely that this thought requires all its thinkers to be in the same brain state, to have identical neuronal activity), but they will also have the thought in relation to a variable network of other beliefs and assumptions (and at the level of words, concepts, and sentences we must assume that the differential systems are conceptual and belief systems; how could they be anything else?), as the thought is held and articulated by, say, the dogcatcher, the dog fancier, the parent, the chef, or by a single individual at different times and in different moods.

NEW HISTORICISM AND CULTURAL POETICS

In the preceding I have focused chiefly on the doctrines and the principles and assumptions informing deconstruction because, despite the sharp decline since the mid-1980s in membership in the deconstruction denomination, these doctrines and principles have in large measure been carried by the lapsarians to their new houses of worship—feminism, gender studies,

Lacanian psychoanalysis, postcolonial studies, queer studies, Althusserian Marxism, Bakhtinian dialogism, new historicism, cultural materialism, and so on. Even as new approaches are adopted or new topics gain prominence, however, former methods of argument (primarily analogical) are employed and prior conceptions of language (principally those of post-Saussurean linguistics) are retained, along with their epistemological assumptions about truth and their metaphysical assumptions about reality (or the Transcendental Signified).[11] In all the newer or emergent critical sects, if ideology achieves prominence (as it does), the discussion of ideological matters proceeds largely along lines that deconstructive linguistics has dictated, with the emphases being placed on relations among symbolic units of social significance within texts and across discourses, as well as on those between verbal products and other cultural markers of power disparities. In one form or another we have in this newer criticism avatars of matters of special concern to item (d), such as culturally, socially, politically, ideologically freighted signifiers chasing culturally, socially, politically, ideologically freighted signifiers; socially constructed texts either referring to other socially constructed texts or representationally embodying political/social conflicts and tensions within themselves. What many, rightly or wrongly, took to be the sterile apolitical formalism of deconstruction has taken root and brachiated in the socially constructed soil of politics and ideology. Or, troped differently, we have in this newer criticism the connubial felicity occasioned by the vow-taking of Continental social/political philosophy and Continental post-Saussurean linguistics. The special quality of this union of politics and language is happily captured in a snappy jingle: in this criticism attention is focused, as Louis Montrose has memorably put it, on "The historicity of texts and the textuality of history."[12]

In brief, texts are located in and products of particular social and cultural eras, and history in any given era is a reflection of the terms and categories or, as some would have it, the symbolic energies that determine the prevailing power relations and constitute what counts as knowledge, truth, reality, the natural, the normal, the right, and the just in that era. Much of the operational force behind such a conception derives at least in part from the long Hegelian tradition on the Continent, in which "the role of social institutions in shaping the individual and the content of his thought" has dominated philosophical discussions.[13] To this tradition has been brought the peculiar insights that come from the recognition that everything is textual, is a matter of signs and their relations, especially as they are organized into various cultural formations of power. History, then, is not a complex set of stable or objective facts and events that have occurred at some prior time in some extratextual world, but an indefinite set of "texts" (i.e., systems of signifying elements) open to various readings, and, like all texts (including literary texts, with which history interacts in various ways), these "texts"— while appearing to reflect or represent extralinguistic, external facts, events, actions, and states of affairs—are simply configurations of signs that invest the ideological propensities of particular eras with "effective" definition and authority, establishing relatively clear divisions of control and subordination that distinguish the privileged and powerful *us* from the justly oppressed and powerless *them*, the *same* (and good) from the *other* (and bad or despised). These investitures of power, make no mistake about it, have real consequences for real human folks, but the "realities" identified have, oddly, no ontological significance, no metaphysical (or even empirical) grounding, in that they traffic only in the "truths" and "facts" of conceptual relativism; the "realities" confronted are constructed socially at particular times and in particular places by moving the signifying resources about. Some of these movings about have our approval; some (most—i.e., all those in which minorities, the poor, and women are deprived of power, opportunity, or freedom, and especially those movings about that characterize or epitomize Western, white, European cultures) do not.

Like many name brands, "new historicism," (a.k.a. "cultural poetics," or "cultural materialism") comes in a number of varieties, some endowing authors with more control over effects than others and each having its own distinct flavor. Nevertheless, something of its essence (if you'll pardon the term) is captured in the following remarks by Stephen Greenblatt, Foucauldian legatee and paterfamilias of new historicism, United States branch:

> In any culture there is a general symbolic economy made up of the myriad signs that excite human desire, fear, and aggression. . . . literary artists are skilled at manipulating this economy. They take symbolic materials from one zone of the culture and move them to another, augmenting their emotional force, altering their significance, linking them with other materials taken from a different zone, changing their place in a larger social design. [Consequently,] A nuanced cultural analysis [of *King Lear*, for example] will be concerned with the various matrices from which Shakespeare derives his materials, and hence will be drawn outside the formal boundary of the play—toward the legal arrangements, for example, that elderly parents in the Renaissance made with their children, or toward child-rearing practices in the period, or toward political debates about when, if ever, disobeying a legitimate ruler was justified, or toward predictions of the imminent end of the world.[14]

This brief enumeration of what appears to be a potentially endless series of "towards" toward which a "nuanced cultural analysis" could be drawn calls attention, inadvertently but nonetheless conspicuously, I think, to what has the unhandsome look of a major flaw—the "let's-head-out-in-no-matter-what-direction flaw" or the "any-matrice-in-a-storm flaw," about which more momentarily.

But before turning to the matrices of social energy in circulation in every distinguishable culture, to those various matrices with which the elements of literary works may interact, we should note that, unlike some of his associates in the cultural poetics enterprise, Greenblatt appears to endow literary artists with considerable power to gather and then to organize cultural materials into powerful works of art. He admits that he has "written at moments as if art always reinforces the dominant beliefs and social structures of its culture, as if culture is always harmonious rather than shifting and conflict-ridden, and as if there necessarily is a mutually affirmative relation between artistic production and the other modes of production and reproduction that make up a society." But Greenblatt assures us that, though defined as a self by the dominant culture and obliged to work with the symbolic resources authorized by the existing regime of power, the literary artist is not necessarily, per order of sociolinguistic law, the tool, flunkey, or lackey of that regime. No, "the ability of artists to assemble and shape the forces of their culture in novel ways so that elements powerfully interact that rarely have commerce with one another in the general [symbolic] economy has the potential to unsettle this affirmative relation," this positive, collusive relation between artistic production and the dominant beliefs and structures.[15]

Furthermore, the artist's capacity to unsettle may expand to a giant's bulk and take on the fearsome look of subversion. For instance, a work that on the surface is openly pandering to the interests of, say, the aristocracy may simultaneously, albeit surreptitiously, champion the interests of the bourgeoisie "to which it was supposedly opposed," as Jean Howard, another historicist/culturist critic, attests.[16] Indeed, Howard further asserts that the stage can "embody and negotiate among a variety of competing ideological interests, rather than being the captive of one."[17] Of course, for some critics—many Marxist critics and some Bakhtinians, for example—the chief value of any play is its registration of the conflicts intrinsic to any social structure or ideological formation.[18] Howard, on the other hand, like so many charter members of the "always historicize, always politicize" sodality, is fond of the "smiling-(bowing, scraping)-on-the-outside/snarling-(plotting insurrection)-on-the-inside" scenario, in which texts overtly support but covertly subvert the interests of the dominant culture. Although authors have their share in the assembling and shaping of the elements of social energy, as Greenblatt insists, texts have this (with deepest apologies to Keats) "negative capability" to unravel their own ravelments, to say "no" while expressing "yes" largely as a consequence of the differential nature of language itself, as a result of the trace of the "not said" in any "saying," as a result of what is *latently* contained in the *manifest* content.

Moreover, despite the attention directed to authors in some historicist/ ideological studies (especially those determined to show that Shakespeare or Marlowe or Pope or whoever was complicit in one or another form of domination or colonial oppression), authors, if functional at all, are generally (usually) subordinated to the operations of the impersonal mechanisms of which they are themselves the product. Indeed, as Greenblatt himself insists at the very beginning of *Shakespearean Negotiations*, "There can be no appeals to genius as the sole origin of the energies of great art."[19] Further, literary works—like all cultural products—draw attention primarily not as unique products of artistic making, as unified wholes, as ethically valuable, emotionally powerful, intellectually engaging systems of intentionality or rationality (as discussed in the previous chapters of this book), but as reflections of deeper political and social conditions, as emblematic way stations of circulating social energy on the era's communication line. In the "historicist" approaches the elements or parts of the work are not considered in terms of their contribution to the workingness of the whole system of intentionality that is, say, *Hamlet*; rather, each identified element is treated as at once exemplifying and partially defining (as well as potentially altering) the symbolic economy of the culture at large. In short, in this mode of criticism, authors are ultimately not central to the enterprise; the principal aim is, to borrow another of Greenblatt's terms, "cultural poetics," which, in essence, entails a grasp of the symbolic organization of the culture as a whole as determined by the relationships among signifiers with social significance. The critic is chiefly interested in coming to understand the nature (as well as the variety) of the ideological work that is being accomplished by the prevailing, culturally defining signifying system.

In a recent article, Donald Pizer makes a cognate or comparable point, while highlighting a similarity (albeit with a striking and telling difference) between historicist studies and the old "New Criticism," in which "the critic viewed all the language of a literary work as deeply implicated in a complex effort to achieve thematic and formal unity." Pizer observes that

What was earlier the critical practice of "poetics," the attempt to describe the structure or form of the literary work as it arises from the distinctive purpose of the work, is now . . . "cultural poetics," the attempt to describe the interaction between the culture and the literary work as that interaction is expressed through the similar yet dissimilar symbolic constructs of both entities.[20]

To all this the historicist critic could appropriately respond that, if there are methodological similarities linking the practices of the New and newer critics in analyzing, respectively, whole works and whole cultures, the newer criticism not only rejects the core beliefs of its predecessor (e.g., the arid formalism implicit in its belief in the self-sufficient, autotelic universe of the work of art), but also serves as a corrective to its focus on the work itself and its consequent isolation of works of literature from the historical/ideological conditions of their very possibility. To the New Critics' sense of the richly interimplicated verbal texture of texts, the newer criticism brings the essential insight that all texts are historically conditioned by the symbolic economy of the era in which they appear. Let me bring this paragraph to summary conclusion by citing Greenblatt's corroborating opinion, which amounts to a less pithy expression of Montrose's bumper-sticker-ready view that the newer criticism is concerned with "the historicity of texts and the textuality of history":

[Liberal arts education formerly separated] the study of history from the study of literature, as if the two were entirely distinct enterprises, but historians have become increasingly sensitive to the symbolic dimensions of social practice [the textuality of history], while literary critics have in recent years turned with growing interest to the social and historical dimensions of symbolic practice [the historicity of texts]. Hence it is more possible [and here we get to the essential point or goal of the newer criticism], both in terms of individual courses and of overall programs of study, for students to reach toward a sense of the complex whole [not of a particular practice, a specific work, but] of a particular culture.[21]

The Selfish Meme

Quite independently of—indeed, a few years prior to—the elaboration of that body of ideas characterizing new historicism or cultural poetics in literary studies, Richard Dawkins, in *The Selfish Gene*, put into circulation the notion of the "meme" as a cultural analogue to the biological gene, arguing that whereas biological evolution proceeds by means of the transmission of genes, cultural evolution proceeds, analogously, by means of the transmission of "memes," units of cultural significance passed from brain to brain, person to person, very much as genes are spread from body to body. This social evolutionary view of cultural transmission is not ideology-based or focused on uncovering the hegemonic apparatuses of state control or delineating the symbolic economy of a whole culture; nor is it underwritten by a poststructuralist conception of language and sign relations, but, like new historicism, it does stress the circulation of packets of social energy in discriminable time periods. Thus it is my hope that a discussion of common features will lead to a brief account of what I take to be some of the special weaknesses of the cultural poetics position.[22]

Briefly, to the zoologist Dawkins, "memes" are units of social transmission, and although they come in various sizes and forms, each meme must be a single transmissible unit, one capable of being "replicated" in new contexts. Dawkins gives as examples of memes such items as "tunes, ideas, catch-phrases, clothes fashions, ways of making pots or of building arches." And, "just as genes propagate themselves in the gene pool by leaping from body to body via sperm and egg, so memes propagate themselves in the meme pool by leaping from brain to brain via a process which, in the broad sense, can be called imitation."[23] Dawkins asks us to take the notion of memic evolution quite literally. Clarifying this aspect of the theory, a recent supporter of Dawkins's view, Daniel Dennett, asserts that in this system "Meme evolution is not just analogous to biological or genic evolution, not just a process that can be metaphorically described in these evolutionary idioms, but a phenomenon that obeys the laws of natural selection exactly." Dennett goes on to explain that

just as the genes for animals could not come into existence on this planet until the evolution of plants had paved the way (creating the oxygen-rich atmosphere and ready supply of convertible nutrients), so the evolution of memes could not get started until the evolution of animals had paved the way by creating a species—*Homo sapiens*—with brains that could provide shelter, and habits of communication that could provide transmission media, for memes.[24]

Most readers, I suspect, would have difficulty yielding to or supporting the notion of a strict or literal, rather than a metaphoric, correlation between genic evolution and memic "evolution," if only because identifying the environmental or cognitive conditions to which fashions in clothes and in tunes, say, are the useful or appropriate adaptations seems not to be a task falling within the range of do-ability, or because natural selection does not seem to be a concept readily applicable to changes in the ways pots are made, arches are constructed, tunes or hemlines are accommodated to popular taste. Unquestionably, fashions have their seasons, and ideas are spread from head to head for a time, until a new ideation contagion takes over, but adaptation, natural selection, survival value, terms relevant to genic changes, do not seem to be suitable traveling companions for persuasion, choice, will, atavism (as in neo-primitivism, neo-realism, neo-Aristotelianism), intentionality, whim, mistake, and so on, terms relevant to memic adaptations and changes.

What we have, at best, is a ground of similarity between two quite distinct forms of dissemination; we have, in short, a metaphoric or analogical relationship between evolution (genic, biological) and "evolution" (memic, social). I suppose we may, if we wish, talk about "fads" in biological structures and forms and about "phenotypical" ideas and modes of dress, but we do so only to accentuate or to give vivid freshness to certain material or formal saliencies in objects of interest to us, not to *equate* an object of interest with what it is in some restricted respects like. My love is a red, red rose, in that, like the rose, she is (from one perspective) vitally alive, beautiful, delicate, and so on or (from a more jaded or mordant perspective) prickly, untouchable, mortal, and so on. But when we get down to the unvarnished blonde-wood, brown-shoe, peas and carrots sense of things, my love is not really a rose (even though you'll never really know what she's like until you know what she's like). So, memic spread and genic spread have something in common, but memes do not literally evolve, though thinking of their peregrinations in terms of evolution—rather than in terms, say, of movements of chess pieces—may provide some vivid understanding of what memic dissemination is like.

Of course, metaphors can mislead as well as illuminate, and if at the literal

level evolution makes little sense as applied to memes, it is also misleading
(or potentially so) at the metaphoric level, if, in addition to obscuring differences in the process of highlighting similarities, it tends to cancel a difference that makes all the difference between evolution and "evolution,"
most notably, the role of intentionality, motivation, and reason in memic
transmission. On just this point, John Searle, addressing himself to Dennett's exposition and elaboration of Dawkins's views, insists that

> It misses the point of Darwin's account of the origin of species to lump the two sorts
> of processes together. Darwin's greatest achievement was to show that the appearance
> of purpose, planning, teleology, and intentionality in the origin and development of
> human and animal species was entirely an illusion. . . . But the spread of ideas
> through imitation requires the whole apparatus of human consciousness and inten-
> tionality. Ideas have to be understood and interpreted. And they have to be under-
> stood and judged as desirable undesirable, in order to be treated as candidates for
> imitation or rejection. Imitation typically requires a conscious effort on the part of
> the imitator.[25]

To the issue of intentionality and planning I will return shortly, but it is
now time to make good on the promise made a few pages back to consider
problems inherent in determining what counts as a meme or, in Greenblatt's
system, a unit of social significance in the symbolic economy of a period and
in ascertaining what "matrices" or "zones" of culture will be appealed to in
a "cultural analysis" of any particular work.

Memes and Cultural Poetics

Knowing when you are in the company of a meme or a unit of social
significance is not quite as easy as knowing when you are in the company
of Smith or Jones. In the first place, memes and units of social significance
show up in various sizes, shapes, and clusters, outfitted in universal and
particular habiliments. For example, memes may appear not only as (in
Dawkins's examples) tunes, ideas, catchphrases, and so on, but also as (in
Dennett's extensions) "cooperation, music, writing, education, environmental awareness," and so on, as well as "shopping malls, fast food, advertising
on television" and "anti-Semitism, hijacking airliners, computer viruses,
spray-paint graffiti."[26] It begins to seem that nothing within the range of
nomination or activity falls outside the boundary of the memic. In the second place, since, as was explained in earlier chapters, all seeing is a seeing-
as, a seeing of this or that under this or that aspect, from this or that
perspective, or under the governance of this or that conception or belief,
and since there is no easily determinable limit to the number of aspects
under which this or that may be seen or described, the appearance of the

"same" symbolic element in different sentences or contexts provides no guarantee that the same cultural unit of symbolic energy is enjoying multiple incarnations. For example, the person over there who is (or means or functions as) the cat burglar to one audience is kindly, old Uncle Bob to a different audience; and what is bad news in Providence (i.e., lots of dogs) to the dogcatcher is good news to the dog fancier.

Furthermore, since the number of relations in which one thing may stand to another is virtually infinite, and since presentential units or elements of the culture (or, indeed, of the language) have no meaning or significance (or, what amounts to the same thing, too many meaning possibilities and, hence, no determinable meaning) independently of the sentence meaning of which they are functional parts and from which they derive their functions, there is virtually no limit to the "effective" functions the elements can perform, the meanings they can subserve. (The preceding is just another way of saying that meaning determines reference, and that words have meaning in the context of a sentence, just as sentences have meaning in the context of a whole text, i.e., of the justification conditions informing the whole work or symbol structure.) Also (and enough on this aspect of the issue for now), because any isolable feature of a text—from a sound or graph pattern, to a word, a phrase, an image, a group of images, an idea, a motif, a thesis, and so on—may have qualities of value or attributes of cultural significance attached to it, and because, as we have noted above, there is an extensive range of diverse, disparate, incommensurable, even conflicting values that each feature may comfortably wear, there would appear to be absolutely no (or precious few) restraints on what any text could say or on the alignments it could forge to who knows how many symbolic economies, especially if, to all the above, we allow some presence to absence and admit the force of the trace on the current effect.

Whenever a connection could be made or a relationship established between an element of the literary text under scrutiny and some element in another text or in some cultural practice or artifact (and when could such a connection not be made, given the malleable and quite accommodating nature of symbols?), a distinctive feature of the symbolic economy of the period would be discriminated. Or, put another way, if one begins analysis with a prior conception of how the era has arranged its social/political energies (as, unfortunately, many of our cultural materialist theorists seem to have done), then one can easily show how elements from quite disparate zones of energy participate in reinforcing the interests of—and, hence, the symbolic economy of—the dominant class. Because the real object of study is ultimately not the literary work but the culture at large (because the end is not the analysis or interpretation of unique products of artistic intentionality, but the elucidation of the "general symbolic economy" of a culture), the literary critic is free to roam in the culture at large for materials relevant to his discussion of, say, *King Lear*. Indeed, if the critic hopes to show how

Lear reflects, contributes to, or alters the general symbolic economy, she is absolutely compelled to consider the text in relation to, as Greenblatt suggests, the "legal arrangements . . . that elderly parents made with their children, . . . [to the] child-rearing practices in the period, . . . [to the] political debates about when, if ever, disobeying a legitimate ruler was justified, . . . [to the] predictions of the imminent end of the world," or to any number of other things as well.[27]

Whatever benefits this historicist or cultural materialist approach has for the illumination of the social energies of the culture, its benefits for the critic are enormous: it frees up the interpretive (or rather, the speculative) energies of the critic, allowing him to "discover" new relationships and associations never dreamed of in Horatio's philosophy. As Donald Pizer has quite sensibly observed, the critic is released "from the confines of the literary work itself, or, rather, the work itself explodes into an almost infinite number of associations with its culture, since almost every facet of its language has some cultural association and can be explored for the relationship of this association to its manifestation in the culture, to its participation, that is, in what Greenblatt calls the 'symbolic economy' of all expression." Moreover, as Pizer goes to say, "this movement back and forth of symbolic expression, from the work to the culture and from the culture to the work, can produce fresh and radical readings . . . , because the heavy freight of cultural implication which the transferred 'symbolic materials' bear in the literary work has often not been discussed or realized," has not ever entered into anyone else's imagination, however inventive, turbulent, perfervid, or eager for distinction that imagination.[28]

Of course, the more than danger—the virtual inevitability—of this ingenious moving about by the critic of "symbolic materials" from what Greenblatt calls "one zone of the culture to another" is that ingenuity barks the shins of credibility or, on the other hand, that everything yields to one's predetermined notions of the social/political entanglements of the period. In short, the danger is, as Pizer notes, that the approach leads to "forced, ingenious, and essentially worthless interpretations as the critic . . . locates transfers which have little support in the work but do confirm his preconceived notion of the cultural design expressed by the work."[29] There seems to be no end, in short, to the number of meaningful relations in which the elements of the culture (as identified by each critic) can stand to the elements of the text (as also identified by the critic). Also, there would seem to be no end to the number of political/ideological directions in which the critic could set out from the text to the culture or from the culture to the text, though, in practice, critics usually have a pretty clear sense of the operative power relations in the social world before inquiry begins, and, as far as gender, class, and race are concerned, a pretty uniform one at that— hence, the diversity of evidence and examples culminating in the homogeneity of the conclusions about power structures in any given period and, indeed, across many periods. The state of modern theory is such that it is no country for whites, males, and Europeans, and, alas, there is no Byzantium toward which they can set sail (even though many of them believe, with Yeats's old-timer, that there are monuments of unaging intellect).

CULTURAL POETICS IN PRINCIPLE AND IN PRACTICE

By now it should be sufficiently clear why I and others—that is, all those who find nothing abhorrent to our common understanding and daily practices in the views about meaning and intelligibility articulated in previous chapters—might have problems with critical endeavors operating under the aegis of item (d), under, that is, the "signifiers chasing signifiers" warrant. But even when we put aside those objections that are grounded in a fundamentally different conception of how meanings are formed and contents are determined (to which I shall return at the end of this chapter), a number of compelling reasons to reject or at least to resist the claims and insinuations of item (d), especially in its historicist incarnations, suggest themselves. Initially, there are the problems connected with identifying what signifiers are significant and what kind of significance they have, given their manifold relational ties to other signifiers. Then, of course, there are problems associated with the task of determining the boundary conditions or the defining characteristics of the "era" or "period" under discussion. The time continuum—like nature or reality—has no contentful states, no intrinsic divisions. Furthermore, no period or era, however demarcated (whether by century—the eighteenth, nineteenth, etc.; by monarchy—Caroline, Victorian, Henrician, etc.; or by epitomizing trait—atomic age, information age, the age of anxiety, the late capitalist age, etc.), has self-nominating capacities; nomination is a selection process in which from the class of eligible and fully qualified defining traits only a limited few are chosen by the critic (with selection too often being a reflex of the critic's antecedent assumptions about the principal components or forces of historical/political development, as in many Marxist and neo-marxist studies).

When examined in an up-close and detailed way, however, every nominated period or era is, despite its nomination, a buzzing hive of confusion, a hive, that is, of multiple, diverse, disparate, conflicting, contradictory, antithetical traits, tenets, impulses, attitudes, convictions, beliefs, aspirations, commitments, and so on (even, it seems, those eras or periods that we were formerly too willing to see as unified in terms of their mind- and life-spaces by authoritarian regimes in church or state)—which is perhaps why it is always easier to say exactly what age "they" lived in than what age "we" are living in. No matter how apt the designation may be, no matter how happily it captures salient features or tendencies of our period, it is always insufficient to the many complex and variegated worlds of experience in which we find ourselves immersed. If it is impossible to describe completely, fully, and finally a bike, a shoe, a car (as I and many others believe it is), it is infinitely more difficult than impossible (and, you must admit, that's pretty darn difficult) to grab a "period" by the scruff of its "beingness" (its, if you'll pardon the expression, essence) and call it by its right name.

Furthermore, because memes or elements of social/political significance may be misunderstood and hence misused, because, additionally, such elements may have for particular writers personal, idiosyncratic, even "unconscious" significance rather than political significance, and because they may be used quite deliberately in ways that are totally separated from and indifferent to their role in what is taken to be the symbolic economy of the period, because all this (and more) is so, the meaning or significance of such "memes" or "elements" in specific contexts of use cannot necessarily be incorporated within, resolved into, or deduced from the pattern of symbolic energies that has the critic's favor.[30] The "memes" as locally used may belong, in short, to another system of relationships altogether, another order of intelligibility, and, consequently, may be more fruitfully discussed relative to that system, one that may be uniquely constructed for quite immediate, local purposes. Finally, even when we take the author and his inadvertent, deliberate, and unconscious choices completely out of the picture, the fact remains that because, as we have seen again and again, there would appear to be no limits on the capacity of signs to hook up with other signs by virtue of some relation or other, every text would seem to be an equal opportunity employer of interpretive possibilities, accommodating many and rejecting few.

Still, as I indicated earlier, it is also true that the notion that a given culture might have something not unlike a distinctive symbolic economy is one not completely offensive to common experience or wide learning. (To be more accurate, we should perhaps say economies, in the plural; we should not expect the enormous diversity of culture-distinguishing symbolic units, deriving from many "zones" or "matrices" of cultural interest, to achieve the kind of coherence that the term "cultural poetics" implies, with its clear suggestion that it does unto the culture at large what "poetics" does unto the literary work, i.e., disclose the distinctive structure or form of the whole design, the whole culture in this case.) Unquestionably, the terrain appears to contain far fewer asperities, the landscape to be more easily traversable, the rivers to be more surely navigable from the Boeing 747 than from the Conestoga wagon, but what is missed at the level of gritty experience finds a compensatory benefit in what is gained at the "higher" level of experience, the one best suited to reveal those larger, more widespread shapes, patterns, tendencies, and relationships that are unavailable to the eye of the wagoneer.

Wherever we direct our glance—whether to politics, finance, agriculture, business, painting, architecture, gender relations, religion, science, technology, or whatever—we find in every period, however discriminated, singular preoccupations with a distinctive body of ideas, values, terms, categories, priorities, and so on that give the period, however identified, its peculiar character or flavor. There can be no question, for example, that eighteenth-century English "culture" had some rather distinctive takes on punishment, genius, taste, the sublime, stockjobbing and market capitalism, latitudinarianism, enclosure, trade, class distinctions and privileges, commerce, medicine, legal rights, and much else besides. In all these areas, preferences, convictions, and prejudices found expression in distinctive symbolic forms. Moreover, it is clear that assumptions about one thing—property rights, for example—reflected assumptions about other things—class and gender distinctions, for example—and governed one's behavior and decisions in such apparently tangential areas as business and social life. Also clear, I assume, is the fact that every person writing in this period was influenced in varying degrees, consciously and unconsciously, by a considerable number of the topics, categories, terms, values, and priorities in social circulation, the particular range of the writer's interests (and, hence, indebtedness) depending on such things as education, class rank, professional responsibilities, personal proclivities, birth order, parental background, family loyalties (both political and social), the achievements of predecessors and active competitors, the state of contemporary debate, and so much else. And it is reasonable to suppose that of the innumerable ideas, things, and events exerting their influence, consciously or unconsciously, on the writer many would inevitably be exhibited directly or indirectly, intentionally or inadvertently, in the writings, shaken or stirred in a multitude of ways to produce, in the end, unforeseen combinations and linkages among the memes or socially significant elements of the culture. Just as clearly, then, every text could profitably be mined for information about how and what units of social energy, from a vast assortment of "matrices" or "zones" of concern, get into circulation, and thereby manage both to reflect and, potentially, to alter the dynamics of the symbolic economy of the period.

From a cultural analysis of, say, Fielding's *Joseph Andrews* or Austen's *Pride and Prejudice*, much undoubtedly can be learned about a vast number of things germane to the poetics of the culture, but only remotely relevant to the ostensible interests of the novel, to the poetics of the work. But this is all as it should be, if one is primarily a historicist or cultural materialist, since as such one's aims are to illuminate and elucidate the culture, not the text. We are all deeply indebted to those historicist critics who have provided genuine insights into hitherto unrecognized lines of affiliation among verbal and other units of cultural significance and hitherto neglected patterns of social/cultural meaning and who have, perhaps especially, enabled us better to understand how disparate and apparently benign features of the symbolic economy are complicit in maintaining, reinforcing, and promoting the power relations characterizing and underpinning the social order as a whole.

In fairness, however, it must be said that if the historicist/cultural materialist approach to literary texts has, in some instances, opened up to view previously obscured aspects of culture at large, it has also tended to etiolate its interpretive gains by (1) working within too narrow a band of topics, interests, and possible symbolic relations (almost exclusively those concerned with race, class, and gender in one or more of their bearings on power, domination, oppression, or with ideology in one or more of its myriad manifestations); by (2) playing a very limited number of tunes on the interpretive instruments (basically, variations on these four: a text or practice supports the dominant power structure; subverts or undermines that structure; appears to undermine only to reinforce it in the end; or lets the contestatory elements subsist in dynamic tension with their horns locked and smoke in their nostrils); and by (3) coming to every inquiry with a prior understanding of what the power relations informing society are and of how the narrative of history plays out, so that the inherence in texts of this or that quality or value depends on a habit of reading determined by one's prior commitments, depends, in short, on begging the question. The consequence of all this is that we have an enormous diversity of quite ingenious, indeed, brilliant readings of essentially the same story involving the same agon.

For purposes of illustration, I will yield the floor momentarily to Louis Montrose, who will provide us with a felicitous example of the dynamic tension version of the story. Explaining his procedure at the beginning of *The Purpose of Playing: Shakespeare and the Cultural Politics of the Elizabethan Theatre*, Montrose notes that in analysis,

Sufficient allowance must be made for the manifold mediations involved in the production, reproduction, and appropriation of an ideological dominance; for the collective, sectional, and individual agency of the state's subjects; and for the specific resources, conventions, and modes of production and distribution of the representational forms that they employ. By representing ideology as a dynamic, agonistic, and temporal process—a ceaseless interplay of continuity and change, of identity and difference—this concept of culture opens poetics to politics and to history.[31]

Once beyond the presentation of his theoretical bona fides, his historicist conception of the cultural poetics/politics of a period, Montrose settles into an analysis of *A Midsummer Night's Dream*, a work that concerns itself, in his reading, with, among other ideological things, Elizabethan constructions of gender and sexuality, and, consequently and ineluctably, with "ideological appropriations" and "relationships of power." In this play, patriarchy (represented by Theseus, Oberon, and Egeus), always susceptible to destabilization as a result of counterdiscourse, is contested or challenged by women's power (represented chiefly by Titania, Hippolyta, and Queen Elizabeth). The contest remains unresolved, and we witness throughout the play the ways in which male authority and female power are first asserted and then undermined or subverted, the whole giving expression to the sexual dynamics of the culture at large. Nothing here gives clear evidence of the more than occasional brilliance of Montrose's analysis, unfortunately, but this overview is not, I think, criminally unfair to the broad features of the argumentative design.

At the end of this discussion of historicist and cultural materialist approaches and their implicit assumptions about language and meaning, we should bear in mind that in these approaches the discriminable elements of any literary work are not understood in terms of their contribution to the workingness of the whole work; they are not, in other words, considered as essential properties of the proper functioning of the work as a particular system of intentionality. Rather, each socially significant element, however determined (and where is there an element that cannot have a social significance applied to it?), is emblematic in some way or another of the extra-artifactual social tensions or circumstances that they are taken to exemplify or, in some cases, to influence or alter. Briefly, the elements are not seen as subordinated to—as deriving their specific functions from—some end in view, some author-generated purpose, from which they obtain their emphasis, value, meaning, and significance. Instead, the elements are understood as signs, consequences, or instances of preexisting conditions. Constraint on meaning and value derives from those conditions of possibility determined by the ideological formations or power relations characterizing the society at large. Specific content, then, is based on a prior analysis or prior understanding of the society's representational system—otherwise, it would be impossible to know what textual elements had clout or meaningful content. Thus, in general, it does not matter from what direction the historicist critics set out or in what direction they move, they always end up at the same ideological site from which they began their analytic journeys.

Entailed in all this, of course, is the view that history, as well as each particular era or culture into which it is partitioned, is a text (or is textual) and that every text—historical, legal, literary, or otherwise—is historical, determined by the representational capacities of the era's prevailing ideological proclivities (of which we somehow have knowledge). Entailed as well are attitudes toward relativism and truth that are inconsistent and incompatible with, indeed, antagonistic and antithetical to those promoted in this book. In the post-Saussure-via-Derrida world all facts are facts of representational systems, and there is nothing outside such systems qualified to serve as makers good or makers true of what is made or asserted. By and large, truth reduces to persuasion, and persuasion to power, in that, in the end, what counts as true or right or natural or fitting is determined by the power structure obtaining in any given era, which controls the concepts, categories, and terms of the various *discourses* in circulation. Despite the considerable diversity of views within the historicist perspective (about, for example, the ability of authors to alter, rather than merely to reflect, the existing power relations), when push comes to shove and the nitty gets gritty, this perspective simply cannot acknowledge that there is a way that things are independently of our era-specific, power-determined representations of them that might serve as a content control mechanism on our beliefs, propositions, sentences.

And even when authors and specific literary works are foregrounded, the former (authors) are not considered as creators of unique artistic products nor the latter (works) as unified structures whose parts are justified and functional relative to a system of intentionality, the origin, meaning, and significance of the parts of which system derive from the creative acts of a rational agent (not from the ambient ideological atmosphere). Moreover, however diverse in focus and emphasis they may be, these historicist approaches, in keeping with their linguistic loyalties, tend to focus generally on the permutational possibilities of subsentential units of meaning (words, images, phrases, and so on) and, if on larger units at all (sentences, groups of sentences), on their meaning possibilities considered in terms of a preconceived ideological framework, not in terms of the immediate, local system of intentionality in which they function and to which they owe their functionality. The upshot of this tendency is that linkages among discourses are often based on semantic possibilities available to or implicated in the words or images or sentences, irrespective of whether those particular possibilities are realized or functional in any of the works under scrutiny. By such means, authors can be shown to be most revolutionary when they express the most traditional views, and the most politically reactionary works can be found complicit in the most subversive plots.

Although new historicists tend not to invoke the authority of post-Saussurean linguistics in defense of their interpretive moves, the assumptions underwriting those moves have their provenance in that linguistics, which assures us that the very iterability of our terms, ideas, or phrases in an unlimited number of different contexts is the surest guarantee of the appropriateness of the meaningful connections, the meaning relations, we choose to emphasize. Indeed, it is the only guarantee, since, in the new linguistic era, we cannot appeal to the way things are for the warrant of our assertions; we cannot appeal to the behavior of things at a distance from us for the justification of our claims, or to the system of intentionality underlying each work for our understanding of the specific content of each work. The only real worlds to which appeals can be made are the socially constructed ones that each era or culture forms by its "representations," by its manipulation of symbols in the ways allowable under the prevailing ideological regime. Basically, then, use does not determine content; rather, preestablished ideological content determines use, determines the connections and relations that may be formed among terms and ideas. Meanings emerge from linguistic relations, and linguistic relations, though various and manifold, have their outside limits set by the power relations of the culture. Innumerable connections or relations may be highlighted and analyzed, and many diverse theses may be advanced, but in the end, all conclusions must be permissible implications of the ideological resources of the culture. Energies may circulate in marvelously variegated ways, but they may not transgress the ideological/political borders of their very possibility.

In a discussion of linguistic relativism (to which all poststructuralist theorists, including, of course, new historicists, subscribe), Marie-Laure Ryan makes a telling point when she challenges the claim of the "Saussure-inspired critique of truth-as-correspondence" that "when using language in a concrete situation, we deal with the full value of words" (that is, all the meaning possibilities that the words have acquired or that a given era allows into circulation). She wisely notes that "it is hard to see how something meaningful (let alone true!) could be said in a sentence predicating a property such as the full Saussurean value of *mortal* (both 'fatal' and 'subject to death') of any entity. *Socrates is mortal* will activate one meaning, and *this wound is mortal* the other."[32] Of course, many words are perverse enough to take on not only different meanings, but also incompatible or contradictory meanings—e.g., "cleave" (to dissever, to split *and* to bring together, to unite), "moot" (that which is debatable *and* that which it is pointless to debate either because the issue is no longer in dispute or because the case is so hypothetical as to be, for all practical purposes, meaningless), and virtually all our terms are both heavy-laden with meanings and battle-ready to function as mercenaries in a multitude of verbal campaigns, to work faithfully in support of a wide range of claims or theses. Ryan's basic point, however—and one endorsed by this book—is that words (as well as images, phrases, and so on) have specific content, specific meaning, value, and emphasis only in contexts of use. She expresses this position, a commonplace for most philosophers of mind and language who reside outside poststructuralism, in these terms: "the predicate 'true' applies to individual expressions and utterances, not to language as a code" [i.e., a system of signs, of "signifiers chasing signifiers"]. "Sentences make truth claims but individual words do not."[33]

These remarks provide an easy transition to the final phase of our examination of the implications and shortcomings of item (d), in that they supply in brief digest an alternative to the conception of language and meaning implicit in item (d) and operative as an intellectual given in new historicist and other poststructuralist criticism and theory. There is undoubtedly no need at this point to review what it has been the burden of previous chapters to establish about content being impossible apart from intentional states; about intentional states (thoughts, propositional attitudes) having satisfaction conditions; about how language does not mirror reality but transforms it into the truth conditions of our assertions; about why, as Putnam says, "accepting the ubiquity of conceptual relativity does not require us to deny that truth genuinely depends on the behavior of things distant from the speaker"[34] (regardless of whether those things are such mind-independent things as stars, mountains, and monkeys, or such mind-dependent things as speeding tickets, social status, or goalposts); about the possibility of objective truth; about the self-refuting nature of relativism, and so on. But as this discussion rounds third and heads for home, it might be useful to recall what Davidson says—echoing as he expands notions expressed by Wittgenstein, Frege, and others—about linguistic meaning:

It is at the sentential level that language connects with the interests and intentions language serves, and this is also the level at which the evidence for interpretation emerges. But just as words have meaning only in the context of a sentence, a sentence has meaning only in the context of use, as part, in some sense, of a particular language. . . . So in the end the only source of linguistic meaning is the intentional production of tokens of sentences. If such acts did not have meanings, nothing would."[35]

Meanings do not emerge from relations among or between signs but, in the alternative scheme endorsed by this book, from the kinds of objects we interact with. As Davidson has elsewhere observed (and as we have noted earlier), "what a person's words mean depends in the most basic cases on the kinds of objects and events that have caused the person to hold the words to be applicable."[36] Objective judgment is possible because the kinds of objects and events we interact with are those that we share with others, and this sharing is grounded in common causal relations with the objects and events that, again in the most basic cases, determine the contents of our words and thoughts. Intersubjectivity, then, is a consequence of our participating in common causal and conceptual relations to objects and events in the world.

Moreover, where there is linguistic meaning, there is, as we have demonstrated earlier, definiteness of content, since the subsentential parts of an utterance acquire their informational or representational functions from the sentence meanings that they subserve. This point is implicitly contained in Davidson's claim above that the "sole source of linguistic meaning is the intentional production of tokens of sentences." What is crucial here is the notion of "tokens of sentences," i.e., sentences used on particular occasions for specific purposes. "Tokens of sentences" are not iterable, though "types of sentences" are. One can find the same type of sentence—the declarative type, say—in many different contexts and have it express a limitless range of opinions, but one cannot move a token sentence from one context to another without altering the functionality of the parts within the sentence or the functionality of the sentence within the new system of intentionality into which it is transported (or both). To illustrate this point earlier I called upon the sentence "I didn't say he stole it," the many meanings of which can be glimpsed by repeating the sentence six times, emphasizing a different word with each repetition, and then delivering each angrily, joyfully, ironically, sardonically, and so on through the entire diapason of moods, tones, and emotions. Clearly, this sentence can be repeated in many contexts (not excluding the serious, the comic, the tragic, the sentimental, and so forth), but each token use conveys a singular meaning.

In most respects, the positions taken in this book on mind, language, relativism, antirealism, the formation and determination of meanings, and so forth are the converse of those adopted and promulgated by virtually all poststructuralist theorists. For the most part, they are precisely those that these theorists situate themselves in opposition to, when they are not simply laughing them out of court or blithely assuming that they were blown out of the water ages ago, when the linguistic turn, exemplified in the interrelated tenets of item (d), was taken, and when, as a result, the nonarbitrary relation among words, thoughts, and things broke down and the true and the real, along with all things else, went immanent, went, that is, into various language systems. And, thanks to Foucault and others, these language systems could now finally be seen for what they in fact were—the devices by which the interests and desires of the dominant classes could be met and satisfied with the happy cooperation and enthusiastic support of the oppressed (who found in the prevalent systems of discourse access to what is "real," "normal," "right," "fitting," and "good"). Because all languages cut up "reality" differently, none, it is assumed, can correspond to reality as it really and truly is in itself. Hence, the *real* is always and only the "real," is always only figural, fictional, scriptural (i.e., written, a kind of writing), never literal, and, as a natural consequence, even the self becomes a "self," first-person authority being subsumed by the discourse in which it finds its expression. Like all things else, "I" and "we" do not write but are written. The moving fingers of discourse or of social energy write and, having written, move on. In briefest and perhaps crudest summary, these are the "truths" implicit in item (d) that exert hegemonic authority in our era and that this book (quite madly, it would seem, if these "truths," in a wonderfully self-annihilating sense, be truths) has had the temerity to challenge or contest (even while granting the ubiquity of conceptual relativity and acknowledging that nothing can be described or expressed without relying on descriptions or expressions).

AUTHORIAL AUTHORITY

The positive alternatives to the prevailing views have been stated most emphatically in the previous chapters, but in this concluding section, it is perhaps useful to underline the importance of the creative agency of the author in the scheme of propositional entailments adopted in this book. Since specific contents, in our view, depend on intentional states, authors and speakers are crucial to the expression of determinate meanings and to our acts of interpretation. The manifold social, political, intellectual, and

mundane experiential factors that impinge on an individual and establish the
range and extent of her life- and mind-space (what we might call her cognitive and conceptual Lebensraum) achieve effective force and meaningful
shape only when they become functional parts of behavior, linguistic or
otherwise. In themselves they are nothing, or, what amounts to essentially
the same thing, they are infinitely many things. They are material conditions
waiting to be informed with contentful value and purpose. As interpreters
of linguistic acts, we strive to come to understand the intentionality that
endows the acts with definite content (i.e., meaning). And, as with all acts,
linguistic acts are rational, done for reasons, which are the causes of the acts.
The basic principle here is, no rationality, no action (or meaning). Now, to
represent speech or writing as a rational activity, according to Michael Dummett, we must describe it as "something on to which the ordinary proce-
dures of estimating overt motive and intention are brought to bear" (a
consideration of belief and desire, for example).[37]

The importance of the immediately preceding discussion for our purposes
becomes clear, I think, when we consider the distinction to which they lead.
Dummett makes the crucial distinction in the following terms:

> The concept of intention [the reasons—mental states—underlying and determining
> the specific nature of the action] can . . . be applied only against the background of
> a distinction between those regularities of which a [writer or] language speaker, act-
> ing as a rational agent engaged in conscious, voluntary action, *makes use* from those
> that may be hidden from him and might be uncovered by a psychologist or neurol-
> ogist [or by, say, a Freudian critic, a cultural materialist or new historicist]; only those
> regularities of which, in speaking [or writing], he makes use characterize the language
> as a language. He can make use only of those regularities of which he may be said
> to be in some degree aware: those, namely, of which he has at least implicit knowl-
> edge.[38]

Of course, trying to establish or, more modestly, to get a handle or purchase
on the nature and extent of the implicit knowledge of which the speaker or
writer is aware is no easy matter (no automatic one, at least). Nevertheless,
our repeated success in understanding what our articulate, carbon-based cohorts utter and write testifies to a capacity to participate imaginatively in a
rich diversity of what Wittgenstein calls "forms of life" and what we might
call "intentional systems."

Every utterance or statement is attached to a body of additional beliefs
and assumptions that are not part of the statement's meaning but that are
absolutely necessary to its conveying and our understanding its meaning.
Simply, to understand the sentence "The mouse ran up the clock," we must
first know, among other things, in what circumstances it appears (whether
in a children's book, an allegory, an everyday situation), and who (what
kind of person, in what state of agitation or calm) said it to whom; addi-

tionally, we must have many ancillary beliefs about the world we are in if we hope to come to a proper understanding of the precise content of the statement—beliefs, for example, about mice as pests, about furniture, time-pieces, locomotion, and on and on through an indefinitely long list of unspoken but operative beliefs. Indeed, the list of necessary ancillary beliefs requisite to understanding changes as the aspects under which the objects are taken change. As the terror of Maple Street, young Sam comes before us trailing a bag of background assumptions and beliefs quite different from the one he trails behind him as Father Mike's most devout altar boy. At any rate, it seems clear that as we gain more experience, we gain, as Samuel Johnson once said, "more principles of reasoning, and found a wider basis of analogy," the cumulative process steadily improving our skill at understanding new meanings, new "forms of life."[39]

Moreover, included within the class of regularities of which the speaker or writer has at least implicit knowledge are all those things that are suggested rather than stated openly, all those inferences that we draw, for instance, from tone, level of diction, and circumstances of expression, all that the saying or doing of such and such may imply, so long as each "implication" contributes to the functioning of the work's system of intentionality, is, indeed, a requisite component of the intentional system, one necessary to the proper understanding of the utterance, statement, work. For example, when King Lear at the very end of the play delivers the line "Pray you undo this button. Thank you sir," as he crouches over the lifeless body of Cordelia, our understanding of its meaning depends, in the first instance, on a host of background assumptions and beliefs that are necessary to but not part of the meaning (beliefs about buttons, shirts, jackets, apparel generally, as distinct from that network of beliefs about buttons in their relations to beliefs about bellies, bodies, anatomy, or their relations to mushrooms, vegetative life generally, or to political campaigns, graft, party platforms, or whatever), and, principally, on our grasp of the massive character transformation that Lear has undergone in the course of the play. Our pity for him at this point is governed by our understanding of his move from blinkered imperiousness and rashness to humble dignity and gracious, generous kindness in the face of intolerable hardship. It is fair to say, I think, that definiteness of content always hinges on the unwritten or unspoken background conditions and beliefs underlying the occasion of local expression, local intentionality.[40]

The reasonably attentive reader will have noticed that Dummett has left open a space through which a variety of critical and interpretive vehicles may comfortably pass by suggesting that in addition to the regularities of which a speaker or writer *makes use*, there are those that "may be hidden from him and [that] might be uncovered by a psychologist or neurologist" (or, for that matter, a Freudian, a Foucauldian, a new historicist, a cultural materialist, and any other-ists who are not interested in works as unique products of art, the informational and representational functionality of which are governed by systems of intentionality that have their effective source in the mental states of particular writers and speakers). If your aim, for example, is to come to an understanding of the "cultural poetics" of an era with a view to exposing the orders of political dominance and oppression implicated in that poetics, then, as we have argued above, discussion can begin anywhere and move in any direction so long as you are pretty certain from the "get-go" what the "political unconscious" or the ineluctable forces of history are up to, since the elements of the cultural "text" under scrutiny are determined in their meanings and values by that "unconscious," by, that is, your prior understanding of the "unconscious" and the power relations that fall within its range of expression. Agency in this mode of analysis is transferred from the conscious mental states of authors or speakers to "social energies" (especially as manifested in class, gender, or race relations), to historical forces, or perhaps the internal dynamics of the unconscious mind.

There are, undoubtedly, less question-begging ways of proceeding (though, in general, one gets the sense in reading these analyses that all roads lead to the imperial city governed by you-know-who—yes, the Wizard of Capitalism). For instance, one could "discover" lines of association or relation in the course of one's research, noting a thread here and, surprisingly, a similar one way over there, and still another one very much like it first here and then there (and so on), until a larger pattern quite suddenly emerged in the carpet. By such meticulous thread trackings (and serendipitous thread discoveries) one is led slowly and inductively to conclusions about the era that the era itself, despite its reticence and evasive ways, has taken pains to disclose, albeit subtly and quite surreptitiously. The discovery of patterns in the fabric of cultures or eras is certainly not to be numbered among the lesser pleasures of intellectual inquiry, and only the congenitally querulous would be inclined to deny that eras, like regular folks, play favorites, take a fancy to some notions, ideas, beliefs, and so on and not others. Nevertheless, all sober, decent-minded, clear-thinking people, like you and me, would quickly note that although eras, cultures, and periods display trends and fashions, they do not really have contentful states or ends in view (except "in a manner of speaking"). We cannot, except in a manner of speaking, transfer agency to language, history, culture, or to anything else incapable of forming and manipulating representational (i.e., informational, contentful) states.

Of course, manners of speaking are handy things. As John Searle observes, "just as we can 'impose' agentive functions on natural phenomena such as sunsets [or rivers, attributing to them a desire to reach the sea, for example], so one can 'discover' nonagentive functions among artifacts."[41] Keeping in mind that *functions* are not intrinsic to either physics or syntax but are "imposed" by our mental states and that artifacts are fashioned in some way or another out of materials with no ends in view by people with ends in view, we can, if we wish, talk about regularities that are, as Dummett has noted, "hidden" from authors and speakers (regularities that analysts and cultural materialists can uncover). Providing an illustration of "nonagentive functions among artifacts," Searle notes that

> If . . . you accept the distinction between latent and manifest functions, and you believe that latent functions are unintended, then the discovery of latent functions of institutions is the discovery of a nonagentive function of an artifact. Thus, for example, if you think that the unintended latent function of money is to maintain a system of oppression, then you will *claim to have discovered* a nonagentive function among the agentive status functions of money.[42]

There is perhaps no criminal degree of exaggeration involved in the claim that today's theorists are specialists in uncovering the hidden sense, the latent meaning, or the presence of the absent signification, particularly those theorists with psychoanalytic loyalties or those operating under the influence of post-Sausurrean linguistics and a post-Foucauldian understanding of power relations in Western capitalist states—in short, all (but a few "reactionary") theorists. But whether natural phenomena (as in setting suns, purpose-driven rivers, pumping hearts, and so forth) or social phenomena (as in circulating social energies, the poetics of a culture, oppression-bent eras, and so forth) are endowed with "agentive" functions, or whether unintended nonagentive "functions" are discovered within the elements of our institutions of language, literature, commerce, government, and so forth, it remains the case that suns know nothing of setting and that cultures have no poetics, and this is so because suns and cultures are not meaning or intending sorts of things.

To those who would object that there is nothing beyond manners of speaking, or who would insist that among manners of speaking there is no choosing based on some ultimate warrant or truth, I can only say please return to page one and start again. Or, if that advice imposes too heavy a burden, perhaps it is sufficient to remember that although nothing can be described without relying on descriptions, we are not left with nothing but descriptions; some descriptions are better, truer, more right, more fitting than others. Moreover, and more relevantly to our current concerns, our only access to structures of meaning and, consequently, to the trends, crotchets, preferences, predilections, biases, unasked questions, and unquestioned assumptions of a given period, era, or culture is through an understanding of the intentional acts of symbol users, an understanding that is especially alert to the specific uses to which common elements are put on the specific occasions of their employment. That the same terms, ideas, images, doctrines, and so on are found in a multitude of texts, say, is no guarantee that they are put to the same uses. Ostensible similarities in doctrine, for example, may conceal real differences in content, in meaning, emphasis, and value, as anyone can plainly see who examines, to take a convenient example, the apparent doctrinal correspondences between Longinus's *On the Sublime* and Sir Joshua Reynolds's *Discourses on Art*. Although both critics concentrate on qualities rather than species of art and share an interest in the faculties of the artist and the emotional effects of art, they are, as critics, advancing radically different conceptions of art. Further, they do not deal with the same critical problem; they make different assumptions, and they pursue different methods of argument. As Elder Olson noted long ago, "Longinus views the products of several arts in terms of a single effect [the sublime]; Reynolds views all the effects of a single art [painting]."[43] Yet a juxtaposition of passages isolated from the principles and assumptions informing each of them with determinate meaning would lead one to believe that they are bringing the same (or very similar) doctrinal offerings to the same altar. The obverse also obtains: ostensible differences in doctrines (terms, phrases, images, etc.) may hide real similarities in viewpoint. And, of course, what applies to these two writers widely separated in time and place applies as well to writers living in the same period, as one can easily see by looking at, for example, the various discussions of taste, genius, and the problem of evil in the eighteenth century. As we get closer to an issue, a problem, a set of concerns, an era or culture, we discover that, though topics and interests are shared, approaches to them vary widely among writers and even within a given writer over time. It is only by attending to the systems of intentionality in which the common elements make their appearances that we can begin to come to an understanding of the richness and complexity of an era or of the many cultures of meaning that make up a culture.

Let me conclude this exploration of the broad implications, of what is at the heart, in the belly and the inspissated gloom of item (d) with a couple of summary observations. First, it is quite true that "language and texts do not represent or refer to extralinguistic or extratextual reality." Language and texts are not referring or representing agents; they have no semantic preferences and no semantic proclivities. Nevertheless, by our intentional use of language and the sentences of our texts in the service of our systems of intentionality, we are able to refer to and represent what is extralinguistic and extratextual. As we have argued long ago, mental states are representational states, and as such, they are directed at and are about something other than the language. Finally, and in partial support of the preceding, I would note that the statement (the text), "A text refers [only] to itself and other texts" does not itself *refer* to itself and other texts (it has no referential function at all apart from some intentionality). Rather, it asserts, that there is an "extratextual" thing called a text that refers to itself and to other texts. Such a statement, in other words, is not an example of what it states is true of texts, if I understand what this text intends to say.

FACT, FICTION, AND METHOD

Chapter 6
Fact, Fiction, Belief, and Emotion

In the preceding chapters, by focusing on the broad issues stated or implied in the current orthodoxies registered as items a, b, c, and d under the first category (somewhat misleadingly labeled "Deconstruction"), I have managed to address, sometimes quite extensively, a substantial number of the views or positions that are to be found under the remaining categories of the "Current Orthodoxies." Consequently, in this and the following chapter, I shall take up issues occasioned by the doctrines itemized in category two and then move quickly to a consideration of the last four categories in chapters eight and nine. As I proceed, I shall attempt to avoid—or at least to minimize—repetition of matters covered elsewhere, though at times rehearsal of key points will be necessary to give force and clarity to local arguments on specific issues. Also, as I consider the remaining items in succession, it is useful to remember that, even though I will occasionally cite and take issue with the views of specific critics, my aim in these chapters, as throughout the book, is not to subject the articulated views of specific theorists to special scrutiny or to provide detailed critiques of particular essays or books (except incidentally), but to consider a host of prevailing principles, assumptions, and doctrines in the light of alternative conceptions of the matters under consideration and to make a case for the superiority of these conceptions to those still in the ascendancy or for their being more felicitously conformable than their current rivals to our experiences and daily (i.e., nonacademic, off-duty) practices. In short, the principal aim is not to provide nuanced accounts and critiques of densely argued and brilliantly executed theoretical documents by this or that theorist. No, the principal aim is to highlight the intellectual or argumentative weaknesses of the major commonplaces that anyone familiar with theoretical discourse in these halcyon days of poststructuralism and late capitalism finds circulating in the ambient intellectual air, and then to show why we would all be much better off if we discarded our radical skepticism and relativism and allowed our critical practices to be informed by the notions of meaning, truth, content, intentionality, correspondence, agency, and so on that this book elucidates and endorses. Baldly put, this book is less concerned with detailing shortcomings than with making a positive case for views not much in favor today. (And, even though determinate meanings and authors seem to be making something of a comeback, they are doing so in advance of any strong philosophic justifications. This book hopes to make some modest contribution to such justifications.)

Under category two rather generally and somewhat misleadingly titled "Skepticism and Irrationalism," we find the following items:

a. There is no direct *or* indirect access to truth.
  i. One implication of (a) is that there is no essential difference between a historical text and a work of fiction ("new historicism").
b. It is impossible to be objective, impartial, to transcend one's biases in taking up a position—there are no innocent, disinterested positions.
c. There is no such thing as a rational method or procedure for arriving at knowledge.
d. Since no position (theory assertion, knowledge claim, perspective) has more rational warrant than any other, "anything goes."

In the first two chapters, I examined the issue of truth and our access to it in some detail, and, thus, there is no need to rehearse previous arguments here. Nevertheless, item (2.a) occasions some additional reflections and comments on the accessibility of truth. An obvious question is immediately provoked by item (a): What is the truth-status of the claim that we have no access to truth? Is the claim true or false? If it is false, then it should be consigned to the Dumpster and never again permitted to trouble the world's peace. (And, of course, if it is false, one thing is certainly true: it is certainly true that it is false.) On the other hand, if it is true, then it is false, because we have somehow gained admittance to that to which we cannot have access. In other words, if it is true, we are in the odd position of having no access to its truth; our plenty makes us poor indeed, since the pot of gold (i.e., the knowledge that there is no pot of gold, the truth that there is no truth) is buried beyond our reach, no matter how deep or how energetically we dig. What is it exactly that one knows when one understands item (a)? In putting this and similar or cognate questions to (a)—and other items of its ilk—one almost always feels a little unclean or embarrassed, feels, for example, the way one would feel if one had taken unfair advantage of or a cheap shot at an adversary, had had the discourtesy or uncouth temerity to call attention to the spinach ort trapped between his teeth, the toilet paper attached to his shoe, the effrontery to note that the emperor was giving new definition to the phrase "scantily clad." But I think it is always fair to ask of any claim whether it applies to itself. Undoubtedly, many a tree, indeed, many a forest, would have lived to enjoy the blessings of maturity had the question been asked early and regularly of many icon-shattering theoretical claims. That the question is easy and obvious takes nothing from its power and muscularity (as has been shown time and again with, for example, positivism and relativism).

Still, there is always the possibility that the question in making its mark misses the mark. Surely, item (a) is not affirming that we are barred from access to an indefinite number of homegrown, socially constructed, theory-laden, scare-quote encased "truths," such as "my car was clocked at seventy miles an hour by the patrolman's radar gun," "the eighteenth president of United States is buried in Grant's tomb," "the largest tree in the yard is an oak," "Samuel Johnson spent many years in London," "there is nothing outside the text," "everything is political," "fish gotta swim," "I had Quaker Oats for breakfast," "quarks have flavors but no hair," and so on through a list of "truths" without end. And, just as certainly, item (a) does not rule out access to a vast host of a priori truths (such as those of arithmetic, geometry, formal logic, and so on) or of definitional or analytic truths—claims that are true simply by virtue of the meanings of the terms employed (such as "all bachelors are unmarried men," "all husbands are male," and so on). No, none of these truths is inaccessible. Lurking within item (a) is a rejection of metaphysical or naive realism and its faithful, indispensable companion, the correspondence theory of truth (and, coordinately, the adoption of linguistic idealism and conceptual relativism). What we do not have direct or indirect access to is TRUTH, the way things just are independently of our perceptions, conceptions, constructions, independently of mind, language, culture, ideology, or episteme. Access is denied to TRUTH, the place where *saying* and *being* enjoy all the rights and privileges of the equivalence or identity relation, where *saying* mirrors or forms a perfect match with *is*. The claim that truth is inaccessible is really a shorthand, attention-grabbing way of saying that what passes for truth is only "truth," that is, "truth" within a discourse, a conceptual scheme, or a way of talking. Since we have no unmediated access to the Transcendental Signified, to reality in itself, and since we, thus, have no way of bringing our sayings and schemes into alignment with the fixed, preexisting order of things (the fixed assemblage of entities, properties, and relations that would provide the ultimate warrant or justification, the supreme maker good and true, of our sayings and schemes), we are condemned to the prison houses of our contingent conceptual schemes, and if as a consequence of our condition we can become acquainted with many varieties of interesting and sometimes conflicting or incompatible truth claims, we are prohibited, it seems, from privileging any.

Of course, as we have seen, from the fact that we have no unmediated access to reality, it does not follow that we have no access to what is genuinely, toe-stubbingly real. Nor, as we have seen, does it follow from the relativity of truth to conceptual scheme that we cannot determine that one scheme is better, truer, more appropriate than another or that we cannot distinguish between true and false, better and worse claims within conceptual schemes. There is clearly no point in rehearsing in detail here what it was the burden of the first two chapters to establish, but because, as Samuel Johnson once observed, we need more often "to be reminded than informed," a quick overview of major points may be in order.[1] First and foremost, it is important to remember that belief in realism—the view that there is a way things are independently of our representations—is entirely compatible with conceptual relativity in that as far as the truth of a representation is concerned, realism avers only that the truth of a statement, in whatever conceptual scheme, is a function of whether what the statement is about is in fact as it is represented to be, of whether what is talked about within a given scheme is as it is said to be.

In other terms, realistic truth insists that truth bearers be tested by truth (or false) makers. Truth, as we recall, is a semantic term, and semantics is concerned with relations between signs and what they are signs *of*, with the representational aspect of signs. Whatever has content has semantic properties, and, hence, semantics is inextricably bound up with intentionality, the capacity of the mind to represent things, to direct attention to something other than itself. Now a *truth bearer* is anything that can be true or false, for instance, a belief, proposition, sentence, or anything else with content (principally, a mental state or a linguistic act). The idea of content is bound up with the normative, in that the content of a belief, say, is the condition under which it is true (if the condition is not met the belief is false), just as the content of a desire is the condition under which it is satisfied. It is true that the eighteenth president of the United States is buried in Grant's tomb and false that the nineteenth is, and my desire for a martini will be satisfied or not depending on whether I get what I want. The condition that justifies the holding of the belief is the truth maker (just as the condition that brings me to what I want or what I want to me is the satisfaction condition).

Worth remembering also is the fact that all intentional states (thoughts, propositional attitudes)—states, that is, with content—have satisfaction conditions. And these conditions are specific to the states (i.e., have specific content), inasmuch as they express or represent their conditions of satisfaction under certain aspects. Our seeing, wanting, intending, fearing, believing, and so on are perspectival, aspectual, are directed toward this, not that, and toward this considered or seen from this, not that angle. Moreover, following from the above and crucial to the view adopted in this book is the recognition that the truth conditions are not internal to the intentional states' system or mode of representation. In other words, saying so is not making so; the truth conditions (the truth makers) are not internal to their representations (the truth bearers). As Hilary Putnam has noted, "truth genuinely depends on the behavior of things distant from the speaker, but the nature of the dependence changes as the kinds of language games [of systems of representation, of conceptual schemes] we invent change."[2] In still other words, we do not make worlds; rather we supply descriptions and representations that the world or "what is the case" does or does not satisfy. We provide conditions of reference, for example, but we cannot make those conditions obtain. We can tell the waiter that there's a fly in our soup, but we cannot produce the fly by enunciating the claim; only a fly (i.e., what we have consented to agree that the term applies to in its insect-designating function, as distinct, say, from its front-of-the-trousers designating function) can satisfy our claim and justify our outrage.

With our mental states and linguistic acts we transform, in Raymond Tallis's terms, "reality into [the] truth conditions of factual assertions."[3] Reality itself, because it has no intentional states, makes no truth claims and has no semantic preferences. Nevertheless, although reality has no legislative power and no disposition to say what's what or to call a spade a spade, it does have veto power when it comes to determining whether what we call a this or a that is a this or a that. And indeed, as John Searle has pithily and accurately remarked; "For every true statement there is a corresponding fact, because that is how these words are defined."[4] The upshot of all this is that we end up believing or we persist in believing only what is true, and we act only on what we believe to be true. The one real world is not some preexisting totality of entities, properties, and relations (if only because an infinite number of real things, events, and states have yet to emerge and because each of us can create on the spot an indefinite number of truths [with their corresponding facts] which have no prior history and for which no accommodation can have been made. For example, it is a fact that an automobile assembled in Marysville, Ohio, is parked in my garage, (and the statement of that fact is a true statement); it is a true fact that a quark is humorless, though never dyspeptic, that "London" is not spelled "London" in French, and so on and so on ad infinitum. Rather, the world or external reality is, as I have argued earlier, the formal or logical condition of the possibility of making true statements. If our representations represent things the way they are, regardless of whether they are mind-dependent or mind-independent things, then those representations are true, fit, appropriate, accurate. And we know we have access to truth, because we know what it is for some of our beliefs to turn out to be false, some of our representations to get things wrong or not to be fit, appropriate, or accurate, given the way things are. For a more extended treatment of our access to truth (and its relation to how things are), the intrepid and boredom-resistant reader can always peruse again the first two chapters, where, following Davidson, I argue that compelling sense can be made of the view that we have direct access to truth, inasmuch as words and thoughts emerge simultaneously with their truth conditions—words and thoughts take their meaning from the objects and events to which they are applicable. That said, I am finished with item (2.a).

Well, almost finished. The rider attached to (2.a) as (i)—"One implication of (a) is that there is no essential difference between a historical text and a work of fiction"—assumes (and depends, in large measure, upon our acknowledging) that we have no direct or indirect access to truth because we are locked within the borders of language relations and language systems. Thus, there is no essential difference between historical and fictional texts because all texts, by virtue of being texts, are fictional, in the sense that they are not referentially or otherwise connected to something independent of language, something real. Since no text can tell us what is really the case, all texts are fictional, are constructs of one or another linguistic community, are, in short, made up, factitious, not factual. The assumption underlying this rider has been adequately dealt with, I hope, in the first two chapters of the book and the opening of this chapter, and much that is relevant to the substance of the rider (hereafter "a.i.") can be found in the discussion of the "textuality of history and the historicity of texts" in the immediately preceding chapter, which subjects to review and examination certain distinctive aspects of new historicism or cultural poetics.

In the next few pages, rather than thrashing again what to me is the dead-horse view that there can be no difference, essential or otherwise, between historical and fictional texts because all texts are "made up," are fictions debarred of access to the way things really are in themselves apart from any taint of the human, I would like to seize the occasion of (a.i.) to consider in a cursory fashion some few of the striking similarities and differences between "real" and fictional accounts of things and between our responses to these distinct accounts, giving special attention to the appropriateness of applying "true" or "truth" to aspects of each kind of text. Of course, a full or even adequate discussion of the manifold relations subsisting between art and reality or, more restrictedly, between fictional works and the nonfictional world of things, actions, and events is beyond the scope and ambition of this chapter (and perhaps the ability of this writer), but it is possible, I think, to make a couple of points on these relations that are usefully consonant with the ongoing interests of this book.[5]

One clear problem with fictions—one separating them from "real" narratives or accounts of things—is that their meanings and references have no identifiable existent conditions of satisfaction; their assertions, claims, posits, people, and places have no truth or satisfaction conditions. There are no existent people, places, or things that can serve to establish the meanings or references of our terms or to guarantee or warrant the applicability of our terms. There are, in short, no existent conditions that can function as the causes of the application of our terms. And there never were or will be any such conditions for fictional people, places, or things. If, as I have elsewhere maintained, the content of a belief is the condition under which it is true, then a great number of the referents in our fictions would seem to have no contents or, otherwise put, no truth-satisfying conditions. It would be as vain and fruitless to look for Santa's guiding of a sleigh in the evening sky as it would be to look for Hamlet's stabbing of Polonius in Gertrude's chamber, or Ahab's searching for the white whale in the ocean's vastness.

Although some distinctions do not seem to make much of a difference, in the general course of things, whenever or wherever we mark a distinction or difference, we do so because a difference is felt or understood, as is the case with the distinction marked by the terms "fiction" and "nonfiction." I'm not sure that the difference we acknowledge to subsist between "a historical text and a work of fiction" is an "essential" difference, but it is taken, I think, to be a real difference, with at least some not insignificant attitudinal consequences for the reader. However richly enhanced and embellished with fictional or novelistic features and techniques designed to heighten interest in action, character, or scene, Truman Capote's *In Cold Blood* and Norman Mailer's *The Executioner's Song*, for example, would be seen to be considerably less estimable as achievements if we were to learn that these accounts of murderers and of their thoughts and activities had been created out of the whole cloth of perfervid imagination and had no basis in actual people or events. Similarly, Boswell's unparalleled accomplishment as a biographer would be more than a little sullied if we were to learn that the *Life of Johnson* had no "real-life" person as its model (we here assume, of course, no independent testimonies to Johnson's existence in the era for which he not so long ago provided the eponymic identification). Similarly, it seems equally clear that if in a coda to an interesting and deeply moving story we were suddenly informed—in a kind of Paul Harvey "and-now-you-know-the-rest-of-the-story" revelation—that everything narrated had actually happened to the narrator's relatives during the Second World War, we would undoubtedly experience a not unremarkable change in our attitudinal state. Something significant would be added to our apprehension of and response to the narrative.

What exactly would be added to this narrative or what exactly would be taken away from the Capote, Mailer, and Boswell writings, it is difficult to say, but once we know that what we had taken to be "real" is "made up" or what we had taken to be "made up" is "real," we experience those changes in our condition that follow directly from the difference between confrontation with what might or could have been the case and what was in fact the case. The experienced differences are, loosely speaking, more quantitative than qualitative, matters of degree rather than of kind, with the "real" events registering generally at the higher intensities, assuming comparable degrees of artistry in the telling of the real and fictional events, such as the betrayal of a friend or the reunion of long-separated lovers. Furthermore, in terms of probability, coherence, strict concatenation of events, or consistency of character, we will, within certain ranges, tolerate in the telling of the "true" story what we would find unacceptable at best or reprehensible at worst in the "fabricated" story. (The "true" story has more *give* to it; we allow "real life" more irregularity when it comes to probability, coherence, consistency, regular concatenation of events, and so forth.) What would destroy or severely weaken the pleasure we derive from the fiction could have little or no effect on that which we derive from the true account.

Basically, at this point, all I would insist upon is the rather innocuous and obvious point that where there is a difference in our state of knowledge relative to people, places, and things there is a difference in our response to or experience of them. Of course, matters become infinitely more complicated when the view of the city before us shifts from the perspective from afar, where neatness of pattern prevails, to the scene from within the gates, where streets, buildings, alleys, shops, and other manifestations of urban complexity overwhelm the senses and tax the understanding. In other words, our responses to actual works are complicated by the admixture of fact and fiction in virtually all narratives, perhaps especially in those such as E. L. Doctorow's *Ragtime*, in which "real" events and characters intermingle rather promiscuously with fictional events and characters, Mailer's *Armies of the Night*, which announces itself as "history as a novel; the novel as history," and countless other, mostly modern (or postmodern) works that cross borders with sometimes alarming frequency. And of course, even works that are nominally and preeminently fictional frequently make more than occasional reference to "real" people, places, and things (such as Queen Elizabeth, Dover, France, cargo, shoes, and so on). Moreover, all this is further complicated by the fact that all narratives, including those that are straightforwardly historical or biographical, are presented from a particular perspective and under the guidance of certain governing assumptions, predilections, biases, and beliefs, with considerable discretion being left in the hands of writers to select, order, and emphasize the materials of the text.

All texts, then, are factitious, that is, made up, and as several wags have noted, there are histories, but no history—no one true account of the way things are or were. The same facts can be variously weighted, and the same events variously reported, so that we can have many accounts—many true though competing and conflicting accounts—of, say, the war for American independence or the English war to suppress the American insurrection. Actions and events are coordinated and concatenated and are determined to be probable, possible, or inevitable according to this or that writer's conceptions of things and relations among them. Inaccessible thoughts, motives, rationales, emotions, and intentions are regularly supplied to agents by writers in an effort to justify or explain small- and large-scale effects. To explain why this or that happened writers commonly reason back from effects to what they suppose to be the mental states responsible for them (or, alternatively, they endow social or economic forces and conditions with agentive functions).

Alas, for a substantial number of the narratives that we take to be factual accounts of real events we often have no authority other than trust or faith. Most or many of them could be fictions, root and branch. Some that the faithful take to be true and factual accounts of real events other readers (e.g., skeptics, agnostics, atheists, show-me Missourians) take to be mythic reports designed to gratify the credulous and advance the powerful or the powers that be—or would be. But putting aside the blandishments or inducements of faith or doubt, there seems to be no way to determine once and for all whether the credulous or the incredulous are in the right simply by looking very hard at the details of the narrative itself. In these and countless other cases, there would seem to be no device or technique of representation, no way of using language or of arranging events in texts that is peculiar to "real" accounts (or fictional accounts), thereby distinguishing them from fictional accounts (or "real" ones).

The upshot would seem to be that factual accounts are often not clearly distinguishable from fictional accounts—by their vestments we cannot separate the true princes from the pretenders. Consequently, we are obliged, it seems, to admit what our common sense required us to deny, namely, the truth of (a.i.): "there is no essential difference between a historical text and a work of fiction." Both kinds are "made up" and made up of the same kinds of materials. And, it is unquestionably true that we can be and sometimes are taken in by appearances, that we readily extend to the pretender the welcome we had prepared for the prince; that is, we sometimes mistake a fictional for a factual narrative. Yet, when we are not stretched to full intellectual rotundity by some grand theoretical afflatus—by the invigorating and wonderfully transgressive view that we have no access to anything that is *not* made up by us, that is *not* a product of our own making and doing, our own linguistic dexterity—we can tell "a hawk from a handsaw," as Hamlet says. In other words, when we are functioning as common citizens of the world and not in our official capacity as theorists, we routinely differentiate fictional from factual accounts, even when we must do so from sentence to sentence or from paragraph to paragraph within a single work. Moreover, even the most dedicated theorist has no trouble making and using the distinction to good practical effect in the course of a day's reading or during a trip to the local bookstore.

In the mundane, practical, brown-shoe, workaday world of decision-making, we generally have very little trouble determining whether the text (or the portion of the text) before us is dealing with what we conveniently, conventionally, and quite routinely think of as real or factual matters or with what we think of as fictional ones, regardless of our on-duty philosophical or metaphysical convictions. By and large, we treat as factual what is represented as such or what we have compelling or sufficient reason to suppose is factual or have no overriding reason to suppose is not so. As always, our understandings and reactions are controlled by what we have reason to believe is the case. (For the theorists, the trouble comes when people start thinking the "real" account has some special metaphysical or ontological privilege, some transcendent warrant or justification.) Of course, we can be duped into thinking that the fictional is factual, as we have seen, and of course, many fictional works shamelessly proclaim that they are relating true events in the voices of the very people who have witnessed or experienced them, notable examples, selected from what in full extension would be an extraordinarily long list, being Defoe's *Moll Flanders*, Swift's *Gulliver's Travels*, Lardner's "Haircut," and Faulkner's "Spotted Horses." Yet it is fairly safe to say that virtually every reader understands that these are fictional works, in large measure because of some subsidiary awareness of another controlling intelligence at work (usually in the selection and arrangement of elements according to principles of coherence, probability, and consistency—principles, in short, necessary to the achievement of maximum artistic effect);[6] because of the presence of fantastic or otherwise "unreal" elements; because of the moral or intellectual obtuseness of the writer, which encourages as it endorses the recognition that the evaluative center of the piece—the first-person narrator—is himself under evaluation, or because of other signs of untrustworthiness or fictional construction.

Although coming to a proper understanding of the fictional or factual status of the work before us is an unremarkable and rather commonplace achievement, there is nothing automatic about it. Nor is there any algorithm or formula that we can follow to ensure a correct understanding of the fictional or factual status of any work. Rather, such understanding depends on a form of abduction, that is, inference to the best explanation, given the available information. However spontaneous, sudden, or automatic the judgment of status might appear to be, it is, at least for the time being, the most satisfying working hypothesis (or guess) about the system of the text's intentionality that we can imagine, most satisfying, that is, in terms of explanatory power and relative to any possible alternative that could be formed at this stage in our encounter with the text.

It is not surprising, I suppose, that we would be such adepts at understanding and interpreting narratives of various kinds, since as people we are to the manner (or to the genre of narrative representation) born, constructing our selves in the authorial mode and transforming our sequential experiences into various narratives, some more fanciful or fictional than others. It seems that we are fabulists and historians congenitally, by native endowment. When asked who we are, where we're going or coming from, what we plan to do with our lives, what we did last night, over the weekend, on our summer vacation, and countless other questions, we tell stories, some tall but most of average height. On a correlative issue, John Searle has wisely observed that "just as our particular experiences occur to us as aspectual, i.e., with aspectual shapes, so there is a narrative shape to sequences of experiences."[7] Moreover, there is nothing idiosyncratic in this view; we can trust Owen Flanagan when he notes that "many thinkers have converged on the insight that a narrative conception of self is the 'essential genre' of self-representation."[8] And the "self that is the 'center of narrative gravity' . . . is a complex construct. It is both expressed and created in the process of self-representation."[9] Let me bring this brief digression on our natural affinity for narrative to conclusion by noting an interesting implication and necessary consequence of the view that the (or a) self is the gravitational center of the personal narrative. As Flanagan remarks, this view entails a conception of personal identity "as a scalar relation [i.e., one admitting of degrees] of continuity and connectedness caused in part by the agent's own activity in light of [his conception of his past and] his . . . visions for his [subsequent] development." And "thinking of identity in terms of agency makes sense of future concern . . . and allows the possibility that I may participate authorially in the creation of a changed person to whom I am nonetheless narratively connected at each point in the reclamation and transformation project."[10] Whatever else it may be, the self is unquestionably an agent dedicated (perhaps in a strict biological sense) to representation and narration, to giving functional form to how things are, might be, could be when considered from this or that factual or fictional perspective (with factual and fictional being understood in their quite ordinary, commonplace sense).

Clearly, the issues embedded in item (2.a.i.) are large in number and extensive in scope, but, fortunately, I can satisfy the interests of our inquiry by looking quickly in my concluding remarks at a couple of similarities between factual and fictional accounts, similarities that preserve the distinction between the two (indeed, depend on its preservation), while also reinforcing our earned understanding that factual accounts can tell the truth about people, places, and things, can get things right and be, well, really true. To get to these similarities, however, I must first revisit what I had to say about fictional content many paragraphs ago, at the opening of this discussion. There, after noting that the only things with content are mental states (e.g., propositional attitudes, intentional states) and linguistic acts and that all intentional states have truth or satisfaction conditions, I seemed to suggest that one clear difference between fictional and factual people, places, and things is that the items referred to in fictions had no content, because the conditions to which the terms were applied simply did not obtain. There simply is no Desdemona or Othello, no Booby Hall (in *Joseph Andrews*) or Pemberley (in *Pride and Prejudice*), and what is represented as taking place cannot take place, because there are no "real" people to take action or thought in any "real" setting.

The immediately preceding remarks seem wrong, if true; they are affronts to our experience and understanding, for if we know anything at all, we know that *Emma, Bleak House, Tristram Shandy, Crime and Punishment, Titus Andronicus, Huckleberry Finn, Sula*, and countless other fictions are chock-full of contents, are content-laden artifacts that have incalculably enriched and augmented our understanding of what's what, of what carbon-based creatures like ourselves can know, feel, believe, think about, and so on. Any reader of any fictional narrative can provide a very detailed account of the contents of the text that she has just read. The problem of content as presented here is in fact a pseudo-problem; the closed room in which we find ourselves has an unlocked door allowing easy egress. And the way out is through our working notion of intentionality.

To refer to anything, we must be able to think about it (and, as we know, what we think about we think about in certain ways, under specific aspects). Now, intentionality is that ability of the mind to represent things other than itself; "it is that feature of representations by which they are about something or directed at something."[11] With very little imaginative effort we can think about and, hence, refer to a limitless number of things for which the "real world" has made and can make no accommodation, including elves, satyrs, Martians, griffins, unicorns, and so on, and not excluding Santa, the tooth fairy, Jocasta, Madame Bovary, and on and on. Our mental contents are not restricted in terms of reference to preexisting entities, concepts, and relations. Furthermore, at the quotidian level (rather than the purely imaginative level), we can have as our intentional object a smoking pipe that is no pipe but only a mirror reflection or a trompe l'oeil—or even a hallucinatory—image of one, and we can feel real pain in a phantom limb—and feel it at a specific site on the limb, not at a site of specific electrochemical activity in the brain (feel it, that is, where it is not and not feel it where it, in some sense, is). The illusionary and phantom limb examples are special cases and need not concern us here, but at the imaginative level there are remarkably few restrictions on reference, on what can be referred to or thought about, though our flights of fanciful representation must have at least some tenuous ties to what falls within the range of extrapolation from existent things and concepts—those we can believe to be true, those for which there are satisfaction conditions that can be met.

About the last point, I would note that it applies even to our most fantastic, surreal, and otherworldly representations that are rich in ogres, sprites, aliens, ghosts, wizards, and benign "fairy-tale" figures, such as Santa and the tooth fairy. All such creatures are compounds of materials or features with which we are familiar—tails, skin, teeth, wings, scales, hair, red suits, and so on. Moreover, much of what I know to be true, I cannot verify or show to be true, cannot supply the truth conditions on which the truth of my knowledge depends; for example, I know, but cannot confirm, that (nonexistent) witches fly through the night on broomsticks. I know what witches are definitionally (or analytically), simply by virtue of knowing what the word "witch" means (by virtue of how witches are represented as configurations of such-and-such features, with such and such powers and moral propensities), and I understand the sentence because I have a wide acquaintance with the concepts of night, flying, and broomsticks (as well as with the representative features and behaviors of witches). A comparable point is made by Hilary Putnam when, in support of the view that it is not the case that we must know how to confirm or verify every statement that we understand to be true, he writes:

even if we take a statement we do not at all know how to confirm [say, "there are no intelligent Martians"], the fact is that the concepts which it employs are concepts which figure in other and simpler statements that we do know how to verify. Our ability to understand such an "unverifiable" statement is not a *free standing* ability. [And, although] I do not believe that truth can be *defined* in terms of verification . . . understanding what truth is in any given case and understanding what confirmation is are interwoven abilities.[12]

For our mental states (our intentional states) to have content, they must have semantic properties such as meaning, reference, and truth conditions, since semantic relations are principally matters of the relations of signs to what they are signs of (are intimately tied to intentionality, to what signs are directed to or about), and what the signs are *of* or *about* is their content. But what they are about need not be true or "real"; what they are about, however, must be intelligible, or refer-to-able in terms that are publicly understandable. In other words, the reader or listener must be able to determine whether in their application the terms are being used correctly, appropriately, or acceptably; use must satisfy correctness conditions. Only those intentional states involving belief have truth as their satisfaction conditions, and we do not *believe* in the real existence of fictional people, places, or things, though we certainly can and do refer to them. The assertion that "there are unicorns prancing in my garden" is both intelligible and false. Contentful mental states are not dependent upon particular existent "realities," though it is fair to say that such states would be impossible if there were *no* mind- or language-independent conditions to which our terms could be applied.

To some, it may seem that we have traveled a great distance to establish what few, if any, have doubted, namely, that fictions do indeed have contents (and, subsidiarily, that we do not *believe* that fictional people, places, and things have truth conditions), but, in my view, the trip is necessary to the following brief discussion of some aspects of the appropriateness of thinking of belief and truth in relation to works of fiction.

If at times we cannot tell the difference between historical (and other nonfictional) texts and works of fiction, that inability is not a consequence of the fact that all works are fictional (that there can simply be no objective facts capable of serving as the truth conditions of our sentences, assertions, or beliefs), as our postmodern skeptics and linguistic idealists would insist; rather, it is a consequence of the fact that in all our verbal representations of matters of interest to us we depend on the same linguistic and conceptual resources. Such truth-functional operators as "not," "and," "but," "if . . . then," "not only . . . but also," and so on do their assigned work of negation, conjunction, qualification, and so on whether they appear in legal statute, biography, public service announcement, or in this or that drama, novel, or other work of fiction. And, as Donald Davidson has acutely observed, most "of the words in a literary work have an ordinary extension in the world," in that "predicates, adjectives, verbs, common nouns, and adverbs do not lose their normal ties to real objects and events when they are employed in fiction." He goes on to make the crucial point that if they did in fact dissever such ties in fiction, their meanings would change radically, and "if their meanings changed we would not understand them."[13] This linguistic and conceptual overlap is requisite to the intelligibility of all our texts. Whether the text in front of us is fictional or nonfictional, the fact is that in both kinds of texts "trees" refers to *trees,* "houses" to *houses,* "smiles" to *smiles,* "anger" to *anger;* "very" functions as an intensifier, and "walks," "jumps," "bites," and all the other markers of action do their customary work.

It sometimes happens among naive readers or spectators that works professedly or generally understood to be fictional are treated in some or all— usually some—of their aspects as representations of actual people and events, as when warnings to characters are shouted out in the theater, when actors are berated on the street for their behavior on stage or in a soap opera, or, to bring such instances to an end, when authors are consulted by correspondents about the current activities and whereabouts of their characters. Naive as these responses may be, they usefully show, I think, that concepts and referents, as well as our evaluations of their moral weight and value, can be transported back and forth quite easily across the border separating fiction and nonfiction, and that it is quite possible—indeed, it is quite common—to draw on the same inferential and interpretive skills when dealing with both kinds of works. Of course, except in special cases, we are usually conscious of the fictionality of fiction and (almost) always so in the theater (if we thought what we were witnessing on the stage were real, we would often be criminally negligent or at least morally deficient if we did not intervene in some way with what was taking place on the other side of the footlights; one or two properly interjected disclosures could do much to alleviate the witnessed distress). We usually do not mistake fiction for fact. Yet, we deploy the same skills, understand essentially the same meanings and references, and make essentially the same inferences as the naive reader when we read our various texts.

Nevertheless, unlike the naive reader, our consciousness of fiction—whether evoked by an identifying marker on the title page, such as the word "novel," by one or another "genre" clue, or by some other means—sustains throughout the reading experience the conviction that we are dealing not with representations of real people and events but with representations of hypothetically possible real people and events, with, as Samuel Johnson said long ago in the "Preface to Shakespeare," "just picture[s] of real original[s]." We are dealing with such realities as are possible to people with our physical, cognitive, and emotive endowments and our manifold interests and proclivities. We deal not with realities, but with what is, if you will, "thought-experimentally real." In other words, our concern here is with those works of fiction in which people like us, armed only with such intellectual and emotional resources as are possible to us, are represented in situations to which we could be exposed. And by "thought-experimentally real," I mean only that our thoughts (our contentful mental states) are directed toward such people, situations, events, dilemmas, and so on as can be imagined to fall within the range of our endowment and experience.

Aristotle, focusing primarily on drama, called such works imitations, because they "imitated" possible lives, exhibited the actions, characters, and thoughts of possible people in a concatenated sequence of events governed by some principle of form, some end in view. Writing many centuries later, Samuel Johnson observed that "imitations produce pain or pleasure, not because they are mistaken for realities, but because they bring realities to mind"; they bring before the mind what is, in my terms, "thought-experimentally real." In the brief section of the "Preface to Shakespeare" that has our interest here, Johnson is addressing, among other things, the credibility of fictional representations of life, addressing, more exactly, the question of how drama can move us if it is not believed to be a true depiction of the way things are. To Johnson, the answer, as we have partly seen above, is that "it is credited with all the credit due to a drama. It is credited, whenever it moves, as a just picture of a real original." In Johnson's view, as spectators, we are always in our senses; that is, we are conscious of fiction, but we are moved by exactly the same beliefs and inferences that affect us in our "real" lives. We do not take the representation for reality; it is, rather, an image of reality. As Johnson says,

the reflection that strikes the heart is not, that the evils before us are real evils, but that they are evils to which we ourselves may be exposed. If there be any fallacy, it is not that we fancy the players, but that we fancy ourselves unhappy for a moment; but we rather lament the possibility than suppose the presence of misery, as a mother weeps over her babe, when she remembers that death may take it from her.[14]

The analogy that Johnson uses to give vivid emphasis to his point—the mother's weeping in response to the imagined death of her child—is, I think, deeply instructive. What the mother does, she does (admittedly, as *Johnson* represents her) in real life in a moment as she imagines (i.e., thought-experimentally depicts) the actual death of her real child, thereby subtly enforcing the conclusion that there is nothing formally or contentfully distinctive about the beliefs and emotions that occur in the "real" setting that could effectively serve to distinguish or differentiate them from those occurring in a fictional setting. Now, as we have elsewhere seen, we believe only what is true (or, if you'll allow a not entirely lazy or inane tautology, what we believe is true), and a belief is something that we are prepared to act upon. For example, I believe that beer exists, I want a beer, I believe, further, that there is a can of beer in the fridge; hence, I *go, walk, run, move at a gallop* to the fridge, where conditions are such to make my belief true and to satisfy my desire. Had the conditions in the fridge been different, that is, had the fridge been beerless, my belief would have been false and my desire unsatisfied. Now, if I tell you a story about a character named Bill who believed and did as I believed and did, we would have in the fictional, the imagined, the thought-experimental case exactly the same set of conditions that obtained in the real case—well, almost exactly the same set, the only difference being the fictionality of one set. Whether this constitutes an *essential* difference between "a historical text and a work of fiction," I am reluctant to say, but it does mark a real difference, one that makes a differ- ence. In other words, it is not the case that there is no difference between historical texts and works of fiction because all works are fictional (as many theorists would have it); rather, it is the case that there is no interpretive or affective difference between the two kinds *because* one kind has genuine truth conditions and the other kind has those same conditions in a hypo- thetical mode. Moreover, it is also the case—and this is crucial—that the fictional kind interests and moves us *because* there are true conditions that we can imaginatively represent. It is the truth of the factual accounts that gives the fictional accounts their force upon us and their relevance to us. All this may seem rather simple, obvious, and even silly stuff, but sometimes you have to make a fool of yourself when you take it upon yourself to announce, in opposition to those who are content to think otherwise, that the emperor is not, as we might say, suitably attired, is not more handsomely invested than your common jaybird.

Moreover, when we are dealing with fictional representations there is no question of suspending disbelief, since the reader or spectator is, as we have seen, always (or usually) in her senses, always (or usually) conscious of the fiction. The fiction is not taken to be real; rather the fiction brings realities to mind. That said, however, it is clear that what is brought to mind is very much the same sort of thing that is brought to mind when we read or witness true events, with one slight difference: in the fictional case, we do not supplement our inferences and judgments with the belief that the events are existentially real or true. On a companionable issue, Elder Olson many years ago convincingly argued that our emotions are based on our opinions, that is, on how we understand or size up situations and that the only difference between our reactions to fiction and reality is grounded in the "additional reflection" that the real events are existentially real, since it constitutes the sole difference between the fictional and the real that affect thought or belief.[15]

Without an opinion or belief about the object of our emotion, there would be no emotion; in other words, as Bijoy Boruah has put it, "a suitable belief about the object of an emotion is not only conceptually necessary for the emotion to be what it is, but is also causally efficacious in producing that emotion."[16] Boruah goes on to distinguish between evaluative belief (e.g., the emotion of fear depends on the evaluative belief that, say, something confronting us is dangerous) and existential belief (e.g., the fear has an immediate, local, and real object of attention), insisting, further, that the evaluative belief is necessary and prior to the actual emotion (the lion in front of us does not evoke the emotion of fear unless we evaluate it as dangerous, believe it to be dangerous). And since this is the case, then fictional characters and events can evoke the same emotional response that the "real" ones evoke, because in both cases the evaluative, though not the existential, beliefs are the same or have the same content. Summing up one major line of his argument, Boruah writes,

Our emotional response to fiction is a reflection of our normal emotional response to incidents of real life. Fictional emotions are rooted in the normal emotional reality of our daily life. They are the extended, and sometimes sophisticated expressions of the very attitudes to life and the world which underlie the occurrence of real-life emotions. What accounts for this common root, and the essential continuity of the former [the fictional] with the latter [real-life] is the *enduring doxastic repertoire*, which is carried along by us as we enter into a fictional world.[17]

Boruah subsequently observes that "this conceptual bond [i.e., the doxastic repertoire that endures across fictional and real-life worlds] . . . explains our ultimate anchorage in reality."[18] And what is true of our emotions, of the beliefs requisite to our emotional responses, is true also of the meanings and references that we ascribe as we read or witness works of fiction. It is the anchorage in reality—in what is true, in what it is appropriate to believe in the represented circumstances—that gives our fictions their interest and emotional power. In the end, it "is not fictional persons but thoughts about persons fictionally depicted by which we are moved."[19]

When we are not in the grip of some *parti pris*, some overriding view of things through which everything is filtered, our beliefs—and, hence, our emotions—are governed by that system of intentionality that is responsible not only for the peculiar aspectual features of the details of the text but also for their logical relations and semantic implications. Of course, that specific system of intentionality upon which our evaluative beliefs and, hence, our emotional responses depend derives from the intentional, representational acts of an agent, whom it would not be an instance of egregious contumacy to call an author. From the preceding, I want to draw out an incidental but extremely significant point, namely, that if our emotional responses are functions of the author's represented system of values and are regulated by that system (as I believe they are), then it follows that no work can have a value that transcends the dignity or worth of its underlying conception. Hence, even assuming flawless skill in the selection and ordering of the elements of the text, we still evaluate works—determining that some are better, richer, deeper, more humanly valuable and significant than others—in terms of the value of the ends to which that artisanal skill is subservient, in terms of the value of our reading experience.[20]

There is, of course, no firmly fixed, universally accepted, Good House-keeping–approved scale of values to which we can appeal in making our judgments, but there seems, nevertheless, to be a strict proportionality between our pleasure (our satisfaction) and the richness of the ethical and intellectual challenges with which we are asked to engage imaginatively, with the greatest pleasure being evoked by those ethically and intellectually rich works that unravel their perplexities and achieve their resolutions without taxing the credibility of the reader or violating the conditions of their own integrity. Just as people fond of puzzles prefer difficult ones, because their solution provides greater satisfaction than the solution of easy puzzles, and just as those who like to solve mathematical problems (or any problems, for that matter) prefer tough problems to easy ones because the pleasure that solution brings increases in proportion to the challenge surmounted, so readers—at least those who go in for deep pleasures—derive pleasure from fictions in proportion to the extent that they give fair, accurate, and vivid representation to those perplexities and dilemmas to which we might be exposed or those challenges with which we, given our bodily constitution, our cognitive equipment, and our emotional propensities, might be confronted. In short, we are pleased in proportion to the value and richness, as well as the seriousness and importance, of the *realities* that are brought to our minds. And no work can transcend the value of its informing conception (though we, of course, may value it for things other than its internally constituted value—for, say, its social or political importance, or for countless other extrinsic values, not excluding its value as a doorstop or for holding open a window).[21]

Expanding on this point would undoubtedly take us far afield, but a simple illustration of how we could progressively raise the moral and intellectual ante of a fictional representation might be helpful here. Suppose, then, that we have a contest between two characters played out in a game of cards, with the winner taking the pot; now raise the stakes incrementally from a heap of money, to a piece of property, to a loved one, to one's own life, thereby augmenting the interest and seriousness of the wager as we change the stakes. Or suppose the antagonists are engaged in a battle to the death; make the adversaries first enemies, then friends, then relatives (cousins, say), then near relations (brothers, father and son, etc.), adding new moral complexity to the confrontation with each change. Of course, the focus here is on but one kind of possible enhancement of interest and pleasure; any richly pleasurable work of fiction will strive to maximize the effectiveness of each of its parts so that they all function cooperatively in the interest of that system of intentionality to which they owe whatever meaning and value they have. The story of star-crossed lovers as represented by the "rude mechanicals" in their drama, "Pyramus and Thisbe" (in *A Midsummer Night's Dream*), is an exceedingly comical "tragedy," but when what is essentially the same story is presented under a radically different controlling conception as *Romeo and Juliet*, it is a deeply moving tragedy, a work whose moral and artistic value far surpasses that of its rival—though, admittedly, in its place, "Pyramus and Thisbe" contributes marvelously well to the effectiveness and value of the work it supports.

At the end of our discussion of (2.a.i.), we can perhaps best express our disagreement with its claim by assenting to it: we agree, then, that "there is [a real but] no *essential* difference between a historical text and a work of fiction." But we must immediately hasten to add that the sameness derives not from some all-inclusive fictionality but, on the contrary, from the persistent durability of a way that things are independently of our representations, a way that can serve as the condition of the possibility of our descriptions and representations, and that our doxastic repertoire can get right or wrong (or, more exactly, can be right or wrong about). Works of fiction would not be "thought-experimentally true," would not bring realities to mind, if we could not distinguish what is true from what is false. Further, and finally, without an anchorage in reality, in what is true, fictions simply would not move and would not be.

Chapter 7

Incommensurability, Rational Method, and "Anything Goes"

Item (2.b.) in our second category is pretty much a staple of current theory; indeed, it seems to be a working premise or assumption, in one or another more or less sophisticated form, of a substantial number of those people today who are professionally engaged in the thinking-about-things business, inside and outside the academy and inside and outside the humanities. Boldly and baldly put, (b) states, "It is impossible to be objective, impartial, to transcend one's biases in taking up a position—there are no innocent, disinterested positions." Once again, of any broad claim it is perhaps a wise initial policy to ask whether it applies to itself. Applying the self-application policy to (b) has the consequence, it seems, of dumping us into the mind-boggling quagmire of deep paradox (the claim is false, if true) and the claim itself into the pit of self-refutation. In short, the claim seems to be simply another of the many forms that shape-shifting relativism can take. To see this, one has only to ask from what position this position on positions is made. The claim does not itself appear to be one made from *within* a position, but one made *about* positions, about the impossibility of taking a position that is not already positioned within a position. Moreover, despite its open-faced denials and notwithstanding its temerarious proclamations of impossibilities, item (b) seems to express itself in an "objective, impartial" manner and to speak quite "innocently" and "disinterestedly." At any rate, no one who had the least regard for probity would ever accuse item (b) of being "subjective," "partial," or of taking up a "biased," "interested position."

GETTING BEYOND INCOMMENSURABILITY

What gives item (b) whatever plausibility it has, what allows it, indeed, to pass among some (and those some are, alas, legion today) as a commonplace beyond question are its undergirding assumptions, namely, that all observation is theory-laden; that all descriptions are from a point of view; that there is no way to stand outside our culture or language game to get a look at how our terms match up with how things really are, and, because all this is so, that our various ways of seeing and describing are incommensurable. The incommensurability thesis is for most theorists today an ineluctable consequence of the view that our many different theories or paradigms not only see things differently but also see different things. The different theories do not and cannot communicate with one another because they do not share either meanings or, more important, referents.

As I have grown fond of insisting, it is ineluctably true that we cannot describe anything without relying on descriptions, that all our seeing is aspectual (we *see* everything *as* this or that, under this or that aspect or from this or that perspective), and that, consequently, all our explanations are, in a sense, theory-informed. But as we have seen (in the first two chapters), the aspectual or theory-laden nature of our observations and descriptions supplies no obstacle to our giving objectively true accounts of things or to our deriving real satisfaction from situations (as we have configured them). For our statements, beliefs, and propositions to be true—objectively and genuinely true—it is only necessary that things actually be as we represent them to be. The statement that I have a nickel in my pocket is true if and only if it is the case that I have a nickel in my pocket, since the nickel in my pocket is the objective truth condition (the truth maker) of the statement (the truth bearer). And, quite significantly, the normative nature of such contentful linguistic acts as "I have a nickel in my pocket" allows the possibility of error; the statement would be absolutely false if it turned out that there was no nickel in my pocket. Saying so doesn't make it so; or truth conditions are not made in the process of articulating claims (except, of course, in special cases, such as performative linguistic acts, in which the expression creates the condition that obtains, as in, for example, "I promise," "I appoint," "I resign," "I dub thee knight," "you're out," "you're safe," and so on).[1] Moving from the mundane (though not the ridiculous) to the sublime (or at least the other- or upper-worldly), we can provide a perhaps more striking instance of how the theory-ladenness of our observations supplies absolutely no hindrance to the objective and noncircular confirmation or rejection—the truth or falsity—of our theories by enlisting the aid of Thomas Nagel, who, on this issue, writes,

It may require some theory, of telescopes or of photography, to interpret the astronomical photographs that show the bending of the light rays by the sun's gravitational field, but the crucial observation—that the images of the stars near the sun are displaced outward—is not dependent on the theory which it confirms—namely, the general theory of relativity.[2]

Indeed, had the displacement been different—had there been, for example, no displacement—the theory would not have been confirmed but falsified. Once again, then, our theories, views, and beliefs are confirmed or made true by a way things are independently of our theories, views, beliefs, and so on. And because this is the case, we can arrive at objective knowledge of a great many matters of interest to us.

On the matter of incommensurability, it is quite true, of course, that two positions are incommensurable if they have different takes on the same objects, events, or states of affairs, if they provide different accounts of the same thing. But to be in a position to say that two accounts are incommensurable we must be operating outside either position, inasmuch as such a judgment is not and cannot be an internal feature of either account.[3] In short, we are not locked within the prison houses of our language systems or conceptual schemes. With any scheme, we can always go "meta"; that is, we can always talk *about* what we talk *with*, can always say what the scheme is interested in and how it goes about expressing that interest. What we cannot do, of course, is *talk about* what we *talk with* from *within* the *talking with* system, inasmuch as, in that case, we would not be talking about it, but with it. Interestingly, then, to say that something is true or right or fitting within a conceptual scheme or according to the priorities or interests of a dominant ideology is to say something objectively true (if, of course, what one says about the scheme or interests is true) *about* the scheme or interests, but something that is not itself relative to the scheme or the interests. This is not to suggest, however, that we have found a way to some completely "disinterested" position from which we can talk *about* "interested" positions. Not at all. When we talk about a scheme's or a language game's interests, we do so in a language that has its own interests, a language that has an interest in fairly describing the scheme's interests but does not presuppose the worth, truth, legitimacy, or whatever of those interests. For example, I can easily describe what the Ptolemaic view of the relation of sun and earth is and contrast that view to the Copernican view, being fair to both views and partial to neither. I can state clearly and fairly what the views are trying to explain and how they go about the job of explanation. Relative to the views described, however, my description of them is not only objective and impartial but also, well, disinterested and, in some appropriate and agreeable sense of the term, innocent.

Moreover, not only can I talk about rival views, but I can also compare the two and make judgments about the superiority of one to another. Of course, for comparison to be possible at all the competing, conflicting, or rival theories would of necessity have to have some object of concern in common; they would have to share a common subject matter or have common referents. Otherwise, there would be no contest, no rivalry, no conflict, and there would be between the two nothing up for grabs. And, as one writer has observed, "the shared beliefs need not be important, interesting, or numerous"; it is enough that some referents be shared. Speaking of Greek, medieval, and modern astronomers' reflections on stars, this writer goes on to note that "It is the common beliefs shared by the temporally distant astronomers which fix the common subject matter of their theories and which underlie our conviction that [the differences exhibit] a case of theory-change, rather than meaning-change."[4] Further, to illustrate the point that theories do not have to share meanings but only referents to be compared and evaluated, Michael Devitt and Kim Sterelny provide a simple but instructive case:

we can compare the "theories," "the evening star is closer than the Earth to the Sun" and "the morning star is not closer than the Earth to the Sun," even though the terms, "the evening star" and "the morning star" differ in meaning [i.e., one means "the star visible in the evening," whereas the other means "the star visible in the morning"]. We can do so because the terms are co-referential [refer to the same thing]. Given this fact, we can see that the two theories cannot both be true; one refutes the other. So we can set aside talk of meaning and concentrate on reference.[5]

What is crucial to the adjudication or evaluation of the claims of rival theories or views, in addition to their sharing a common subject matter, is that the outcome of the issue or matter to be decided is not inherent in what is shared. Less darkly, what is shared allows both views and is not predisposed to favor one or the other, and, in the case where one is confirmed and the other rejected, the observations or whatever that make adjudication possible do not presuppose the truth or superiority of one of the rivals. Both conditions are essential to the process of comparison and adjudication; the allowance condition is necessary to comparison and competition, and the neutrality of the observations is necessary to the objectivity of the evaluation of the rightness or fitness of the theories. In a discussion of the first condition, John D. Greenwood gives as an example the competing theories of "evolution" according to "punctuated equilibrium" on the one hand, and "continuity" on the other: noteworthy is the fact that although "both competing theories presuppose the same theoretical characterization of 'evolution' (in terms of adaptive changes, etc.) . . . neither explanatory theory is presupposed by it." To illustrate the second condition—that even though "the critical observations that frequently enable scientists to adjudicate between competing theories are frequently theoretically informed, they are rarely informed by the competing theories"—Greenwood presents two exemplary cases:

the telescopic observations of the stellar parallax that enabled scientists to adjudicate between geocentric and heliocentric theories [both allowed by belief about shared referents] were informed by the theory of the telescope, but did not presuppose the accuracy of either the geocentric or heliocentric theory. [Moreover], the X-ray diffraction discriminations of the structure of DNA that supported the Watson-Crick theory of the structure of DNA over its rivals were informed by the theory of X-ray diffraction but did not presuppose the accuracy of the Watson-Crick theory or any of its rivals.[6]

Whatever one's biases as a witness may be going into one of these debates, the observations or criteria that both parties accept as decisive (and, importantly, as neutral relative to the matter at issue) force one to transcend one's biases and to accept the decision of the impartial—though theory-informed—referee, much to the consternation, we must assume, of the supporters of item (2.b.). In the end, there may be no uninterested positions, but when our interests are not prejudicial to the issues at stake, they can be crucial to disinterested judgment and evaluation.

One of the most—perhaps the most—persistent, intransigent, and common errors committed by many current literary theorists is the assumption that any attempt to discuss conflicting views impartially necessarily presupposes an ability to get outside mind and language and take a look at things from the perspective of eternity, of epistemological and ontological neutrality. Regulating my ambition by a painfully keen sense of human limitations of mind and constitution, I only affirm, in all modesty, that the language used to describe rival claims can be at once fair to both claims without being partial to either and partial to some interests without being unfair to the competing interests of the rival claims; thus, the language of description and evaluation is fair and impartial without being uninterested. It is just that its interests are not prejudicial to either of the claims seeking a hearing and wishing to have its interests prevail. The speed gun's interests in measuring the speed of cars, buses, bikes, rollerbladers, hikers, and fast-balls can be disinterestedly and impartially decisive in determining whether the state's theory or your theory of how fast your car was moving prevails before the magistrate.

Having tapped the heavens, the genetic code, and the courtroom for assistance in the task of taking some of the boldness out of item (b)'s temerity, I would like to conclude these reflections on (b)'s effrontery, gall, cheek by using a conflict between "new criticism" and "Chicago criticism" as my final illustrative example of how fair description and impartial evaluation might work. Both the New Critics and the so-called Chicago critics were identified as "formalists," and both were interested in and used the term "form," yet they developed incompatible theoretical positions. For the New Critics "form" made a pair with and found its antithesis in "content," and this binary unit (form/content) was often paired or exchanged with such other similar binary units as "style"/"content," "the poetic"/"the discursive," "irrelevant texture"/"logical structure," and "image"/"idea." On the other hand, for the Chicago critics "form" was what gave "matter" its structure and function, and a text was a regulated, hierarchical sequence of form-matter relationships with the "form" of one level becoming the "matter" of the next higher level, all the way up to the synthesizing principle of form for the whole text. As many literary historians have shown, it is quite possible to describe accurately *how* these critics variously used the same terms, *what* they sought to explain, and *how* they went about their explanations without resorting to language partial to either critical position. Indeed, I have just provided such a description, albeit a sketchy one.

Furthermore, in this particular case, it is possible, I think, not only to compare the theories but to determine the superiority of one view to the other. Assuming a common interest in accounting for the "full formal integrity" of any given literary work and, thus, the appropriateness of "comprehensiveness" as an evaluative standard (everyone familiar with the contests of these "mighty opposites" will acknowledge the legitimacy of our assumption here), we can say unequivocally, I think, that relative to the Chicago position, the New Critical one is limited or partial, in that it is concerned with and can make accommodations for fewer *commonly recognized textual particulars* than its rival—being focused on the dynamic tension or paradoxical relation of terms, ideas, images, symbols, and themes, while subordinating or neglecting such things as character, action, and manner of representation. Consequently, the Chicago position, in accounting for more *commonly recognized particulars* than its rival (including those for which the New Critics also made accommodation), is superior in explanatory power to that of the New Critics. Generally speaking, the New Critics subsume many works (virtually all works) under a single structure, finding the same system—though different manifestations—of tensions between "logical structure" and "poetic meaning" in (virtually) all works, whereas the Chicago critics distinguish among many *kinds* of structures and seek, further, to identify the peculiar "principle of form" underlying each particular work of any kind. Of course, this is an "illustration" of how comparison, evaluation, and judgment of rival critical theories could proceed, not a full-scale argument in defense of our "illustrative" conclusion. In other words, the reader need not accede to the conclusion to consent to the explanatory authority of the example. Enough has been accomplished, however, if the reader—after bracketing, as we say, the incoherent, self-refuting nature of (b)—can no longer comfortably yield to the seductive charms of (b)'s conventional wisdom-violating claims about the impossibility of objectivity, impartiality, and disinterestedness. I offer no brief for our innocence (our ability, that is, to adopt "innocent positions"), but I believe we can still tell a jaybird from a jailbird and sometimes know when we get things right and when one view is better than another.

RATIONALITY AND METHOD

The last two items enrolled under the second category can be and will be handled with some dispatch, in part because they raise few issues that haven't already been examined in detail and in part because the conceptual and practical issues that they entail do not invite extensive treatment. Item (2.c) avers that "There is no such thing as a rational method or procedure for arriving at knowledge," and item (d) provides the welcome assurance that "Since no position (theory, assertion, knowledge-claim, perspective) has more rational warrant than any other, 'anything goes.' " In this concluding section of this chapter, I shall consider each briefly and in the order in which they are listed. With (c), we could shorten the workday by simply noting that if there is any method at all for arriving at knowledge it would have to be a rational one, inasmuch as rationality is implicated in method by definition (is a constitutive feature of anything going under the name of "method"). An irrational method is not an oxymoron (in which the terms, though ostensibly or genuinely antithetical, are perfectly appropriate to the things or circumstances to which they are immediately applied—as applied to the rude mechanicals' "Pyramus and Thisbe," the apparently self-annihilating phrase "lamentable comedy" or "tragical mirth" is happily apt, and despite the apparent native antagonism of the conjoined terms, understanding winces not a bit when introduced to such couples as "military intelligence," "benevolent dean," "obedient child," or "happy marriage"). No, an *irrational method* is not an oxymoron but a flat contradiction in terms that cannot be resolved by any special circumstances or exceptional cases. There may be some madness in Hamlet's method, but where there is method in it, there is no irrationality; even the mad have their reasons and act under the guidance of beliefs and desires and intentions (frequently, alas, against their own best interests).

At any rate, if a method *is* a method only to the extent that it is purposeful activity (i.e., activity requiring agents to take certain steps or make certain moves that have as their end the realization of the purposes of the activity), then any method is by definition rational. Indeed, a method is rational to the extent that it is or involves activity, since actions, unlike mere motions or movements, are performed for reasons, and are explained in terms of the reasons for them. As one philosophical wag has put the case, "Such behavior as does arise from beliefs and desires—actions—must, of course be rational, given those beliefs and desires. That is what it is for behavior to be an action."[7] Put as simply and as pithily as possible, a method is rational simply by virtue of what it means to be a method.

Of course, none of this is to deny that we often—all of us some of the time, some of us, if not most, at least a great deal of the time—behave irrationally, take steps, and make moves that retard rather than advance our best interests, or take the nickel today that forethought and prudence would have transformed into a dollar tomorrow. And no one would deny us the capacity to choose—deliberately but anything but wisely—benefits that cancel one another out, as when, for example, we enjoy our first smoke of the day while jogging on the treadmill or when we indulge our disdain for the dean during the presentation of our grant proposal. Moreover, our interests are often divided, our desires conflicted, and our beliefs unsettled or unstable, and when these conditions obtain, we have a tendency to act not rationally but impulsively, preferring even a bad outcome to the anxiety of neurasthenic indecision. Additionally, we know that weakness of will—that ability to discern what we ought to do, what is right to do, what is best to do, and then to do otherwise (usually for some temporary gain or, well, just for the hell of it, just because it's not like us to do so)—always stands ready to dog our steps and, in the usual event, to impede our progress. And, standing on our elevated perch, we can see that our associates below sometimes are mistaken in their beliefs and corrupt in their desires (i.e., that they believe what is untrue and want what is harmful), and that, consequently, they act in ways that only the self-deluded would consider rational. But irrational as such actions are when viewed from the balcony or the pedestal, they are rational in some sense of the term, since, like all actions, they are rationalized by the contents of the mental states that cause them, that are the reasons for the actions; they are rational, given those beliefs and desires. (At least they are so when they are not purely whimsical or impulsive.)

Are we then obliged to enroll under the rational any action whatsoever, however mean, malicious, destructive, however bizarre, turning the "rational" thereby into a category capable of accommodating all acts, rational and irrational? Well, yes and no. Yes, if what we mean by rational action is one undertaken under the guidance or sponsorship of some beliefs and desires, some mental states causative of the action and, hence, explainable in terms of such states; the action is rational to the extent that it is explicable in terms of mental states functioning as its reasons or causes. But no, if by accepting the "rationality" of all actions we thereby feel compelled by the force of logic to abandon our right and obligation to call this or that action irrational. As a descriptive term, rationality applies to all actions, but as a normative term, rationality implies its opposite, irrationality. Just as what one truly and sincerely believes need not be true, so what one "rationally" does (what one does for reasons) need not be rational (as judged from, say, a "disinterested" perspective, one, that is, not blinded by self-interest). An action performed under a mistaken belief is not rendered wise, good, beneficial, or rational because it has its reasons. We must distinguish, as we have seen in an earlier chapter, between rationality as a condition of the possibility of any thought (and action) whatsoever and the rationality (or wisdom, rightness, and so on) of some specific action taken. Moreover, and this is a crucial point, the fact that rationality in its broad, descriptive sense can and does make accommodations for both rational and irrational actions does not mean that it is finally a null or empty category.

Much that is pointedly relevant to our understanding of the foundational shortcomings of the current orthodoxies, of much postmodern theorizing, follows from the view that rationality is the condition of the possibility of thought, meaning, and action (including, of course, verbal or linguistic action). For instance, where there is rationality, there is of necessity (as we have noted above) agency. Agreeing with Davidson, Devitt, and others cited elsewhere in this book, Christopher Cherniak writes that "The most basic law of psychology is a rationality constraint on an agent's beliefs, desires and actions. No rationality, no agent."[8] What is more, where there is no rationality, there is no content, no determinate meaning or reference, no objective truth. Upon our acknowledgment of the ubiquity of rationality in discourse and other action, then, much depends.

The immediately preceding paragraphs are somewhat digressive, I suppose, when considered in the light of item (2.c)'s broad pronouncement, but they achieve a certain pertinency when we recognize that so much of what fuels the current orthodoxies is the denial or diminishment of the importance of the agent (i.e., the writer, the author) in the determination of the literary work's effects and meanings.[9] To greater and lesser degrees, postmodern theorists either diminish or deny the role of the author in the making and shaping of the literary work and in determining its meanings, effects, emphases, and moral dimensions, reducing the author to an "author function" and giving priority to the ways in which language as such proliferates meanings or in which historical, cultural, social, or political forces or conditions of power govern the possibilities of expression (and thus, the writer's functional role) and the nature of class, gender, race, and sexual relations. Of course, in opposition to such postmodern theorists as Derrida, Foucault, Barthes, Greenblatt, Jameson, Lyotard, Lacan, and legions of others, I have attempted both here and elsewhere to submit a brief on behalf of the inextricability of content, rationality, and the mental states of agents. At the moment, however, my limited aim is to locate or uncover the possible underlying assumptions to which in a pinch item (c) might appeal by way of justifying what on its face is a patently absurd position, here supposing, for the benefit of item (c), that those who would deny or diminish the significance of the author—of agents and their agency—would as a matter of course or logical necessity have no use for rationality and, a fortiori, rational method.

In a further attempt to satisfy this retrograde ambition to give intellectual legs to this lame position, I could find a way to give partial assent to an aspect of item (c) if the emphasis of the claim were put on the "arriving at knowledge" phrase ("There is no such thing as a rational method or procedure for *arriving at knowledge*") and the point of the whole claim was to affirm that there can be no logarithm for creativity, for the intuitive leap to a fruitful hypothesis, for that sudden insight which, like a bolt out of the blue or an apple on the head, with gestalt suddenness removes the darkness from obscurity, untangles the perplexed, gives form to the shapeless, and society to our jumbled, unsociable ideas. "Live and learn," it is said by us and to us, and yet if experience is a great pedagogue, it frequently happens that what we learn from experience requires a leap of understanding, an inference based on information that is limited in examples and uncertain in its predictive powers (in its ability to assure us that things will be in the future as they were in the past or that this will follow with comforting regularity from that). Thus, we are fond of noting that our theories are underdetermined by the evidence or our observations, and our observations are overdetermined by or heavy-laden with theory. And it seems to be the case that whereas we have a pretty complete picture of what the formal rules of deductive logic are, we have no such picture for inductive logic, for induction or abduction (i.e., inference to the best explanation). But, of course, not only do we arrive at hypotheses (by one inspired or uninspired means or another) but we also attempt to confirm them. And confirmation (or disconfirmation), whose result is knowledge, depends upon method—and hence, rationality and rational procedure. As before, saying so or thinking so does not make so, and only some of our theories are satisfied by truth conditions. If wishes were ponies, it would be Christmas every day of the year. But alas, some of our theories run bump into recalcitrant conditions, and it's blue Monday all over again.[10]

Item (2.c) has undoubtedly taken up more time and attention than it deserves, but let me take one last shot at what might lie behind its attraction for adherents (if indeed it has any). In passing I should note that offhand I cannot think of any theorists who state the position quite as starkly as item (c) puts it, though it is also clear that there are few proponents of rational method among those who align themselves with what we are for convenience calling the current orthodoxies. In brief, to the supporters of item (c), if it is rational, it is tied up with reason. And if it is connected with reason, then it is inevitably part of the Enlightenment project, which, as many theorists tell us, is the source of all the woes of Western culture. Man's reason, which finds perhaps its most fitting symbolic representation in Blake's demon Urizen, is the instrument of oppression and subjugation and the means by which the powerful define the conditions of right, justice, order, nature, and truth. From reason, as from the head of Satan, spring objectivity, determinate meaning, capitalism, science, and all manner of unpleasant things. Accurately and informatively describing salient features of some current theorists' "radical questioning" of the importance of the concepts of intentionality and action to the explanation of human behavior, Paisley Livingston writes,

[These theorists] entertain the possibility that all notions of human agency are products of some purely contingent and factitious ideology or discourse, behind the back of which are the unknown . . . forces. As this story goes, the concept of individual agency is basically a theological hangover produced by the Enlightenment which, drunk on reason, sought to secularize the notion of God's divine will. [In place of this human agent] . . . what we need [they say] is a historical perspective on the emergence and future disappearance of what is taken to be the "problematic philosopheme of agency."[11]

On the matter of reason, objectivity, and the Enlightenment, one current theorist, Gayle Greene—self-identified as a feminist—taking issue with an antediluvian who has defended all three, says,

I think all this talk about *objectivity* betrays a kind of nostalgia for a simpler past when the world seemed knowable and manageable. Yes, feminists are suspicious of a standard which has brought the planet to its present disastrous condition, of that "*reason*" which has arrogated to itself so much power, the control not only of women but of as much of the world's resources and population as it has been able to grab. So was Shakespeare—his villains use *reason* to mask the most appalling irrationality— and he rightly identified such rationality with the new order, the "brave new world" he saw on the horizon, the *Enlightenment* perhaps, whose spirit of protestantism and capitalism, he suspected, did not bode well.[12]

For illustrative purposes one could hardly ask for a quotation more congenial to the interests of my argument here. It is perhaps ungracious, therefore, to note that Greene seems to have a pretty clear fix on Shakespeare's intentionality and to know objectively and with absolute certainty not only what Shakespeare intended but what he "suspected" to be on the horizon.

Now, as I said, I can guess, but I don't really know exactly what congeries of assumptions and beliefs undergird item (2.c) and aspire to endow it with plausibility, if not authority, but I do know that as an article of faith it will not withstand much scrutiny. Moreover, I also know that however ingenious and intellectually sophisticated the case for it might be, it cannot be very sturdy if the whisper of the most naive and obvious objection may topple it. In response to the claim that "There is no such thing as a rational method or procedure for arriving at knowledge," we do not need to enlist the aid of the countless kinds of knowledge we securely own as a result of the diligent application of what has come to be called, rather loosely, the scientific method or, more generally, to provide examples of the utility of the hypothetico-deductive method to those seeking knowledge in various areas of social, political, anthropological, historical inquiry. No, to say that there is "no such thing as a rational method or procedure for arriving at knowledge" is to deny that upon which I—like all my carbon-based, symbol-using cohorts—rely most of the days of my life, when, for example, I set out to locate my misplaced keys, when I track down the source or date of a poem, when I plot out an escape route at a cocktail party, and so on and so on. We are always right, I think, to reject any view that would make impossible that without which we could not do, that upon which our getting by, day by day, depends.

IN PRINCIPLE AT LEAST, "ANYTHING GOES"

The final item in this category, item (2.d), puts its case with Spartan economy: "Since no position (theory, assertion, knowledge-claim, perspective) has more rational warrant than any other, 'anything goes.' " At the outset, we should note that this phrasing gives us a current orthodoxy from the seamy side out, from, that is, the critic's perspective. The idea from the reviewer's and judge's seat is this: if, as the faithful repeatedly affirm, truth (along with determinate meaning, objective fit, and so on) can never make an appearance in any public forum without being adorned in scare quotes ("truth"), if truth (right, fit, meaning, etc.) is always contingent, theory-laden, relative to the language game in play, to culture, class, era, or whatever and never *really true* (fitting, and so on) for you and for me, now and later, then—and here the judge of the faithful makes his pronouncement—it would seem to follow as night follows day, Costello follows Abbott (tock follows tick, grief, marriage), that anything goes, that there are no defeasibility criteria or normative standards to which appeal could be made to determine the rightness or acceptability of this or that position, to establish its truth or falsity, or to settle disputes between contending theories, views, and interpretations (with the award going to the superior, better, or best litigant). In other words, because no position can present truth (etc.) unbedecked in scare quotes, all, or most, arriving at the ball must be welcomed as if they were to the manor born, must be greeted as princes and princesses. In other words, the "anything goes" charge is leveled by the critics of relativism against the relativism that is a pervasive feature of the prevailing theoretical orthodoxy, because it seems naturally to follow from any position that asserts that there can be no objective fit between our sayings or writings and what is really the case, or that affirms that an interpretation cannot be regulated by or brought into conformity with authorial intention, or that meaning is not determined (i.e., determinately fixed) by the intentional states of the author, or that there are, on the one hand, no worldly constraints or, on the other, no noncontingent, transparadigmatic logical (or rationality) constraints on our expressions.

Of course, the "anything goes" charge is persistently and adamantly rejected (when it is not simply ignored) by those against whom it is leveled, though, not surprisingly, the charge has never to my knowledge been successfully refuted. Before taking a quick look at one such attempt to refute the charge, however, I would note that by and large the proponents of current critical theory have not gone in much for sustained intellectual debate of complex theoretical issues or for responding to the sharp challenges that their adversaries have put to their principles, assumptions, and arguments. Rather than engaging in genuine debate with their opponents, adherents of the current orthodoxies have for the most part chosen to dismiss them out of hand or to neglect them (perhaps finding it safer to starve than to besiege or confront them). Moreover, over the course of the last twenty years or so, as one critical wave after another has broken over its predecessor and one ism after another has solicited their attention and allegiance, literary teachers, critics, and theorists (making up not three, but one class of folks) have been assimilators of one and all, not sifters or winnowers of the good, the bad, and the intellectually or argumentatively ugly. That is, they have not subjected the arguments of the successive appellants to severe scrutiny. Putting what is absolutely the best possible face on the common practice, Annette Kolodny has dubbed it, honorifically, a "playful pluralism, responsible to the possibilities of multiple critical schools and methods, but captive to none."[13]

In fact, these assimilators have made accommodations for a relatively narrow band of possibilities within the available range; and it is not unfair to say that within that band they have been captive to all, but critical of none. In truth, within that band, they have been equal opportunity employers and, collectively, the Ellis Island of the academic community, offering refuge to all varieties of ideas and claims, however tired or weak, and to all applicants so long as they had letters of introduction from, for example, Derrida, Barthes, Foucault, Bourdieu, Lyotard, Freud (via Lacan, of course), Marx (via Althusser and others), Greenblatt (via Foucault), and so on. The ready adoption of this and that aspect of the views of these and those (mostly French) intellectuals in one or another mix-and-match, Chinese-menu combination is not particularly surprising finally, since the progenitors of the adopted views (and thus, the acolytes) share a great many assumptions about language, reality, the social construction of meaning, the correspondence theory, and much else. Still, the unfortunate result of the neglect of contrary or opposing voices and arguments and the relatively unquestioned adoption and application of a fairly extensive but nevertheless very selective and restrictive body of assumptions, principles, and claims has been a dearth of the sort of tough-minded and rigorous debate that has led not only to heat but also to light in the so-called "hard" sciences, in philosophy (where tough arguments have as their mighty opposites other tough arguments), and in many other disciplines not dominated by the orthodoxies under review. As Brian Vickers has recently remarked, "in effect, a gulf exists between the critics of poststructuralism and its proponents, who simply ignore all critical voices. What might have been an important debate has never taken place."[14]

All of which is not to say, of course, that there have not been some significant controversies conducted in print (Vickers is speaking generally—

and speaking truly). One can immediately recall, for instance, lively and not unheated exchanges between John Searle and Jacques Derrida, M. H. Abrams and J. Hillis Miller, Stanley Fish and Ralph Rader, Fish and Walter Davis, Richard Levin and a platoon of angry social critics, and, if one searches deep into the hidden crevices within the memory bank or assiduously examines the bibliographical archives, perhaps a few other noteworthy debates. But for the most part, there is on one side a richly variegated landscape, that is, a long line of argumentatively cogent and intellectually informed critiques and trenchant analyses of the philosophical and practical limitations or shortcomings of the theories and views that have achieved virtually hegemonic authority in literary studies (and, increasingly, in every branch of the humanities and social sciences) and on the other side an arid plain and deafening silence, or, perhaps more exactly, a busy and bustling band of entrepreneurs alert to sales and demographic figures but remarkably indifferent to reports of product defects.[15]

Of the current theoretical scene it is also worth remarking, I think, that the adherents of the current orthodoxies have been not only starkly indifferent to the bone-dissolving critiques of their most fundamental doctrines and assumptions but also wonderfully ignorant of or uninterested in the broad range of inquiries going on in fields in which they presumably would have a strong intellectual investment, given the alacrity with which they pronounce of matters of history, economics, society, mind, culture, language, and so on. For example, although a not insubstantial number of critics have shown how Saussure's views have been misappropriated and otherwise mangled and mishandled by Derrida and others following in his wake, and although a not unimpressive list of philosophers and linguists has shown that, even if we take Saussure in pure, undiluted or uncontaminated form, we still do not have a very handsome body of insights into language, the only linguistics that has a purchase in theory is the Saussure-via-Derrida linguistics, modestly supplemented and adapted to special interests by Lacan, Barthes, Foucault, and others.[16] One looks largely in vain in the texts, notes, or bibliographies of these theorists for references to (let alone discussions of) recent developments in cognitive psychology, linguistics, the philosophy of mind and language, economics, political theory, and so on.

Thus, it is clear that in a very important sense anything does not go with these theorists. There is no room in the current orthodoxies, for example, for most of the positions on language, mind, determinate meaning, the correspondence theory, relativism, the possibility of objective truth, valid interpretations, and so forth that it has been the business of this book to elucidate and defend. So, although our theorists are short on defeasibility criteria, on standards to which appeal could be made to rule theories, views, meanings, interpretations, and so forth, in or out, right or wrong, fitting or unfitting, warranted or unwarranted, they are long on startling and indefensible opinions. They are absolutely certain, for instance, that there is no truth, only "truth," no stable, determinate meanings, only shifting, historically or culturally determined, contingent meanings, and so on. To misappropriate the language of item (d), what definitely does not go with our theorists, then, is the position that some "position (theory, assertion, knowledge-claim, perspective) can be objectively demonstrated to have more rational warrant than another." More expansively, what certainly does not go is anything that rubs the grain of anything stated or implied in the current orthodoxies in the painful way, that rubs against rather than with the grain of orthodoxy's foundational beliefs.

To bring this excursus on "anything goes" to conclusion, I would like to take a brief look at how Barbara Herrnstein Smith more or less defends postmodern theory against the charge. At the outset of her case, she insists that "a rejection of the idea of objectively determinate meaning [does not imply] that anything goes in the domain of verbal practices: that we can say whatever comes into our heads [no one, to my knowledge, has made this claim]; that all literary interpretations are equally valid, . . . and so forth." Everything does not go because our verbal behavior is constrained and limited in practice by what she calls "reciprocal effectivity." Smith, however, is obliged to recognize that, given the theoretical machinery from which she and others within the fold operate, anything could go *in principle*, but the fact is that *in practice* local effectivity keeps us within bounds. As she herself clearly puts it, "Indeed, the idea of reciprocal effectivity suggests why, although perhaps[17] anything always *could* go in principle, not everything ever *does* go in fact, either in language or in any other domain of social practice." Crucial to our understanding of how verbal or other practices are constrained, then, is a grasp of reciprocal effectivity, which, in so many words, is explicated as follows:

What are commonly posited as the laws, rules, maxims, principles, or innate hardwirings that constrain, or are presupposed by, verbal practices can be seen as reifications (that is, hypostatized abstractions) of the *relatively stable patterns* of those practices themselves: that is [and here we get to the heart of the matter], the patterns of coordinated verbal action and re-action that emerge from the ongoing practices of interacting speakers and listeners and are stabilized by their differential consequences for them as verbal agents.

Perhaps sensing that this verbal field is a bit too crowded with locutionary asperities, Smith takes another run at definition: "In other words, what keeps us more or less in line as verbal citizens is neither any abstract regulative force [e.g., such regulative ideals as coherence, consistency, logic, or rationality, essential to the expression of any thought or thesis] *nor* any biologically inscribed internal necessity,[18] but the fact that producing and responding to verbal forms in certain ways rather than other ways works out for us, on the whole, better rather than worse."[19]

In essence, Smith is offering here a slightly more subtilized version of the kind of pragmatic relativism that Stanley Fish formerly sold under the "interpretive communities" label; the basic idea is that the contingent standards of a local, historically or culturally situated speech community function as overseers of our sayings and writings.[20] What we say (or write) is true (or right or justified or warranted) if it accords with the standards of our culture, group, or speech community, if it is permissible within the language game we are playing or the interpretive community to which we belong. Truth, meaning, and reference are locally determined by the conditions of possibility inherent in one's historically established language game. If one does not play the game properly, then what one says is not "true," what one wants is not granted, and what one does is "wrong"; our sayings, wantings, and doings, then, have "differential consequences" for agents, depending on whether or not we play by the "rules" of our community or culture. Thus, within the culture or community, it is simply not the case that everything is up for grabs and that "anything goes." On the other hand, however, since nothing outside the local system can monitor our sayings and doings, since there are no external constraints (i.e., extracommunity constraints) on our sayings and doings, and since, consequently, no system can justly claim privileged status, it turns out, as Smith intimated, that *in principle* anything and everything could go.

There is no need here to rehearse in detail the arguments of previous chapters against relativism and radical skepticism about establishing truth, but as this discussion of item (d) and of the category as a whole comes to a close, it is perhaps useful to remember that, from the point of view advanced in this book, it is because there is a world independent of our representations that our representations can be true or false, accurate or inaccurate. And it is because you and I and the rest of our kind are causally and conceptually linked to that world in pretty much the same way that we can share understandings and arrive at the objective truth of things.[21] And although it is true that we cannot say things without using language or describe anything without relying on descriptive terms, we can articulate innumerable statements and claims whose truth is acceptable to members of various communities, ancient and modern, and in no way depends on the imprimatur of any particular, historically contingent speech or interpretive community. Birds gotta fly, fish gotta swim. These are truths in all cultures in which birds and fish have intelligible reference and in which flying and swimming are not mysterious concepts. Similarly, it is a truth universally acknowledged that you cannot enjoy the fruits of autumn while indulging in the visual and aromatic pleasures of the blossoms of spring, and that you cannot drink from the mouth and the source of the Nile at the same time.[22] Moreover, as we have repeatedly seen, there are worldly, linguistic, biological, logical, rational, and psychological constraints on our sayings and doings, all of which transcend, even as they work within, the constraints of our particular speech communities. And for the most part (except when we are dealing with analytic truths or those claims that are true simply by virtue of what the words mean or how the terms of the claim are defined), what *is true* depends on *what is the case*, and what is the case is not up to the community (except, again, in special performative or definitional cases).

Furthermore, on the interpretive side, there are constraints on meaning that derive from the intentional states of speakers with purposes, goals, ends in view. As we have elsewhere seen, only mental states and linguistic acts have content; contentful states are representational states, and representations are aspectual, that is, determinate in their content. Thus, where there is meaning, there are correctness or justification conditions, for as Colin McGinn has wisely observed "there is no such thing as meaning something by a word [or a sentence] and it being undetermined what counts as a correct utterance [or use] of the word [or sentence]."[23] Therefore, our interpretations are conformable to the represented intentionality or they are not. In the end, then, we can say that there are both external and internal constraints on the expression and interpretation of meanings (and, more generally, on what we can say or do)—external, worldly constraints and internal, psychological, intentional constraints, which are necessary prior conditions of any speech and are independent of any speech community. In principle *and* in practice not everything goes. Of course, nothing in all this automatically prevents a reader from misreading or overreading any text or speech, and every reader remains free to read each and every text in the light of her special interests or to relate the text in whole or in part, on the basis of any ground of similarity or affiliation, to any number of concerns—political, cultural, legal, racial, or whatever—that engage her energies and purposes. Of course, what the reader then says or writes will have, like the original text, a determinate meaning, one that also can be misconstrued in wonderfully baroque ways and applied in whole or in part to any number of matters of absolutely no interest to the reader-turned-writer/critic/interpreter.

SECTION THREE

INTERPRETATION, POLITICS, AND LITERARY VALUES

Chapter 8

Agents, Makings, and Meanings

Although in the preceding chapters we have ostensibly dealt with but two of the six major categories on the "Current Orthodoxies" sheet, the plain fact of the matter is that in dealing with these two (and with their conceptual entailments or implications), we have been obliged to confront more and less directly virtually all the major conceptual issues raised by or implicit in the list of orthodoxies. To subject each of the remaining categories to the same degree of scrutiny that we have directed to the previous two, then, would be tantamount to adding suspenders to an already securely belted pair of trousers, would be to indulge in a form of criminal supererogation. Thus, in the next two chapters, the remaining categories will be briefly considered (categories three and four in this chapter, and five and six in the next chapter), with special attention being given to those that raise new or complicate old issues, provide opportunities to give additional weight and force to previous arguments, or otherwise draw interest by irresistible attraction. Finally, because an issue that is almost lost in a throwaway, parenthetical aside (in category four)—antihumanism—figures centrally in current theory, it will be the focus of the concluding chapter; more exactly, the last chapter, working with the conceptual blocks established in the preceding chapters, will build a defense of a pragmatic, pluralistic humanism, showing in the end that such a humanism is not an option but an inevitability for creatures with our biological and cognitive endowment.

READERS MAKING MEANINGS

With the preceding as background, we can begin the discussion of categories three and four. The third category on our list is "Reception Theory," and enrolled under its heading is item (a): "A text has no intrinsic meaning but means what a given reader/audience takes it to mean." I think it is fair to say that the conceptual issues that this item raises have been dealt with at sufficient length in chapters two and three, in which the self-refuting nature of relativism and the dependence of meaning on contentful intentional states were discussed in detail. Nevertheless, it is perhaps worth noting that item (3.a) provides us with one more instance of a statement that cannot pass the self-application test; in other words, the claim made by (a) cannot be applied to (a). Indeed, the claim exhibits another variation on self-refuting relativism, in that the intelligibility of the statement is not dependent on the conditions it specifies for the intelligibility of statements (texts). It is a text whose meaning is not dependent on what a given reader or audience takes it to mean, and thus, like its relativistic associates, it is false, if true. We are asked to believe what we cannot believe if the text of item (a) is true; that is, item (a) expresses a general, universal truth about texts for you and for me, for every reader, now and in the time to come (and expresses that truth in the process of denying its possibility). I understand the meaning of the text as you and you and you understand it. Any claim that immolates itself in the course of its expression would not seem to provide the *petra* upon which a durable faith could be founded. All this, of course, is not to deny that every reader has an unalienable, constitutionally protected right to read any text in any damn way she pleases; nor is it to deny that different readers sometimes (quite frequently, alarmingly frequently, even) read the same text differently. About these different readings, I shall have more to say shortly. For now, enough is accomplished if item (3.a) can be used against itself to establish not the mere possibility but the undeniable reality of durable, determinate meanings.

Whether the determinacy and stability of meaning are being undermined by the nature of language as such (by its always being caught up in an endless system of differences and, hence, deferrals of meaning) or by the varying psychological and social forces to which it is answerable and in terms of which it is mediated, the fact remains that current theorists have little use for determinate meaning or for what was formerly understood to be the ground, basis, or center of that determinacy—the writer, speaker, author. At any rate, reception theory, a form of or kissing cousin to reader-response theory, is committed by definition to multiple readings, since it transfers the source of meaning from authors to readers, only in whose interpretations do textual meanings emerge and only in whose evaluations do texts achieve their aesthetic merit or social/political significance. If reader-response theory gives prominence, indeed priority to the sequential, moment by moment interpretive responses of the single reader, reception theory focuses on the varying interpretive and evaluative judgments of readers over time, within and across eras or periods. As a necessary consequence of their principal assumptions about the dependence of meaning and value on the interpretive and evaluative practices of readers, both response and reception theories, although in some instances willing to acknowledge the persistence of certain material features of texts, can make no accommodations for the sort of determinate meaning that has its origin and source in the intentional acts of speakers/writers and that this book has consistently endorsed and supported.[1]

It is undoubtedly unnecessary here to rehearse the arguments employed earlier to demonstrate that meanings must be determinate because of what it is to be a meaning, but it cannot be a serious breach of civil behavior to remind readers that there is no content apart from intentional states (mental states are representational states) and that intentional states represent their conditions of satisfaction only under certain aspects, those aspects of interest to the representer (things are represented under certain, under specific aspectual shapes). Moreover, as we have seen, correctness conditions attach to our use of words. Under the prevailing conditions of representation (under the operative justification conditions, in the present context of use), the words are applied to the proper things or they are not; they function correctly or they do not. Further, as we have also seen, words have meaning only in the context of a sentence; it is at the level of the sentence that the accumulated latencies of meaning enfolded in individual words achieve specific functionality (i.e., specific use and meaning). Less cryptically, the various meaning possibilities that have accreted, for example, to the word "bill" over the years as a result of being used in different ways in different contexts (as a bill of lading, a bill on a cap, a bill on a duck, and so on), achieve single, specific meaning and functionality in a given sentence expressed on a particular occasion in a particular context (in the hardware store context, the bill must be paid, not have crumbs of bread tossed in its direction). And if our words acquire meaning in the context of a sentence, sentences (and hence words) acquire meaning only in a broader context of use, only within a system of intentionality—a whole work, say, or a practice, a "form of life," in Wittgenstein's terms. Thus, it is, as Davidson has informed us, that "in the end the only source of linguistic meaning is the intentional production of tokens of sentences."[2] The emphasis here falls on "tokens of sentences" (as distinct from "types of sentences"), of course, because tokens, unlike types, involve specific use and, hence, specific—definite, determinate—content.

SAME TEXT, DIFFERENT MEANINGS; SAME MEANING, DIFFERENT TEXTS

With such reminders we can leave item (3.a) and move on to a quick examination of what is registered as (i) under (a). Item (3.a.i.) states, "One implication of (a) is that the same text may be construed to have different meanings and different texts may be construed to have the same meaning." If man is the measure of all things, as Socrates's foil, Protagoras, insists, and each man measures differently, then we would not be surprised to learn that the same thing has been construed to be of different lengths. Similarly, if texts have no intrinsic, determinate meaning and mean what different readers take them to mean, then we would not be shocked to learn that the same text has been construed to have many different meanings. Nor, under these conditions of meaning determination, would we be disinclined to believe that different texts have been construed to have the same meaning, though this eventuality seems to be more a matter of probability (of statistical probability) than of likelihood or inevitability. In other words, it is more likely that the same text will be read differently by different readers than that radically different texts will be construed to have the same meaning by different readers (though this result clearly is a possibility, given the vagaries of the interpreting species—and, in particular cases, a virtual certainty, given the tendency of many current theorists to read many or most texts in light of a single historical or political metanarrative or a single set of power relations). At any rate, the first possibility—same text, different reading—follows quite naturally from the reception theory premise, whereas the second possibility—different texts, same attributed meaning—does not.

One need not be a devout member of any particular interpretive sect or in thrall to any current orthodoxy, of course, to recognize that the same text can be read differently and that different texts can be understood to have the same meaning. It is with interpretive diversity or identity as it is with marriage. Asked about one's belief in either, about whether one believes in such diversity or in marriage, one can faithfully reply, "Believe in it? Hell, I've seen it." As have we all. Indeed, members of the same hermeneutic circle, citizens of the same interpretive community, despite their common adherence to the same doctrines and dogmas, can take the same given (the same text) in different ways, can give very different spins to the same work. On the other hand, nothing is perhaps more common than the ability of critics who share the same conception of prevailing power relations or ideological formations to find the *one* story embedded in the many literary (and other) products of the culture or era, to read the many as one. In these cases, the alchemical elixir by which the many are transformed into one is a compound of preconception and begging the question. By the diligent application of this compound two or more texts (or other cultural products)— dealing apparently (and actually) with very different topics, subject matters, referents, and so on—are revealed to be expressing essentially the same meaning (e.g., the commodification of personal values, the oppression of whatever is alien or other, the hegemony of the capitalist ruling class, the conflict of love and honor, appearance and reality, justice and mercy, and so on).

On a more mundane level, we can readily see that different texts can be understood to convey the same meaning when we consider, for example, these two very different sentences: "Joe hugged the tree" and "The tree was hugged by Joe"; or these, "The mad bulldogs are coming" and "Here come the mad bulldogs," or these, "The evening star is visible now" and "The morning star is visible now," and so on indefinitely. In each of these cases, the texts are manifestly different, yet in each the referents and truth conditions are the same. In each case, the same state of worldly affairs is the truth maker of the assertion, the truth bearer. Briefly, then, every reader— even this one, who is not a reception theorist or a poststructuralist of any kind—can with a free heart and clear conscience agree with (a.i); it is certainly, beyond any shadow of a doubt, true "that the same text may be construed to have different meanings and different texts may be construed to have the same meaning," but, I hasten to add, not *because* the text "has no intrinsic meaning" and can be taken to mean "what a given reader/ audience takes it to mean."

Comity, however, is short-lived, for what all current theorists, by prior theoretical commitment, cannot believe in or acknowledge is that the *meaning taken* can be (and for some purposes—namely, interpretive purposes— should be) squared with, or accurately reflective of, the *meaning given*, that there is a recoverable intentional meaning embedded in the text, of which the interpreter can provide a faithful and true account. Arriving at a correct reading, however, is no easy, certainly no automatic matter; a correct interpretation of meaning does not come to the understanding as easily as leaves come to the tree. Nevertheless, the fact is that in most of our encounters with texts day by day and in most of our conversational exchanges with our fellow symbol users we have the good fortune to take what is given in the sense it was given. Notwithstanding what we have heard about the capacity of language-as-such to defer meaning indefinitely and about the paradigm-driven or theory-laden character of all linguistic usages (about how we are all locked in the prison houses of our particular conceptual schemes), we somehow manage to understand the joke told, to get the point of the essay read, to follow the directions given, and to be appropriately affected by the tale related. We do all this as a consequence of our ability to get a grip on the system of intentionality underlying and determining the articulated content of the speech or writing.

Still, getting that grip and holding on to it are often difficult matters, largely because there is no way of telling what the functional values of the words constituting a speech or text are simply by looking long and hard at them. In an earlier chapter, I supported the point by observing, with the help of Hilary Putnam, that "the assertibility conditions of an arbitrary sentence [such as 'I didn't say he stole it'] are not surveyable."[3] That is, the sentence could be appropriately expressed on many different occasions, under various conditions of intentionality, with meaning shifts taking place as occasions and conditions changed. Any sentence, separated from or considered apart from the system of intentionality endowing it with specific meaning, can support a rich variety of meanings, and a cursory glance at the history of the critical response to any work that has attracted the attention of more than two or three academics reveals that a single text is open to many diverse, even contradictory readings. Exaggeration has a small stake in the claim that *Hamlet*, say, has nearly as many interpretations as readers.

And sometimes, even when we are fairly confident that we are working within the system of the text's or speech's own intentionality, we run bump into recalcitrance, into a term or phrase that seems on its face to upset our ongoing understanding of the workingness of the whole and, consequently, to cast in doubt our operative interpretation. For example, the modern reader of "The Pleasures of the Imagination," Mark Akenside's eighteenth-century poem, who comes across the phrase "God's plastic arm" may suddenly be brought up short in his interpretive progress. The phrase cannot be accommodated to his understanding of the poem, and it seems, at least momentarily, that what he had taken to be a serious poem linking the divine with the human imagination is in fact a satiric or sacrilegious poem. But once he thinks of plastic, not in terms of an oil by-product (not in terms of garden hoses and a host of other modern artifacts), but in terms of the plastic arts and plastic or reconstructive surgery, he can restore the molding, shaping, creating arm to dignity and power and reinstate his former operating conception of the formal dynamics of the poem. At any rate, the fact is that in spite of this proliferation of meanings and interpretations and the difficulty of holding on to the informing system of intentionality in the face of recalcitrant material, we are sustained in our ability to recover intended meanings by our knowledge that there is no meaning apart from intentionality and by our manifold successes in getting things right, in seeing how the parts fit one another.

The fact of our success is easier to state than to account for, however. There is no algorithmic procedure that we can use to discover or to narrow in on—by triangulation, the process of elimination, or any other established method—a correct interpretation (i.e., one consonant with the representational and expressive import of a text's intentional system), just as there is none for invention or creativity. Each text presents a new challenge to our interpretive skills, but as we gain more experience and found, as Samuel Johnson says, a wider basis of analogy, we become increasingly adept at forming interpretive hypotheses and testing them against alternative possibilities. Moreover, success builds upon success, and as we become familiar with more and more possibilities of use through our exposure to more and more texts and through our daily encounters with fellow symbol users in a variety of contexts, we not only increase our doxastic repertoire but extend our familiarity with all the tropic potentialities of symbols (our familiarity, that is, with the ways of metaphor, simile, synecdoche, irony, and so forth), thereby enhancing our ability to make informed guesses about the nature and kind of meaning we are encountering. Our chief advantage, however, derives from our "preintentional capacity to symbolize," our capacity, that is, "to attach a sense, a symbolic function to an object that does not have that sense intrinsically."[4] All our language uses (as well as language itself) depend upon this capacity, and our developed and complicated uses are the elaborated manifestations of this capacity.

In the end, then, although a single text may be construed to have different meanings by different readers and many texts may be construed by many readers to have the same meaning, the vagaries of interpretive practice cannot change the fact that meaning arises only in specific contexts of use and only within a particular structure of intentionality. Texts may come to mean different things to different readers and construed meanings may be used in the service of a variety of issues of importance to the reader, but as systems of intentionality texts cannot mean many different things, though they may certainly express richly complex meanings. The assertibility conditions of a text, like those of a sentence, may not be surveyable and we may not be able to formalize our methods for grasping those conditions, but we learn them, as Putnam goes on to suggest (concurring with Michael Dummett and others), "by acquiring a practice," by learning how to work within a form of life, a system of intentionality.[5] In Davidson's view, an "interpreter of another's words and thoughts must depend on scattered information, fortunate training, and imaginative surmise in coming to understand the other."[6] And, of course, the information, the training, and the imaginative surmising are all grounded in our cumulative experience with the varieties of symbolic uses outlined above. That said, I can leave category three, knowing full well that I have said what I meant and meant what I said and believing that the reader has understood my meaning (even if she disagrees with it—disagreement presupposing, of course, knowing my meaning, catching my drift exactly; some meaning must be shared for disagreement to exist at all).

DEWEY DEFEATS TRUMAN: THE AUTHOR'S NEAR-DEATH EXPERIENCE

Because the conceptual issues raised by category four have, for the most part, been considered in great detail in the first three chapters of this book, they will not be subjected to extensive reexamination here. At the outset, however, the category mentions with by-the-by casualness, in what is tantamount to a whispered theatrical aside, a large and important issue, the antihumanism endemic to current theory, an issue with ramifications extending beyond the concerns of category four. Indeed, the concerns of category four might properly be considered as lesser included elements of the overarching antihumanistic program of much (most) contemporary theory.

Rather than addressing here what I take to be the intellectual shortcomings of and the conceptual problems inherent in the antihumanistic thrust of much current theorizing and then outlining a kind of pluralistic, practical humanism that is consonant with the priniciples and assumptions underlying this study as a whole, I shall focus in this chapter on some points relating to agency and authorship that were neglected earlier or that deserve under- scoring, reserving for the final chapter a discussion of why I take humanism to be inevitable and indispensable, rather than contingent and disposable. One final procedural note: in what follows, I shall examine category four all at once, so to speak, not item by item, under the assumption that one argument in support of the dependence of content on the intentionality of an agent, a speaker, or writer is sufficient to silence the hostile murmurs of all demurrers.

To begin, then, category four, which centers on current orthodoxies re- lating to writers/speakers/subjects, reads as follows:

4. Death of the Author, Subject
   a. Personal agency is denied (antihumanism)
      i. "Language speaks man"—denial that the author generates the text. Some- how the text generates itself, or is generated by language itself, using the individual as its vehicle.
      ii. The subject [i.e., the individual writer or speaker] is "decentered"—unity of the subject, capable of making free, informed, rationally based choices, is denied.

Who or what is better equipped to take deep satisfaction in such claims as these than you and I and others just like us? It is difficult to imagine a machine, however intelligent, capable of subsuming itself so *willingly* and *gleefully* to the play of impersonal forces, whether they be those electro- chemical forces in neural networks so much in favor with certain eliminativ- ists or those forces of language-as-such or of ideology so much in favor with certain literary and cultural theorists, a machine capable, that is, not simply of recognizing and accepting its place in a system of movements (rather than of actions), but of deriving genuine pleasure from contemplating its place in such a system and especially from announcing it to others who are similarly placed.

Apparently, we alone are creatures eminently and peculiarly qualified to covet and enjoy the heresies of paradox (to take pleasure in learning that things are not at all what they seemed to be, what everyone had taken them to be). Thus, we should not be disappointed to learn that in recognizing and accepting our place (i.e., *believing* that we have it) and then announcing it to others (i.e., *acting* on our belief) for the sheer pleasure of being first with the distressing news (i.e., in the interest of gratifying our desire for, among other things, distinction), we are more than well on our way to being the originator of an action, the author, the agent of an action based on and caused by our intentional states. In this delightful case, one heresy (i.e., that we are agents) drives out another (i.e., that we are not agents), making room for the appearance of the former heresy, which can again be driven out by the new one, and so on indefinitely, in a continuous loop of loopy delights. But alas, this round of joy is illusory, since to the extent that we believe and choose to act on our belief in our incapacity to be the generator and origin of our apostasy, we undermine the validity of that incapacity in the process of articulating it. In short, the heresy of agency trumps the heresy of passivity. This is so, at least, if we are right in arguing that there is no content at all in the absence of rationality and no rationality in the absence of the agency of an agent. As I have argued at length in earlier chapters, there is no representational or expressive content apart from the mental states of agents and, hence, no way for the heretical views of the current theorists to obtain a hearing in the minds of the theorists themselves—or for a correct interpretation to be achieved in the minds of their readers—unless the conditions of the possibility of meaning are other than the theorists state them to be.

Still, to see how the arguments expressed earlier apply to the doctrines of category four, it is important to understand exactly what underlies the denial of personal agency in the fixing of meanings. When Roland Barthes, in his article "The Death of the Author" (1968), and Michel Foucault, in his article "What Is an Author?" (1969), proclaimed the "disappearance" (Foucault) and "death" (Barthes) of the author, they were *not* saying that the author (the agent, the human person) had no role in the sequence of events that eventuated in a text; what they were denying was that the individual writer had the role that traditional criticism, conventional wisdom, or common understanding had assigned to her.[7] Over the course of time that role had been variously characterized, though in its multiple forms it invariably entailed—at least in Western thought (which is, at any rate, the primary object of attack in most current theory)—the postulation or assumption of some unique individual, who was the source and origin of meaning, the "center" and basis of productive activity, the maker of distinct forms, the purposive agent responsible for determinate meanings, the *vates* or seer who by means of his prophetic vision and creative capacity gives the rest of us access to truths and realities otherwise passing our understanding, or, in that mode favored by, among others, Lord Shaftesbury (especially in *Advice to an Author*), William Collins (especially in "Ode on the Poetical Character"), Samuel Coleridge (especially in *Biographia Literaria*), and August Schlegel (notably in *Vorlesungen über schöne Literatur und Kunst*), the artistic genius, the true poet, the products of whose imagination find their only analogue in the creative effects of the infinite I AM, the divine maker.

According to this last view, the poet's imaginative processes and creative activities are repetitions or echoes in the finite mind of those imaginative and shaping powers definitive of the divine mind, the infinite I AM, God. In Coleridge's scheme the universe is the product of God's continuous process of creation, and this process has its analogue in our continuing perception of the world around us, in the perceptual capacities of all human minds. This everyday, perceptual activity is the product of the "primary imagination." It is at the next level, that of the "secondary imagination," that the mind functionally imitates or duplicates the processes and effects of the divine imagination, for here the ordinary products of primary perception are shaped and ordered into a new and unified creation—the work of art. "Fancy," on the other hand, is that capacity of the mind to rearrange the "finites and definites," which, conjoined by association in Humean fashion, come to us prepackaged by perception, and, thus, its products are not exemplary of God's creative energies, but uninspired assemblages of bits and pieces of things ready to hand. It is the secondary imagination, that "esemplastic" power of the mind, that echoes God's original creative process and molds the reimagined products of perception into a new artistic unity.[8]

At any rate, what Foucault and Barthes denied was the validity and legitimacy of the assumed centrality of the individual in the making and shaping of the work of art, whether that individual was envisaged as a mundane craftsman or a simulacrum of God. Attention is directed to those views of the poet's creative acts as analogous to God's world-shaping acts, as exemplified in Coleridge's scheme, because from them it is a short step to idealism, most notably German Idealism, to the loss or absence, in short, of the Transcendental Signified and its guarantor, the Transcendental Signifier. And if God is to the world as the poet is to the poem, the novelist to the novel, the artist to the work of art, then the loss of one entails by analogical necessity the loss of the other, the poet once again assuming the likeness of God, in this case by echoing or repeating His "absence." Just as there is no transcendent Agent determining the materials and form of the world, so there is no single, autonomous, human agent who is the source and determiner of fixed textual meanings.

With the linguistic turn in idealism, accomplished on the continent by turning Derrida loose upon Saussurean linguistics, we enter the labyrinthine maze or abysmal pit of permanently deferred meanings, of local, gauzy, shadowy, evanescent meanings, the temporary "effects" of the play of differences, the diaphanous after-images of "things" that earlier generations had taken to be real substances, to be point-at-able, foot-kickable, tangible things or stuff, put here long ago by God's plastic arm or called into being by the poet's song. This potted intellectual history will certainly not win the plaudits or withstand the sustained scrutiny of those trained as historians of philosophy, but it does bring us a serviceable, handyman's understanding, I think, of where Barthes and Foucault (and, hence, all their myrmidons within the ranks of current theory) are, to employ the vernacular, coming from. What is clear, in any case, is that advocates of the current orthodoxies (certainly those who endorse the doctrines of category four) generally assume that once meanings go immanent (i.e., once things and thoughts go inside conceptual schemes, inside the language that makes them, at least temporarily and "effectually," what they are)—once what *is* becomes only *semes*—then determinate meaning, justification, objectivity go into exile and authors are subordinated to the linguistic (and social) forces of which they are the effects or consequences. Like other apparent stabilities, the author is merely an "effect" or "function" generated by the internal play of language. Alternatively (but compatibly), the author, in Barthes view, is a necessary fiction or hypothetical construct, the progeny of anxiety and prudence, engendered to act as a check or curb on the free play of the meanings inherent in a literary (or any other) text.

Since virtually all modes of contemporary theory and certainly all subscribers to the doctrines of category four treat language-as-such or, more expansively, discourse-as-such as the principal locus of interpretive interest, there are psychoanalytic, Marxist, new historicist, cultural materialist, and so on versions of the loss or decentering of the author. In the psychoanalytic versions, broadly speaking, the speaker or author is not a single integrated consciousness exhibiting continuity over time, though susceptible to change and development in the light of new information, interests, and goals, but a disunified congeries of impulses and compulsions, a product of sociosexual conditioning, a thing spoken (by the terms of its conditioning) rather than a self speaking. And when the focus is on discourse-as-such, as it invariably is in the Foucauldian lineage, which includes, of course, the majority of new historicists and cultural materialists, attention is directed principally to what the era or period speaks, to *on dit*, to, that is, the language put in circulation by the prevalent cultural forces. The writer/speaker—or, more appropriately, the subject—is a construction of the operative ideological formations, a temporary "site" jerry-built out of the conceptual categories and power relations dominant in a given period. Again, language speaks man and the self is decentered. All this is so because everything is textual, and texts, like all things else, are language bound, and language has no center, no anchor in any fully warranted system of things, in the Transcendental Signified.

So, in the end, for these critics, it is not the case that a flesh-and-blood human individual can be eliminated from the process of writing, typing, or word processing a thing we can all consent to call a text; such an individual—whom you could call on the phone, meet at a conference, have dinner with—is a vital, a necessary causal link in the physical production of a text. It is just that this individual has no ontological significance and no genuine power or authority to impose his or her will on the materials of the text to keep them within the narrow limits of some particular intention. The author you have dinner with is, like yourself, a product of the conditions of allowable expression, a self-less agent of language and the powers that be. For

these critics, the author recognized by common understanding and traditional criticism has disappeared (into the surrounding ideological ether) or
died (the author is dead; long live the author-function or the author-effect).

Such, then, in brutal brevity is the story behind the claims of category
four. The tale has our interest primarily because it enables us to see how
extensively this particular network of views about agency and authorship has
spread in the body of current criticism, but also because it fills in some of
the details characterizing a stance that is everywhere rejected in this book.
This brief overview of the role (i.e., the subordinate or nonrole) of the
subject or agent in much current thinking is designed to give distinct shape,
at least in outline, to what stands in opposition to the positive account of
the absolute inseparability of specific meaning from agency that is argued
for earlier.

At this point, it is undoubtedly unnecessary to rehearse previous arguments or to review some of the inherent contradictions, practical inconsistencies, or self-refuting embarrassments naturally accompanying efforts by
symbol-using agents to erase purposive agency on the part of people with
content-involving mental states or to subordinate, at best, agency to the
dynamics of language as such or the circulating energies of one's cultural/
political milieu. I would only remind the reader that if it is only at the level
of the sentence that language performs the functions that language serves,
our sentences perform their functions only on specific occasions of use, and
what they specifically express (the function they specifically perform) very
immediately depends on the intentions of the writer or speaker. Moreover,
the contents of those intentional states cannot be deduced from or resolved
into any set of political or social conditions (if only because those conditions
can support an indefinite number of different, even conflicting pronouncements or theses) or into any of the possible differential or relational maneuvers of language-as-such (or discourse-as-such, if only because such
maneuvers are not and cannot be contentful). The burden of our earlier
arguments has been to demonstrate that Michael Dummett's claim, namely,
that it is "essential both to our use of language and to any faithful account
of the phenomenon of human language that it is a rational activity, and that
we ascribe motives and intentions to speakers" and writers, has strong (intellectual, theoretical, conceptual, polemical) legs to stand on.[9]

To bring these animadversions on the claims of category four to conclusion, then, let me say that I hope those arguments, especially those in chapters two and three, can contribute something to the extension to areas of
literary study of what Hilary Putnam confidently affirms is widely understood elsewhere in the intellectual world: "It is widely recognized that the
interpretation of someone's language must always proceed simultaneously
with the ascription of beliefs and desires to the person being interpreted."[10]
Finally, then, it is the contents of the individual's mental states that are the
reasons and causes of actions, linguistic and otherwise, and although the

circumambient energies circulating about agents unquestionably influence what an individual agent might think about, they cannot determine in any explicit and finite sense what ultimately is specifically thought and expressed.

As a codicil to this section, I would make a few brief observations that those who are not irony challenged might find agreeable to their kidney. With a bow in the direction of Samuel Johnson's Imlac, I would enroll under the rubric "Inconsistencies cannot both be right, but, imputed to man, they may both be true" the following:[11] Just at the time when agents were disappearing and dying, the promoters of their exile or demise were themselves making the strongest claims for notice, drawing attention to their personal and individual contributions to debate, talking about themselves and their fellow luminaries (and bringing administrators around to their way of talking of them) as stars (superstars even), acting as entrepreneurs peddling themselves as commodities on the academic job market, championing merit raises with all the forces of logic and all the weapons of extortion, hunting celebrity with avidity, and changing institutional loyalties with all the alacrity and meretriciousness of a streetwalker with free-agent status. At this very time, for example, Stanley Fish—champion of a form of social constructionism and interpretive-community relativism—was urging the editors of a major journal (perhaps the major journal in the field of language and literature studies), *PMLA*, to abandon their blind submission policy, instituted to ensure that referees would concentrate on the quality of the work submitted and not be influenced by the submittee's reputation (deserved or undeserved, earned or otherwise established) on the grounds that because he and a select few others among the (g)literati were who they were, whatever they had to say would deserve a hearing, if only because the hoi polloi would want to know it was they who were saying it. Whatever the merits of this case, it does have a rather charming way of centering the subject, I think. And, finally, it is interesting that at precisely this time, their theoretical convictions about deliquescing or expired agents notwithstanding, many poststructuralist critics found memoir writing and criticism—heavily seasoned with personal reflections and autobiographical data—especially congenial to their intellectual life. Nothing in these remarks is offered for its argumentative or probative value, of course; I offer them to my readers as lagniappes. Although many more examples could be added to those cited above, what is sufficient is, I think, always enough. On authors and agency, the rest, for me, is silence.

Chapter 9
Human Universals, Politics, and Literary Value

We come now to the penultimate category on the "Current Orthodoxies" list, titled "Relativism and Social Constructivism" and containing the following three maxims:

a. There is no absolute or universal truth—every truth is relative to a conceptual/ linguistic framework ("language game," "discursive practice"), the scientific community, [interpretive community], race, gender, class, or culture, that somehow "constitutes" or "constructs" it (creates it?).
b. Similar considerations apply to moral, ethical, aesthetic values.
c. Reality, nature, the subject, are "socially constructed."

Whether concurring with the views and arguments of this book or not, every reader will agree, I think, that items (5.a) and (5.c) have not suffered the indignity of neglect in this study. Indeed, the positions stated expressly in, as well as the principles and assumptions underlying, items (a) and (c) have been considered at length in earlier chapters (especially chapters three and four), and hence, they do not invite extensive reexamination here. In this section, I shall give special attention to my principal reasons for rejecting what is stated and implied in item (b), making a case in the process for moral universals on grounds similar to those used in defending linguistic (and, to some extent, logical and arithmetic) universals. On the issue of transcultural or transparadigmatic standards of moral value I shall have more to say in the concluding chapter, and I shall defer discussion of standards of aesthetic value until the last section of this chapter.

TRUTH AND SOCIAL CONSTRUCTION

Before taking up item (b), however, I would like to comment briefly on aspects of items (a) and (c), operating here on the assumption that now, as always, we need more often to be reminded than informed. What we notice right off the bat, of course, is that, like the other relativistic statements about truth that we have examined, item (a) is false, if true. The truth claim that "every truth is relative to a conceptual/linguistic framework . . . [to] the race, gender, class, or culture that somehow 'constitutes' . . . it" is not itself relative to any of these, and, thus, if the claim is true, it manages to say the thing that it is not capable of expressing, thereby erasing the truth expressed in the process of expressing it. This statement expresses, it seems, a truth that is not relative to the conditions of truth-making specified in the statement; in short, it expresses what to all appearances is an absolute or universal truth, one that is true independently of the era in which it is expressed and one that does not seem to obtain its validation permit from any one particular conceptual scheme. Well, enough on the intestine difficulties of radical relativism; still, because the avatars of the god of relativism continue to attract attention in each new appearance, it is always helpful to be reminded, I think, that a change of hats does not bring about any alteration in the charlatan's appealing but ultimately self-destructive personality.

On a more substantive aspect of item (5.a), it is useful to remember that even though there is no grand, foundational, bedrock truth, there are many real, genuine truths, a full warehouse of which can be shared by people of both genders, of all races, nationalities, political proclivities, and historical circumstances, including truths by definition or stipulation, logical truths, deductive truths, arithmetic truths, and countless others. Of course, many truths are specific to very narrow conceptual systems; they are determined by those systems and have no existence apart from them, and what one historical era takes to be true may be rejected as false in a subsequent era. Moreover, there are no truths of any kind apart from some representational and conceptual system. After all, content becomes content only within a system of conceptual relationships, and, thus, truth is relative to a conceptual framework. As we have seen, truth is a semantic, not an ontological matter. But in acknowledging the ubiquity of conceptual relativity, we do not as a consequence deny the possibility of objective truth.

And if we cannot formulate or express any truths without relying on some terms, distinctions, descriptions, and categories, the result is not that we are stuck only with terms, descriptions, and so on. Naming something a rock or stone or tree is not an act of creating rocks or stones or trees, and saying there's an even-toed ungulate on my desk does not put one on my desk, though the statement would be absolutely true, for me and for you, if there were in fact one on my desk (and absolutely false if there were not). As Putnam observes, "there would have been stars even if language users had not evolved. . . . There would have been a world all right, but there would not have been any *truths* about the world."[1] And as it is with mind-independent things, so it is with mind-dependent ones: we decide what is or is not a touchdown, but only the crossing of a certain line by a certain spheroid object, under certain conditions will count as a touchdown. When the conditions are right, and only when they are right, the team will have scored a touchdown, and that's the unvarnished truth—a truth of football, mind you, a truth only within the football conceptual scheme, but a real, genuine, bona fide, objective truth nevertheless, a truth for him and her, now and in the time to come, under liberal and conservative adminstrations alike. Finally, to bring this brief commentary on item (a) to an end, I do not have to belong to a particular interpretive community to know what is true for that community or to believe that what it accepts as true is indeed true. Though unaccustomed and generally unwilling to wear your particular linguistic/conceptual glasses, when I put them on I see what you see and see that what you see is true about the world or the text, remarkably different though it is from what I see to be true about the world or text when I have my conceptual lenses on.

Item (5.c) need not detain us long here, since the issue of the "social construction" of reality has been the focus of considerable attention earlier (in chapter five). Nevertheless, it is instructive, I think, to consider the difference between arranging our terms this way, "the social construction of reality," and arranging them thus, "the construction of social reality."[2] The first way—the way of our current theorists—subordinates folks like us to a congeries of social/political/linguistic/cultural forces that determine not only who we are but also what there is to think about and how to go about our thinking of it, whereas the second way—the way of this book and of a goodly number of people outside literature and sociology departments—endows conscious human beings with capacities to talk about real and imagined things in a variety of true and creative ways and to do so with the full cooperation of reality (of the way things are independently of mind, language, and power relations). The preceding formulation undoubtedly puts matters a little too starkly, a little too simply, but there is more than a soupçon of truth in the view that if in the second way, the human being is a maker, shaper, molder, creator, who fashions materials at hand and in mind into forms that are always reflective of her interests, often adequate to reality, and generally gratifying to his desires, in the first way the human being (along with all things else) is a marked woman, a made man, the incidental or inevitable consequence of the play of linguistic or social forces. The human being is the made, not the maker, the shaped, not the shaper, the created, not the creator, the spoken, not the speaker. The individual and the content of her thought (and, thus, what is taken to be real or natural) are shaped by language itself or by social institutions. In short, all that inheres in or adheres to the first way stands in relation to the interests and arguments of this book as fire to the library, as acid to milk, jabberwocky to sweet reason.

Of course, there is a sense in which the idea that we are in no small measure the creatures of our cultures, our environments, our class, race, or social positions is perfectly sane and reasonable. Moreover, we clearly pay attention to the ideas and values that are in circulation in our intellectual neighborhoods, our cognitive spaces, crediting and adopting by and large those that are credited and adopted by our peers and rejecting those that are not. Additionally, we tend for the most part to do our thinking in the terms and categories that have purchasing power and cash value in our communities and to ask those questions that fall within the range of implication of those terms and categories, neglecting—being in fact largely oblivious of—those that do not. Not a little of what we say and think is undoubtedly formulaic or programmatic, that is, pre-scripted by the invisible hand of the culture in which we are obliged to make our way. And if we can come to believe that our terms and categories have no warrant from the way things are, that everything is good or right or true only relative to some conceptual scheme, and that no conceptual scheme is imprinted with reality or truth's own imprimatur, then we are inevitably compelled to look to the cold gruel and hard mattress of relativism and social constructivism for our sustenance and comfort in this state of life.

Yes, in large part, we are the ventriloquist dummies of society/culture, speaking the master's words in our own voice. But, and here's the rub, unlike the showman's artifact, we are also to a not inconsiderable extent free agents, capable of talking back to our masters and imagining things never dreamt of in their philosophies. The old saw has it that nothing succeeds like success, but with us carbon-based, symbol-using, content-involved handicrafters it seems that nothing *surfeits* like success. No sooner does a position or view or idea or opinion manage to stand upright than it is in danger of being knocked over or of being confronted with an opponent. Nothing, at any rate, is better equipped to stir an academic or intellectual into action than the expression of an opinion or thesis or argument by someone other than herself. Opposition, revision, supplementation, refinement, rejection, novelty, and so on are more than mere features of our inquisitive and querulous natures; they are more like ontological imperatives or conceptual pheromones to which our minds are inexorably attracted. With apologies to Alexander Pope and the laws of metrics, let me say that "With varying vanities, from every part, / Academics shift the moving Lexicon of their heart; / Where critics with critics, with theorists theorists strive, / Opinions banish opinions, and ideas ideas drive" out of circulation.[3]

In any case, it is unimpeachably true that we can always talk about what we talk with (i.e., subject to scrutiny and analysis what we say or do, disclosing in the process the principles and assumptions, the motives and aims underlying our practices); can always say "no" to what we have elsewhere affirmed (i.e., we can reject what we had formerly been swayed by); can always imagine how things might be differently expressed or done; can always create new meanings with neologisms or by endowing existing verbal materials with new symbolic functions (i.e., we are not restricted to the terms, meanings, and meaning possibilities in place), and so on. We are not trapped in the linguistic prison houses of our culture or of any ideological formation, for that matter. And finally (on this matter), cultures and languages cannot construct specific meanings, and no matter how heavily freighted terms and phrases may be with accumulated social or ideological significance, the actual meaning of those terms and phrases on specific occasions of use in the service of particular aims or interests cannot be predicted from or determined by their meanings in other contexts, however automatic or conventional those meanings may have seemed to become.

CROSSING SOCIAL LINES: LINGUISTIC AND MORAL UNIVERSALS

In what remains of this chapter, the focus will be on the moral and ethical aspects of item (b): "Similar considerations apply to moral, ethical, aesthetic values." The similar considerations that apply, of course, are these: there are no moral or ethical values that are grounded in what is absolutely right and true; ethical and moral values are culture-relative and culture-specific; what is permissible in one culture or society is prohibited in another; the moral acceptability or rightness of a practice is something that is determined within the culture and something that cannot be assessed as moral or right from the outside in the light of some general standard; there are no transcultural standards, no universal standards to which appeal may be made in judging the moral beliefs and practices of different societies; I'm OK, from where I'm coming from, and you're OK, from where you're coming from; "different strokes for different folks"; and so on. In keeping with my habitual practice with regard to relativism in its manifold guises, I should note at the outset that the judgment that all morality is relative is itself a moral judgment, and one of an expansive, comprehensive kind—one, hence, that cannot be applied to itself. Like others of its family, this judgment is false if true, since it does not derive from a particular culture, a particular moral system. But let's move on to other matters.

Unquestionably, there are divergent social practices across cultures, and no one would deny that what is required, accepted, permitted, tolerated, discouraged, and prohibited varies considerably from country to country, culture to culture, society to society, neighborhood to neighborhood, family to family. Moreover, no one would suggest that some particular culture has access to *the* moral code by which the practices of all cultures should be evaluated (though in the concluding chapter I will argue that because certain moral principles and values are shared across cultures, it is possible while speaking from within one's own culture not only to criticize another culture's practices but to do so in a manner agreeable to that culture's own implicit standards). Despite this diversity, however, there is, I maintain, a core of moral knowledge that is instinct to our species, as much a part of our native endowment as our knowledge of language. In short, we are as predisposed to develop a moral sense as we are to develop a linguistic one. And just as there are linguistic universals underlying an extraordinary range of strikingly different languages, so there are moral universals underpinning a richly diverse range of cultures and societies.

In science and in much of our everyday knowledge of the world, we depend on experience for the establishment of the rules and laws we live by, and if we draw the wrong inference from experience (if we come to believe, say, that not all fires are hot, that objects heavier than air do not always drop, or that putting on a cape enables one to fly), further experience will admonish our inference, will disconfirm our working hypotheses and compel us to revise our beliefs. Of course, all of our true beliefs of this kind are vulnerable to new evidence—in what has become the standard example, our swan theory could be overthrown by the appearance of one black swan. Our laws hold only so long as the succession of experiences tends to confirm them. In this empirical way of knowing, our theories and laws are, notoriously, underdetermined by the evidence or facts (whereas, conversely, our observations are, just as notoriously, overdetermined by our theories; they are, as we say, theory-laden), and we rely on induction (and abduction, i.e., inference to the best explanation) for our tentative security. That is, we assume on the basis of limited evidence that things will behave in the future as they have behaved in the past, knowing in the deep recesses of our consciousness, however, that experience may prove otherwise. To all that we now believe, it is always possible to say "it ain't necessarily so." In this way of knowing, then, skepticism (the belief that things may be other than they seem to be) can be subdued, but not eradicated.

All this has our interest because moral knowledge involves a completely different way and kind of knowing. Such knowledge—like our knowledge of logic, of arithmetic, geometry, and mathematics generally—is a priori, rather than a posteriori, knowledge; it is not based, at any rate, on induction or abduction, and it can be neither proved nor disproved by experience (though it undoubtedly requires experience of some kind to set it in operation). For example, once we grasp the idea that six of these and a half dozen more of them supply us with twelve of them, then we do not need to keep testing the result (with, say, bananas, monkey wrenches, doughnuts, club sandwiches, Red Sox fans, assistant professors, and so forth) to make sure the rule holds, and no subsequent experience with double sixes in any of their possible manifestations will cause the rule to be removed from office. Similarly, once we get our minds around the concepts of, say, stealing, betrayal, false witness, lying, and so on, on one side, and equity, fairness, loyalty, and so on, on the other side, we have access to a kind of knowledge that is not vulnerable to assault from experience. We do not have to witness repeated instances of betrayal to know that it is wrong, and no subsequent instance of betrayal will be able to convince us that betrayal is a form of virtue. (Of course, there are cases in which goods clash, and in which one good must be violated for the sake of a greater one, and so on and so on, through innumerable degrees of moral entanglement and complexity, but the basic point that is at issue here holds.) Further, these arithmetic and moral truths obtain across all cultures, all ideological formations, and for all races, genders, classes, nationalities, and so on.

After discussing the a priori nature of our logical knowledge in *The Problems of Philosophy*, Bertrand Russell goes on to observe,

Perhaps the most important example of non-logical *a priori* knowledge is knowledge as to ethical value. I am not speaking of judgements as to what is useful or as to what is virtuous, for such judgements do require empirical premises; I am speaking of judgements as to the intrinsic desirability of things. . . . We judge, for example, that happiness is more desirable than misery, knowledge than ignorance, goodwill than hatred, and so on. Such judgements must, in part at least, be immediate and *a priori*. Like our previous *a priori* judgements, they may be *elicited* by experience, and indeed they must be; for it seems not possible to judge whether anything is intrinsically valuable unless we have experienced something of the same kind. But it is fairly obvious that they cannot be *proved* by experience; for the fact that a thing exists or does not exist cannot prove either that it is good that it should exist or that it is bad. The pursuit of this subject belongs to ethics. . . . [It is] important to realize that knowledge as to what is intrinsically of value is *a priori* in the same sense in which logic is *a priori*, namely in the sense that the truth of such knowledge can be neither proved nor disproved by experience.[4]

On the basis of precious little experience, we seem to develop very early in our lives a rich complex of moral principles that not only serve us well in the affairs of our everyday lives but also inform the various official codes and rules of the institutions by which our social lives are organized and regulated. Across vast differences in specific cultural practices and in individuals both within a single culture and from culture to culture, there persists, it seems, a huge stock of ethical commonalities, of moral judgments grounded in shared ethical assumptions.

The exact nature of the social and biological conditions responsible for the emergence, growth, and development of our common moral sensibility, of what appears to be a species-wide and species-specific system of ethical principles is not currently known and may forever elude our understanding. Nevertheless, many have seen in our acquisition of language (another system rich in universals, in principles that have effective force in all human languages) something analogous to our acquisition of moral knowledge and principles of ethical assessment and judgment.[5] Our transcultural linguistic and ethical knowledge, at any rate, seems to be the natural product of our native biological and cognitive endowment. Of the many who have commented on the parallels, Noam Chomsky has done so with admirable clarity and brevity in *Language and Problems of Knowledge*, in which, among other things, he notes that what is true of linguistic knowledge is also

true of moral [knowledge]. What its basis may be we do not know, but we can hardly doubt that it is rooted in fundamental human nature. It cannot be merely a matter of convention [or of contingent social or political conditions] that we find some things to be right, others wrong. Growing up in a particular society, a child acquires standards and principles of moral judgement. These are acquired on the basis of limited evidence, but they have broad and often quite precise applicability. It is often though not always true that people can discover or be convinced that their judgements about a particular case are wrong, in the sense that the judgements are inconsistent with the person's own internalized principles. . . . The acquisition of a specific moral and ethical system, wide ranging and often precise in its consequences, cannot simply be the result of "shaping" and "control" by the social environment. As in the case of language, the environment is far too impoverished and indeterminate to provide this system to the child, in its full richness and applicability. . . . it certainly seems reasonable to speculate that the moral and ethical system acquired by the child owes much to some innate human faculty. The environment is relevant, as in the case of language, vision, and so on; thus we can find individual and cultural divergence. But there is surely a common basis, rooted in our nature.[6]

Commenting on this passage, Colin McGinn draws the inescapable conclusion: "the same kind of reasoning that leads to the postulation of an innate language faculty suggests the postulation of an innate moral faculty: poverty of stimulus, richness of result, uniformity of basic principles."[7]

What tends to impress us, I suppose, and what tends to be emphasized in current theoretical discussions are the enormous differences in social practices and in the particulars of moral judgment from era to era, culture to culture, and person to person, but anyone who has read widely and traveled far (or who attends closely to how children arrange the rules of fair play and equity in the games that they create) can easily discern in the enormous variety of our activities the application of judgments based on similar ethical principles. In focusing on the surface differences in occasions and situations, we miss the underlying similarities in moral principles. As an independent a priori ground of knowledge, like logic, arithmetic, and language, ethics cannot be replaced or trumped by ideology or power relations. On just this point, Thomas Nagel writes,

Having the cultural influences on our arithmetical or moral convictions pointed out to us may lead us to reexamine them, but the examination must proceed by first-order arithmetical or ethical reasoning. To take some crude but familiar examples, the only response possible to the charge that a morality of individual rights is nothing but a load of bourgeois ideology, or an instrument of male domination, or that the requirement to love your neighbor is really an expression of fear, hatred, or resentment of your neighbor, is to consider again . . . whether the reasons for respecting individual rights or caring about others can be sustained, or whether they disguise something that is not a reason at all. And this is a new moral question. One cannot just *exit* the domain of moral reflection. . . . All one can do is to proceed with it in light of whatever new historical or psychological evidence may be offered.[8]

It is unquestionably true that our moral capacity is extraordinarily complex and that we are a long way from understanding its nature and workings in their full extent (as we are in understanding our language capacity), but it is a serviceable resource that, like language, is acquired and used in remarkably similar ways by all human beings. In the concluding chapter I shall talk again about human universals. For now, enough has been accomplished if I have been able to show that the radical relativism of item (b) with regard to moral values can be called into question and that across immensely diverse social and political conditions a common fund of moral principles, based on a common human nature, is appealed to and relied on in defining and dealing with our emergent ethical situations and dilemmas. This section can be fittingly brought to a close, I think, with the following remarks by Colin McGinn:

I strongly suspect that sociologists and anthropologists [and, of course, literary theorists] have grossly exaggerated the variations in the moral attitudes of different societies, partly out of misguided philosophical relativism, but also in order to confer greater interest on the practice of those disciplines; for they would hardly seem as full of fascinating surprises if all cultures actually converged in their basic view of life. In the same way the study of alien languages loses some of its interest if all languages turn out to share a basic structure. The human mind is much like the human body in this respect: human bodies clearly differ in all sorts of ways, but it would be an obvious mistake to conclude that there is no fundamental convergence of physiological type in the human species—as a comparison with the bodies of animals of other species shows. . . . There is such a thing as cognitive human nature, as our shared biology suggests; and it seems only reasonable to expect that our moral sense, like our linguistic capacities, will reflect that common nature.[9]

POLITICS, ARTISTIC FORM, AND LITERARY VALUE

With category 6, "Politicization of Texts," we come to the end of the doctrines and maxims identified on the list of "Current Orthodoxies." Breaking with the procedure employed for most of the other categories, I shall here refrain from examining the items of the category singly and in the order of their listing; instead, I shall discuss politics and artistic merit (and value judgments generally) as they figure in the conceptual framework developed in this book, in the system of entailments generated by or implicated in the doctrines, principles, and assumptions endorsed and supported in this book, directing responses to the particular doctrines itemized in the category only as the need or occasion arises.

To contextualize the discussion, however, it is first necessary to present the category with its alphabetized particulars. Under "Politicization of Texts," we find the following six items:

a. All texts (including works of art and music) are treated as essentially political.

b. All texts are treated from a radical leftist perspective, i.e., as instances of "hegemonic discourse" or "counter-hegemonic discourse."

c. Levels of meaning and issues other than political in a text are disregarded.

d. All levels of meaning other than political in a text are treated as having political implications or as somehow symbolizing political doctrines.

e. Different levels of merit in texts are disregarded. Texts are evaluated exclusively on the basis of political content.

f. There is a tendency to equate the value of a text with the level of its popular appeal, regardless of whether or not it has any intrinsic merit. Standards of intrinsic merit are attacked as "elitist."

Obvious to every reader, I suppose, are the intestine difficulties of this list, which present themselves in the form of a body grotesquely swollen by redundancy and pleonasm and crying out for the timely intervention of Dr. Occam's scalpel. Indeed, a neophyte surgeon with some rudimentary training in verbal trimming and sentence combining could easily find a way to ligate (a) and (b), and (c) and (e), or to graft (a) through (e) into one healthy, efficient, message-carrying artery, thereby relieving the list as a whole of its linguistic uremia and reducing it to two robustly pink items, (a) and (f). Its shortcomings notwithstanding, the list focuses our attention on dominant tendencies in critical writing today (exhibited most clearly perhaps in race, class, gender, and postcolonial studies), and any reader even noddingly familiar with critical studies today would be obliged to acknowledge the general legitimacy of the charges enumerated in this category, if not their perfect justice (since they are perhaps a little too free with the peremptory "all," the exceptionless "all"). And, of course, this emphasis on politics—as we have seen in our discussion of new historicism and cultural materialism—seems to be inevitable once meaning goes immanent (once the world—actually worlds—and all the things in it go inside conceptual schemes or linguistic frameworks), once texts are historical and history is textual, since then "reality" and the shapes it can assume are determined by the masters of discourse, by who controls through language the ideological formations of the age.

On the other hand, our progress to the political is not inevitable at all, and it represents but one of the extraordinarily many things in terms of which literary productions may be considered. In our view, there are no meanings at all apart from the contentful intentional states of agents. Intentional states have definite content, because they represent their conditions of satisfaction under certain aspects; intentional states are representational states, and all our representations are aspectual, a "seeing" things "as" this or that or a conceptualizing of matters in this way or that. Linguistic meanings, then, depend upon the intentional production of sentences with specific content, for it is at the level of the sentence that the words achieve functionality, that is, function in the service of the interests and purposes of agents on the specific occasion of their use. And sentences themselves are functional and meaningful within the encompassing practice of which they are a part, within the system of intentionality or "form of life" from which they derive their functionality. In short, sentences express something meaningful only on specific occasions of use.

Because all this is so, as we have argued at length earlier, literary works, like all other verbal products, are systems of intentionality with meaningful content when we encounter them, and, thus, one legitimate task available to us but not to current theorists, given their presuppositions about agency and intentionality, is that of *interpretation*, the recovery of expressed intentionality. Briefly, interpretation involves coming to an understanding of the text's categories of intelligibility (its content) in their functional relations within a system of rationality and justification. Whatever else they may be, works of literature (works of art generally) are artifactual practices, structures of intentionality with recoverable senses, emphases, and values.

At this point in critical history, when the study of literature tends to focus on anything but the work as a unique product of artistic choices—when the focus is on, for example, the preconstructional conditions of the work's possibility in language, history, ideology, gender, race, class, and so on—it is important to remind ourselves that, as Catherine Elgin insists, "we design category schemes [including works of art] with more or less specific purposes in mind and integrate into the scheme such values and priorities [such concepts and details] as we think will serve those purposes."[10] What is worth remembering, it seems to me, is that our texts are first and foremost artistic practices requiring appropriate moves. To borrow from Crispin Wright, a practice can be characterized as "any form of intentional, purposeful activity" and a move as "any action performed within the practice for its characteristic purposes."[11] This notion of practice squares perfectly with a view articulated by Kenneth Burke many years ago and still apt and viable: "the poet makes a poem; and his ways of making the poem are *practices* which implicitly involve principles, or precepts" (or, as I would be inclined to say, justification conditions). "The critic [i.e., the interpreter], in matching the poetry with a poetics, seeks to make these implicit principles explicit."[12] What we strive to understand is the workingness of the details within a system of artistic interest.

Because we have many interests that the texts do not share (or that the texts have on the sly or, as we might say, *unintentionally*), and because so much of the current conversation about literature is dominated by the interests of "theory" (by interests, that is, that are generally hostile to or subversive of authors, texts, and determinate meanings within knowable structures of intentionality, by interests in, for example, the social construction of texts and the radical instability of meanings), it can be useful to distinguish between the internal and external *goods* and the internal and external *causes* of literary works. The notions of internal and external goods I derive, in large measure, from the work of Alasdair MacIntyre, though in what follows I revise and extend them in ways that he would not necessarily endorse. Like the writers cited in the previous paragraph, MacIntyre thinks of artistic activities as practices, and *internal goods*, in his view, are the results of choices that serve the interests of the practice. Basically, a practice is a "coherent and complex form of activity through which goods internal to that form of activity are realized in the course of trying to achieve those standards of excellence which are appropriate to, and partially definitive of, that form of activity."[13] The *external goods* that a practice might bring (wealth, fame, power, for example) can be achieved by many means unrelated to the practice in question, whereas the internal goods are "virtues," to use MacIntyre's term, or features of the practice; they are features, powers, and values within the possibilities of the system's realized intentionality. The nature of *internal* and *external causes* will become apparent, I think, in the process of discussing an example.

Let our example be a portrait, one of a particular individual and one designed to meet the ordinary, person-in-the-street test of verisimilitude or likeness. Since in this case the formal object of intentionality is a "traditional" portrait (of my uncle Bill, say), all the internal goods would be features contributing to the likeness; all the perceptible features of the painting would be functional properties contributing to the realization of the likeness. At this level, the artist would be obliged to get the nose "right," have only one ear on each side of the face, make the chin like Bill's chin, and so on. The internal causes of these internal goods are such material and efficient things as paints, brushstrokes, coloring, shading. On the side of external goods, on the other hand, we have, for example, the current and potential market value of the portrait, its ability to hold open a window or to cover a hole in the wall (these are possible goods of the portrait—goods owing to discernible, real, material features of the portrait—but not goods internal to the functioning of the portrait as a portrait of Bill), the admiration it brings from the family and the general public, and so on.

As a brief aside, I would note what I take to be a cognate or companionable body of ideas in Fred Dretske's recent discussion of "metarepresentation" in *Naturalizing the Mind*; metarepresentation is the *conceptual* representation of something as having a certain, a specific representational content (determined by a particular aim of intentionality). To illustrate his point, Dretske discusses the ways we might represent a photograph of a person, of "Clyde," in his example. He notes that

We can represent it as a piece of paper, as a piece of paper weighing 2 grams, as rectangular, and as having certain colored areas on its surface. We can also represent it as a picture of Clyde (or, simply, as of Clyde, where "Clyde" is understood to be a description of what the picture is a picture of—its representational content). In describing it as a picture of Clyde, I represent the object as a representation. I thus produce a metarepresentation. A description of the picture as weighing 2 grams is not a metarepresentation. It represents a representation, but not as a representation.[14]

Similarly, a description of a literary work that does not represent it in terms of the interests of its system of intentionality—that represents it, say, as an example of the play of language, or as a reflection of power relations in a given era or of the courtship rituals in a society governed by capitalistic exchange values, and so on (assuming that these are not aspects of the functional intentionality of the work, of the artistic intention of author)—is not a metarepresentation of the work.

Returning to the issue of goods and causes, I would note that when we reach external causes, we arrive at the scene where most of the critical and theoretical activity goes on today, where reading is seen principally or exclusively as a matter of *thematizing*, of revealing the themes or ideas that literary works are either expressing or seeking to conceal. Here we are concerned with the preconstructional causes that are operative in the production of anything whatsoever, either at any time or distinctively in some particular historical era (depending on whether our focus is on the general workings of, say, mind or language or on the social/political/ideological preconditions of expression). In short, here we are concerned with the historical, social, ideological, linguistic, cultural, psychological, racial, gender, class determinants of production, which are antecedent to all production but which, alas, can themselves produce nothing in particular. Though necessary to and inevitably entangled with all making and producing, these are not causes into which particular practices can be resolved or from which particular products can be deduced, if only because they cannot inform any work with specific intentionality, with specific content having particular meanings, emphases, or ends in view. Nevertheless, because such causes variously impact on or are variously implicated in specific works, these causes can become independent sources of interest and can variously inform and be modified by specific works.

Indeed, these causes have become more than independent sources of interest to most current theorists; they have become the sole or primary source of interest. Commenting on this tendency in current critical and theoretical writing to think of literature (and all other artifacts, for that matter) solely in terms of its relations to such causes (and, consequently, to value works proportionately to their capacity to illuminate or comment on such causes, especially the political or ideological causes), Herbert F. Tucker, in an editorial preface to a recent special issue of the journal *New Literary History* featuring essays on formal and structural concerns, writes that

For over a decade now, scholarship in the humanities has lavished its attention on contextual relations. Under the banners of historicism and ideological or material cultural studies, the critical understanding of literature has aimed at illuminating the situatedness of the text: its diachronic or synchronic coordination with other texts and, more ambitiously, the co-determinate relation in which the system of literature stands to other cultural systems. . . . The privilege such study accords to the *relational* aspect of literature tends in practice to entail a like privilege . . . for the merely *referential* aspect of literature; the interpretive correlation of the text with its *contexts* [its external or preconstructional causes] typically emerges through a comparison among *contents*. Left to itself, the often politically urgent critique of historical and cultural meanings has a way of approaching literature as if it were information, of regarding a text's formal literariness as if it were a code to be broken and discarded in favor of the message it bears.[15]

Of course, when literature is considered in these terms, the issue of intrinsic merit can hardly arise (if it arises at all, it is generally derided as an elitist or bourgeois concern), because the value of any given work is tied to its relational standing with regard to external issues—political, ideological, racial, class, cultural issues—to how it expresses, illuminates, subverts, endorses, or otherwise evinces the preexisting social or linguistic conditions of its possibility. Thus, it is not surprising that distinctions between high and low art, between greater and lesser, better and worse artistic achievement would be minimized or lost, or even that popular works would be, in many cases, elevated above so-called "classics" or "masterpieces" in critical esteem, since it could be—and frequently is—argued that popularity is itself a powerful testimony to the work's being deeply invested in the views, assumptions, and values of the culture of which it is a member, indeed, a peculiarly representative member. And certainly, relative to how well the work puts into relief or illuminates what you as a critic take to be the special political or social features of the era or what you happen to find especially interesting (whether it be race, sexuality, gender, class, or whatever), a text previously considered mediocre, undistinguished, or merely popular would be better, more interesting, more valuable than a less serviceable text that self-appointed mavens of "high culture" had denominated a "classic," a great work of art, a monument of unaging intellect, or whatever.

Value, after all, is a relative thing, and nothing in itself has a value. That is, no trait is good or bad, valuable or worthless, proper or improper considered in isolation. A "value" is "a relative attribute of something in virtue of certain discernible properties as these relate to something else."[16] For example, a shoe has certain physical properties and is of certain size, but it is a great or little shoe only relative to other shoes, though it is still in virtue of its peculiar physical size that it is great or little. Or, an aspirin has a particular chemical constitution, but it is helpful or harmful relative to something else; it is helpful relative to adults but harmful relative to children, but helpful or harmful still in terms of its chemical constitution. Now, the standard or the something else in relation to which we establish the value of a trait or feature of anything changes as our interests and foci change. A shoe, for example, is a better substitute for a hammer than a sock, or a tie, or a banana. Further, to recur to a former example, relative to seeing and hearing the show, the seats in the first row of the loge are vastly superior, unquestionably better than the seats in the last row of the third balcony, but relative to sharing special moments with someone special free of the glare of unapproving observation, the seats in the third balcony are incalculably better than those in the loge.

The grandly obvious upshot of all this is that literary works, like most things else, can be evaluated, cherished, esteemed relative to a wide, virtually unlimited assortment of standards, both internal and external. Relative to others, some works are more patriotic, more theological, more spiritual, are heavier, smarmier, wordier, more racist, easier to memorize, longer, shorter, and so on through who knows how many comparative measures. But we need to remember also that because literary works are structures of specific content determined by the artistic choices of conscious, rational agents, are unique systems of intentionality with their own distinct correctness or justification conditions, are, like other artifacts, governed by ends of view, ends that determine the nature, number, order, significance, and values of the constituent parts—because all this is so, we need to remember that literary works can be evaluated by formal, internal standards, as well as by an immense variety of external standards. Internally considered, some works are more meritorious than others, and degrees and kinds of intrinsic merit can be distinguished. (Anyone who has graded papers or ranked candidates for this or that award, job, or position by the quality of their work knows this.) Also, because a work of literature is a complex composite of several subordinate structures—of scenes, characters, sequences of action, of linguistic, rhetorical, logical structures, of structures of ideas, images, metaphors, and so on—internal value judgments can be extraordinarily various and made at several levels of evaluation.

Briefly, by the standard of euphony the word "eckcetera" (for et cetera) or the injunction "lug the ugly guts onto the slag heap" is, to be kind, unpleasant, but expressed by a particular person on a specific occasion it would be not only appropriate but perfectly suited to the interests of the scene in which it appeared and, hence, to the work as a whole; it would be an internal good of the overall intentional system. Or, to consider larger units of value, if the three quatrains that make up, along with the concluding couplet, Shakespeare's "Sonnet 73" ("That time of year thou mayst in me behold"), were rearranged in any way, the power and effectiveness of the poem would be severely diminished, even though each quatrain makes essentially the same point about the imminence of the speaker's death. As the poem progresses from quatrain to quatrain, time becomes shorter, space smaller, light dimmer, and so on, so that the approach of death becomes increasingly more imminent as we move toward the couplet.

In this, as in so many works that we have over the years come to value highly, to esteem as "masterpieces" even, we witness the workingness of parts large and small in the service of the whole, of the system of intentionality that both implies and is implied by those parts. And there is a special pleasure in coming to an understanding of the fittingness of things, of how this or that element of the text is just right for the text. Moreover, on the side of teaching, there is a special pleasure that comes from helping students to achieve a rich understanding of the internal dynamics of a text, a result that can be prompted by getting them into the habit of asking of greater and lesser parts either why this or that salient feature of the text is present (what its function, value, or significance is) or how the text would be affected if this rather than that were the case. There is a huge difference between sailing well in a storm and capsizing and between hitting the target and missing it; there are many ways of realizing the latter, but precious few ways of doing the former, and the difference between minor and major writers is that those in the majors know when to tack and how to steady the aim. In short, writing poorly or merely adequately is easy; writing well is difficult, but when it is done well, the satisfaction is proportionate to the difficulty overcome. And nothing is more satisfying to the reader than participating, by means of understanding, in the proper, fitting, and right functioning of the elements of humanly significant systems of intentionality.

Surely, those of us who take an interest in such things can be forgiven for directing some of our attention to the "internal goods"—that is, the satisfied needs of the artistic structure—of texts, to the rather uncommon and remarkable fittingness and workingness of things in certain literary works, once they are understood in terms of their specific justification conditions, their particular system of intentionality. And perhaps we can even be forgiven for valuing more highly than other works those that manage not only to fit much of interest in but also to make so much of what fits in contribute significantly to the working of the whole work. Certainly we can be forgiven, at least condescendingly, for continuing to admire and value highly *King Lear, Paradise Lost,* the *Essay on Man, The Prelude, Pride and Prejudice, Great Expectations, The Waste Land, Ulysses,* and so on as "masterpieces," as monuments of unaging intellect. And, of course, we continue to admire them even though propositionally, as bodies of ideas or systems of thought, they are, if not philosophically bankrupt, at least intellectually undistinguished or suspect, and even though most of what is politically, ideologically, or historically interesting in them can be found in many other earlier, contemporaneous, and later works (both serious and comic, both popular and elite) as well as in other cultural artifacts—such as publishers' account books, legal briefs, trade routes, jokes, dress designs—and undoubtedly in purer, starker, bolder form (and hence, more valuable form).

In addition to admiring these "masterpieces" for the largeness of their conception, the extent of their understanding, the importance of the matters they raise and deal with, we recognize as we applaud in each of them a superior kind of formal or artistic achievement. We discern in each, as I have said, rightnesses and appropriatenesses that are widely distributed and deeply embedded and that, by enhancing the workingness of the whole, make the realized work a rare and, hence, especially valuable achievement. Still, it is necessary to understand that this formal richness is inseparable from the intellectual and moral achievement of the works. The verbal, imagistic, and structural accomplishments are integrally related to (are, in a sense, the conditions of possibility of) the conceptual reach, moral significance, and emotional power of the works. In *Othello*, for example, every scene, virtually every word, not only contributes to the forwarding of the action and to our understanding of the bases and effects of jealousy, but also enhances and enriches our sense of the internal integrity, of the architectonic cohesiveness of the work as a whole. One after another, each image, phrase, or scene finds itself involved with predecessors or successors in a complexly appropriate system of interimplication. In the end, then, it seems fair to say that if the making of such deeply self-satisfied (i.e., integrally coherent), formally and morally rich works as *Othello, Paradise Lost*, and so on is a huge and uncommon accomplishment (as it clearly is when measured against the standard established over the years by the accomplishments of other toilers in the same literary fields), then our participation, by means of understanding, in such achievements *at the level of their interests and justifications* is a huge pleasure (for which we need to make no apology and for which we do not need, for heaven's sake, to ask for any forgiveness).

Let me bring this brief discussion of the "intrinsic merit" of texts, of the value of understanding texts at the level of their interest and intentionality (as distinguished from understanding them in terms of their relations to political/cultural matters) with a few comments on some of the ethical implications of such a focus (at least with regard to some works upon which we have traditionally placed a high value). We have regularly seen that any work—indeed, any differentiable part, any isolable element of the work—can be examined and discussed in connection with any number of things linguistic, social, political, legal, philological, ideological, anthropological, horticultural, economic, patriotic, mechanical, biographical, colonial, pyschoanalytic, or whatever. Nevertheless, high among the interests generated in us by the internal workings of writings not motivated or justified by a system of *ideas* or *themes* but focusing on morally differentiated individuals in humanly interesting situations is an interest in what speaking broadly we can call "ethical quality."

Most of our novels, dramas, narrative poems, as well as the majority of our lyric poems, for example, invite us to note clearly and then to consider carefully, apart from self-interest, what it would be like to think and feel in such and such a frame of mind and to live in such and such circumstances. We are allowed to see vividly and to participate imaginatively in moral perplexities, in situations of moral choice and moral action, confronting those perplexities not as a system of ideas or as a corpus of theses or moral propositions, but as a complex of social, personal, emotional circumstances impinging on or otherwise affecting and affected by particular character or personality. What we witness and are moved by are ethical possibilities of living. We are interested in what it would be like to live in them and live them out (i.e., to know the consequences of their adoption and use). For many simple reasons within easy reach, all of which are undoubtedly connected in some way or another with our insatiable interest in ourselves, we are tirelessly interested in "new" exhibitions of moral perplexity and possibility. Such exhibitions enable us to add to the stock of our conceptual storehouse, to enlarge our understanding of what may be possible to creatures who wear our mortal flesh and share our cognitive capacities, and to fit ourselves for further and future understanding and judgment.

Life is short, and, like Shakespeare's irrepressible Bottom the weaver, we cannot be in all roles or know very much by reflection alone about the roles available or possible. Literary works, however, provide us with "ethical samples" of ethical possibilities, and they are, in a very large and untrivial sense, the schools of our moral sensibilities, teaching us surreptitiously much about the nature and bases of right behavior. As we read these works, the line of our sustained interest is the line of moral entanglement, complication, and, usually, resolution. In other words, the line of *our* interest and satisfaction follows the line of the text's moral concerns, and these concerns supply the categories of rightness and the conditions of justification that make up the text's interest and make for artistic fulfillment (for the satisfaction of the text's internal interests). But as we move beyond the texts we carry from them conceptual resources serviceable in the making and understanding of many new situations and texts, and in the making of the good life (or at least in the understanding of some of the components of human flourishing). Reading literature at the level of its ethical concern (which is, for many works, the level of justification or intentionality) with empathetic understanding will not necessarily make us better people, of course, but it will *exercise our capacity for and improve our skill at moral discrimination*, provide us with concepts useful to the formation of a regulative image of the good life, and, thus, make us better equipped for right action.

To the extent that the current orthodoxies diminish the significance or deny the possibility of intrinsic merit, while affirming that stable, determinate meaning is impossible because of the nature of language as such and that everything is political/cultural/ideological, they either throw themselves on the sword of self-refutation or restrict our focus to too narrow a band of the relational interests and the standards of value in which we may view and by which we may judge literary works (and all other products of human ingenuity and intentionality). By way of concluding this examination of the listed orthodoxies, I would say only that the adoption of most of what is stated or implied in the listed items requires us to violate our earned understanding of what's what and deprives us of the conceptual resources on which we depend every day of our lives to get along in all the worlds we encounter and make.

Chapter 10
Humanism and Intercultural Critique

Although "antihumanism" appears on the list of current orthodoxies only parenthetically in item (a) of category four—"Personal agency is denied (antihumanism)"—among current theorists it is like the snow in Ireland at the end of James Joyce's "The Dead," that is, "general." It is openly avowed or tacitly assumed in virtually all theoretical and critical discourse, since Humanism, also identified as the "Enlightenment project" in some circles, is the subsumptive or covering term for all that is antithetical to current wisdom. Humanism, for example, is identified or associated with belief in realism (i.e., belief in a way that things are independently of our representations), in a correspondence theory of truth, in determinate meanings, in authors as creators of unique artistic products, in human beings as effective agents of social change, in conceptual relativity but not relativism, and so on. Indeed, all that this book has endorsed, supported, and argued for would be anathematized by most current theorists as a form of humanism, as a nostalgic pining for worlds well lost, for mythical kingdoms of the epistemological and metaphysical kind, ultimately, for the assurance that the Transcendental Signifier was in His Scriptorium and all was well with the world.

It is difficult to get a defense of humanism under way in today's critical and theoretical environment, but not because "humanism" is not everywhere derided or because "human universals" (the subsidiary interest of this chapter) are not everywhere discredited. Such universal disdain among theorists supplies my only secure foundation of hope, since I know that nothing pleases an academic more than a defense of the indefensible, an affirmation of the value and truth of what all had come to agree was worthless and false. No, the difficulty arises because the assaults upon both humanism and human universals are so various and so diversely inconsistent that any quick ground-clearing or any expeditious exhibition of the positive case is precluded. Still, something can be done, as I hope to make clear in what follows, to rehabilitate the term and the practice of humanism, to show, in fact, that in its pragmatic and pluralist form humanism is inescapable for creatures with content-involving capacities such as ours. To get to this positive inescapability, it will be helpful to consider two less than meliorative conceptions of humanism's inescapability.

At the outset, however, I must confess that I don't know what "humanism as such" or "in itself" is (indeed, I don't know what anything "in itself" is, what it is, that is, apart from some representation; with most folks today, I assume that we have no access to unconceptualized reality—certainly no linguistically unmediated access to abstractions—though, unlike many literary theorists, I do believe it is possible to refer determinately to things and events outside speakers and outside thought and language, albeit only by means of thought and language—if there is a puzzle in this subordinate clause, its resolution will have to be deferred until later). Just as there is no such thing as history, only histories, so there is no humanism, only humanisms, a confusing, often contradictory, array of humanisms. In the interests of stylistic elegance, however, I will use "humanism" in the singular throughout this chapter and trust to the reader to determine from the immediate context what kind or aspect of humanism is under scrutiny.

INESCAPABILITY ONE: HUMANISM AS WESTERN THOUGHT

In the Western tradition, there is a line of subject matters, as well as a disparate assortment of doctrines, beliefs, attitudes, and ends, that has been associated with humanism in the broadest sense. In one or another conception of the term, humanism stretches from Hellenistic Greece (in the skeptical and relativistic views of Protagoras, in the transcendentally significant Forms of Plato, in the intrinsic and essential properties of matter in Aristotle, and so on) to pre- and post-imperial Rome (in the rhetorically grounded views of, among others, Aulus Gellius, Cicero, and Quintilian, for whom the study of certain subjects—grammar, rhetoric, history, poetry, moral philosophy—was instrumentally necessary to the cultivation of the good citizen, quintessentially, the orator, and the production of the good society; liberal arts produce the liberal man who produces or envisions the liberal society); to fourteenth-century Italy and sixteenth-century England and northern Europe (in Renaissance humanism); to Enlightenment Europe (in, among other things, the new sciences of man—psychology, linguistics, history, and sociology, which established the principles of our common nature on new bases and gave defining immediacy to such inseparably human and unalienable values or regulative ideals as equality, justice, freedom, liberty, and individual rights); to, abbreviating mercilessly, reformist England and France in the nineteenth century (in which social benefits and individual rights were acquired or extended, and Arnold and others fought a defensive action against all that was inimical to liberal studies and in support of "high seriousness," of the great tradition of thought and expression); to twentieth-century New Humanism (in the moral urgency of More, Babbitt, and others), secular humanism (the demon of the American right), and liberal humanism (the capitalist flunky of the academic left).

Of Hellenism, humanism, and Enlightenment we are the legatees; whatever has or can be associated with these can be and has been called humanism or humanistic. Even in this laughably simple and highly condensed overview it is possible to see many humanisms, some defined in opposition to dialectic, some in opposition to state or church, to feudalism, to science, to intolerance, and so on, and some acting in concert with religion, science, the state, and so on. And, wherever we look, we find humanism not only struggling with enemies abroad but also entangled in local squabbles at home, as friends and relatives make claims of their own and revise those of one another. For example, what looks from a distance like a smooth ride in the eighteenth century to a better, deeper, richer understanding of the principles of mind (the foundations of thought and experience) and the principles of language (the universal bases of expression) is, from within the carriage—i.e., when the discussions are examined treatise by treatise—a rough journey over rugged terrain, as John Locke, David Hume, George Berkeley, Thomas Reid, Adam Smith, Dugald Stewart, and others knock one another about and wrestle with all the little devils in the details.

Nevertheless, in all the manifestations of what many have for a variety of reasons been willing to call humanism (by this or some other name), there are recurring and persistent emphases, in various degrees and kinds, on the place (in a metaphysical scheme of things), nature (essence), and ends of human beings; on what is consonant with his nature and agreeable to her reason; on what is worthy of her study and his action. Such emphases, of course, are also found in those forms of humanism going under the name of communism (at least in its concern with abolishing the self-alienation of humans brought about by capitalistic structures of labor and property), Freudianism (at least in its concern with uncovering the universal bases of maturation and action), and existentialism (at least in its preoccupation with the human universe, the one and only universe of human subjectivity). Because it is a big net, a large tent, accommodating great and small and almost one and all, because in no matter what direction you set out you always run into something that has borne or could bear its name, because, indeed, in one form or another it is coextensive with Western intellectual history, humanism is inescapable.

INESCAPABILITY TWO: HUMANISM AS UNIVERSAL SCAPEGOAT

Indeed, it is its coextensiveness with that history that makes it inescapable in a negative sense in most contemporary theoretical discussions, since in those discussions it is the lowly porter of all the newly discredited onto-theophallologocentric baggage of our tradition, the ever-present scapegoat of our collective moral and cognitive sins, or, as Richard Levin has justly informed us, the empty discursive slot into which we can insert anything we find abhorrent.[1] This is not the time or place to provide an extensive review of its inescapability in this sense, but a few reminders of its serviceability are perhaps in order. Above all else, humanism, as outfitted in clownish robes by modern theorists, is the comically impotent foe of the two foundationalist or bedrock truths of postmodernism, namely, that there is no Transcendental Signified that is the guarantor of meaning or reference (i.e., meaning is the transient effect of the play of signifiers in a relational system of differences) and that reality is socially constructed (i.e., is the consequence of knowledge/power relations in various regimes of social discipline). Both truths, of course, diminish or eliminate outright the significance of human beings as agents of making and of social action or reform.

To register a demurrer or to fail to assent to these truths is to be a humanist, it seems. To do either is to support or give aid and comfort to objectivity, rationality, determinate meaning; additionally, one is necessarily committed to belief in the correspondence theory of truth and, consequently, tied to programs of scientific rationality and conceptions of absolutes and universals (tied, for example, to views of the fixed, unchanging, essential nature of things, including human beings), and, thus, one acts in collusion with the subjugation of nature and the oppression of non-Western populations. In short, one is ineluctably a participant in systems of oppression, repression, and exploitation. The Enlightenment values of equality, distributive justice, liberty, democracy, individual rights, the rule of reason over the forces of superstition and arbitrary power in church or state, and so on—these values are nothing more than the sales gimmicks of capitalist greed, competitiveness, and exploitation, the alluring packages within which the real goods are found, namely, means-end rationality, unrestrained individuality, and the will to master, control, dominate, own (liberty, for example, is the liberty of the leveraged buyout, and freedom is the freedom to buy and sell or to capitalize on the labor of others). Thus, in a fairly recent article, a modern theorist, taking his hints from Foucault's analysis of the Enlightenment, finds that the Inquisition, long considered by some as the antithesis or the Other of the Enlightenment, is really the Enlightenment without its modesty on, the Enlightenment in its native ragged toothedness and clawishness, as can be seen especially in the Inquisition's attention to the individual and in its determination to totalize control and to universalize truth.[2] In its own imitable way, this article epitomizes a tendency among theorists to argue that just the reverse of what we had always thought to be true is true. Tired of milking the cow, theorists have with increasing frequency set about to milk the bull, as Samuel Johnson might have said.[3]

I assume it comes as no breaking bulletin that dialectical materialism (in its nonhumanist mode) or cultural materialism is interested in eliminating what we self-deceivingly call natural rights and values but what are really historically constructed bourgeois ideals of liberty, freedom, justice, and individual rights and in reducing mind, consciousness, and reason—more specifically, ideas, beliefs, values, and so on—to the superstructure of the informing material reality. In this scheme, mind or consciousness is nothing apart from the material conditions of production and consumption or from regimes of power and knowledge. As Marx and a host of more recent theorists have taught us, life is not determined by consciousness; rather, consciousness is determined by life, that is, by power relations and the material conditions of existence.[4] There is no fixed human nature that human beings have under all forms of social organization.

Let me bring this coals to Newcastle line of exposition, this rehearsal of everyday's news to conclusion with a few summary remarks and a couple of quotations. So much of what is wrong with what is called humanism by many theorists derives from its commitment to a metaphysics of presence, a belief in our ability to hook our thoughts and language onto things as they really are in themselves, and, on the other hand, its belief in human agency, in human intentionality as the source and origin of meaning and action. Any literary theory that assumes that human authors create structures of determinate meaning relating to matters of human interest and concern that readers can come to understand in their proper emphasis and determinacy is in the grip of the metaphysics of presence and an unwarranted conception of agency. As Foucault, with characteristic zest, says, "To all those who still wish to talk about man, about his reign or his liberation, to all those who still ask themselves questions about what man is in his essence, to all those who wish to take him as their starting-point in their attempts to reach the truth . . . to all these warped and twisted forms of reflection we can only answer with a philosophical laugh"; . . . man is "simply a fold in our knowledge," destined to "disappear as soon as that knowledge has found a new form."[5] Although in the following quotation Joan Wallach Scott is concerned with the relevance of antihumanistic postmodernism to feminist scholarship, she provides a useful epitome of the issues addressed above:

Precisely because it addresses questions of epistemology, relativizes the status of all knowledge, links knowledge and power, and theorizes these in terms of the operations of difference, . . . poststructuralism (or at least some of the approaches generally associated with Michel Foucault and Jacques Derrida) offers feminism [its most] powerful analytic perspective. . . . [Since there is no objective basis for one story rather than another, the only grounds for judging one better than another are] its persuasiveness, its political utility, and its political sincerity.[6]

INESCAPABILITY THREE: PRAGMATIC-PLURALIST HUMANISM

Before explaining briefly why I think humanism in some positive sense is inescapable, let me note by way of disclaimer that the humanist I respect (whom I prefer to call a pragmatic pluralist) would be the last to say that there is not much powerful sense in the critique of the ways in which Enlightenment values such as liberty, freedom, and justice have been used in the service of oppression and domination. These values are vaguely and variously defined and implemented, and they often conflict with one another, as John Rawls and Isaiah Berlin have powerfully evinced: freedom often leads to inequality, and the liberty of one can diminish the freedom of another.[7] Indeed, almost every Supreme Court case involves the conflict of one Enlightenment value with another. Moreover, all would agree, I think, that as historically and culturally situated people our conceptual resources are in various gross and subtle ways determined by our social context. In every period, some answers go unquestioned (some things we assume to be right or true or natural), and many questions go unasked, and it is certainly one of the tasks of criticism to question answers and ask questions and to explain as best we can why "mum" has been the word.

Having said that, let me quickly indicate what I take to be the characteristic assumptions and concerns of the pragmatic-pluralist humanist, the principles and conceptions that make humanism inescapable in a positive sense. Briefly, then, there is the recognition that, as Hilary Putnam remarks, "there are only the various points of view of actual persons which reflect the various interests and purposes that their theories and descriptions subserve."[8] As F.C.S. Schiller observed early in the century in connection with pragmatism, "humanism is merely the perception that the philosophic problem concerns human beings striving to comprehend a world of human experience by the resources of human minds."[9] Moreover, though all our theories and descriptions reflect our interests and values (we don't talk about or describe what we are not interested in), we are committed to the view that some of our theories and descriptions—as well as some of our interests and values— are better (truer, more right, more useful, more satisfying, and so on) than others. Also, though some of our views and values are truer, better, and more right than others, we also recognize that there is no metaphysical guarantee or warrant for these normative judgments. With Putnam, we acknowledge that our views cannot be justified or validated "by anything but their success as judged by the interests and values which evolve and get modified at the same time and in interaction with the evolving views themselves."[10] Finally, still speaking generally, we recognize that as human beings we inhabit a common world, not only or chiefly because we may all "become victims of ecological or nuclear disaster," but primarily because, as Ruth Anna Putnam goes on to say, "to a large extent we share our understanding of that world, and on that basis we can come to further agreements";[11] and we share that understanding because we have object-involving abilities and conceptual capacities in common.

Furthermore, it is worth observing that the attack of contemporary theorists against humanism is addressed to I-Don't-Know-Who. In the humanist, or pragmatist-pluralist, tradition to which I belong, I don't know anybody who is an essentialist or foundationalist, or who believes in a universal, unchanging, human essence. Indeed, as Dewey repeatedly reminded us, those who appeal to "essential human nature," to "the laws of nature," and to what is "agreeable to reason" tend to do so in an effort to rationalize and justify the interests and privileges of the powerful.[12]

Nor do I know anyone in this modern humanist tradition who subscribes to the metaphysics of presence, who believes, say, that we can look at our language or thought from a medium distance and compare it to things and the world as they really are to determine which are the real, intrinsic properties of things in themselves and which are the properties of our human projections. But because we have no access to unconceptualized reality (reference, meaning, and the mental are not ontological but semantic or intentional categories), it does not follow, as one philosopher notes, that "language and thought do not describe something outside themselves, even if that something can only be described by describing it."[13] There is no essence to reference, and though reference is nonsense apart from some conceptual scheme or system of rationality, the objects picked out are no less real and no less independent for being scheme-identified. For the pragmatic-pluralist, the meaningful question is not whether objects or states of affairs "really exist" or not (this, I submit, is an unintelligible question, to the extent that it implies that nature or reality has its own semantic preferences, that it has its own unique language that it is waiting for us to discover or learn); no, the meaningful question, as some philosophical wag in the humanist-pragmatist-pluralist tradition has said, is whether notions such as object or event or states of affairs "are to be conceived of as having a single determinate meaning or whether they are more happily conceived in terms of an open and ever extendable family of uses."[14] What the pragmatist says to the postmodern relativist is that some things are true, reasonable, and warranted (just as many things are false, unreasonable, and unwarranted), but we can only know such things once we have adopted a conceptual scheme or system of rationality.[15]

Truth, as many have pointed out, is not a heavyweight metaphysical notion. It is, like meaning and reference, a semantic-intentional, a conceptual notion. Even so, truth is truth—whether a belief or a descriptive sentence expressing that belief is true or not depends very immediately on whether the conditions external to (though expressed by) my thought or language satisfy or justify that belief. We distinguish, for example, between conditions of reference and reference; that is, we determine under what conditions a chair, say, will be a chair, but we do not determine whether those conditions obtain. And the same is true of "social" as well as "physical" reference: in "Betty is a widow," we determine that "Betty" is "Betty" (has that name) and that "widow" has certain traits, but we don't determine whether those traits apply to any given individual (rather, the condition of the individual determines whether the traits apply to her).

Also, we distinguish between determinate reference (or meaning) and absolute or intrinsic reference; there is no thing or state of affairs that just is what it is in itself, though to be determined as something is to be that something, a chair, say. The skepticism or relativism that characterizes most recent theory seems to be what Hilary Putnam calls the flip side of metaphysical realism; because we have no Transcendental Signified and, hence, no way to hook our words and thoughts onto reality in itself, we have come to believe that we have lost all power to refer at all, to refer to real things and states. But this conclusion does not follow. In fact, because it violates what we consistently and inescapably do all the time, it is an incoherent notion. Who is there who does not know, absolutely and certainly, that martinis are alcoholic drinks and that even-toed ungulates make poor typesetters?[16]

Now the same "state of affairs" can be truly described as a "martini," a "collection of fermions," a "gappy bundle of particles," and so on, but to ask what the state really is, is to ask an incoherent or impossible question; to conclude that because it is not really one thing or another absolutely it cannot be anything but a product of thought and language, a series of ephemeral effects of a system of differential relations, is to be a disappointed metaphysician, a referential skeptic and relativist in danger of missing the special pleasures of a good drink. A brief examination of how true and real states may be truly and really different and alike at the same time may be helpful. Many different worldly conditions can produce the same sensory stimulation (e.g., a "real" glass, a plastic imitation of one, a hallucination). Given different past experiences and present beliefs, the same stimulation can produce different experiences (e.g., I experience the train's leaving with sadness, whereas you experience it with joy). Given other different beliefs, the same experience can lead to different "observational beliefs" (e.g., I see "furniture" in the room, whereas you—a member of a very different culture—see "sources of fuel"). Given different other beliefs, the same "observatonal beliefs" can lead to different "theoretical beliefs" (e.g., different theories of earth-sun-planet relations).[17] As Michael Devitt observes, "each belief is tied to a range of conditions in which, relative to other beliefs, it is justified [as true or right or good] in varying degrees."[18]

Further, where there is any content at all there is, as we have seen, rationality; without reason there is no thought, no content, no facts, things, events, and so on. Citing the content of a statement or utterance is simply giving its function within a system of relationships, a system of justification conditions. Again, as has been demonstrated earlier, coherence, consistency, and logic are the conditions of the very possibility of thought. Moreover, despite postmodern assertions and declarations to the contrary, logic and rationality have no metaphysical presuppositions attached to them. They are those conditions in the absence of which there is no thought or content. Truth is prior to reference, in that our words have meaning only in the context of a sentence, and a sentence has meaning only within a context of use in a particular language, only within a particular system of intentionality. Sentences, then, express something definite, have definite content only as used on particular occasions within a system of justification, and what they express depends, among other things but inescapably, on the intentions of speakers and writers. As Michael Dummett notes, "any adequate philosophical account of language must describe it as a rational activity on the part of creatures to whom can be ascribed intention and purpose."[19]

There is undoubtedly no need at this late stage to rehearse the reasons why I am convinced that this "humanist"-agential view of language is superior to that based either on differential relations or on social construction. But in passing I would simply note, with Nelson Goodman, that the relational becomes categorical in a context of use. For example, in the system of numbers, any number—considered in relational terms—can be both an immediate predecessor and an immediate successor, but when, say, five becomes categorical, becomes, that is, our ground or origin, only four is absolutely and determinately its immediate predecessor and only six is its immediate successor; in this system, five, of course, is only and absolutely the immediate predecessor of six and the immediate successor of four.[20] The trouble with relational views is that there is simply no end to the relations in which one thing can stand to another (the number of relations in which one thing can stand to another is virtually infinite), though theorists, of course, tend to privilege binary or antithetical relations. Any thing at all is like Wittgenstein's rabbit-duck, in that anything can be seen, logically, in many ways. As one philosopher has observed, it is no "exaggeration to say that any piece of information may, in the context of an appropriate epistemic background, be relevant to any particular belief."[21] For example, "A flash of gray glimpsed in the woods may be evidence of the presence of a squirrel, if you take yourself to be in New Jersey, say, but evidence of a wood pigeon, if you take yourself to be in Scotland."[22] Once we give up on metaphysical realism and, more important, the skeptical reaction to its loss that leads to the denial of determinate reference and meaning altogether, we can free ourselves to get on with the sort of referring and meaning we do anyway with a clear conscience.

On the notion of social construction, we can say, yes, we are culturally situated beings who think about and refer to things and values that have cultural standing, but such things and values take on content and determinacy only in contexts of use. Also, what society or culture cannot produce is a particular utterance with definite, specific content, since its stock of terms and phrases is, until used, divorced from the network of intentionality and background assumptions that make them beliefs and give them function and emphasis. Moreover, the closer we get to any culture, the more diverse, disparate, and contradictory are the things we find expressed in it. Some new historicists focus (ostensibly at least) on this diversity within a culture's linguistic economy, of course, but for some reason, it seems that all uses tell essentially the same story about power relations or have essentially the same ideological functions. And because of our capacity both to understand and imagine new structures (otherwise, how would critique and reform ever begin?) we can always transcend the conditions of our conditioning. On just this matter, Steven Winter, defending objectivity as a form of what he calls "transperspectivity," has usefully reminded us that a "physically, historically, socially, and culturally situated self can reflect critically on its own construction of a world and imagine other possible worlds that might be constructed; situated self-consciousness involves the ability to imagine how the world might be constructed differently."[23]

HUMAN UNIVERSALS

It is time to make the final turn, to human universals. Because, as Winter and others make clear, our only access to content is through our participation in systems of justification and intentionality, and because we do so participate, we are obliged to reject all forms of skepticism and relativism. Simply, the possibility of translation entails the falsity of relativism, just as, conversely, the truth of relativism (i.e., of being locked within the prison house of our particular language game or conceptual framework) entails the impossibility of translation. To say that something is true according to the norms of this or that culture or in this or that language game is to say something that is objective about the culture or the language game from outside the culture or game. Similarly, to say that two or more views are incommensurable is to speak truly from outside the contending or conflicting views. The sort of relativism that takes the form of a denial of communication and understanding across paradigms, that assumes that we are locked in the separate prison houses of our language system or that of our interpretive community, or that asserts that interpretations are simply the inventions of the interpreter is, as many have demonstrated, incoherent, inasmuch as "the general position always runs afoul of that actual practice which it claims to be the source of truth and necessity; such relativism is an attempt to view language and thought from the vantage point which it proclaims to be inaccessible."[24] Or, as Susan Hurley has wisely observed, "some aspect of the form of life of the skeptic [or relativist] has implications inconsistent with the content of his view," thus involving him or her in "pragmatic inconsistency."[25] For example, one who argues against or merely asserts an opposition to determinate meaning is necessarily implicated in pragmatic inconsistency, in that the activity not only is inconsistent with the view expressed but also affirms the truth of what is being rejected.

In *Philosophy and an African Culture*, Kwasi Wiredu, a Ghanian philosopher, correctly observes that

Relativism . . . falsely denied the existence of inter-personal criteria of rationality. That is what the denial of objectivity amounts to. Unless at least the basic canons of rational thinking were common to men, they could not even communicate among themselves. Thus, in seeking to foreclose rational discussion, the relativist view is in effect seeking to undermine the foundations of human community.[26]

But, of course, as we have seen, we do translate, and we do know that without recourse to standards of rational acceptability, to the cognitive values of coherence, rationality, instrumental efficacy, and so on, we would not have any content or any world at all.

It is difficult to say—and we will perhaps never be in a position to say definitively—on what exactly our "object-involving abilities" and our conceptual capacities are based (just as we will never have a complete, scientific account of induction), but it is clear, I think, that we share forms of reason and that these shared forms are based on our common bodily makeup and experience and on our common cognitive abilities. It is clear, for example, *that* there is considerable uniformity in our quality spacings (I see red as you see red); *that* our partitioning principles are common and, it seems, innate (I discriminate the boundaries of entities pretty much as you do); *that* we perceive colors only within a certain range of the spectrum and presumably share other perceptual norms, and *that* we cast our identities in some narrative form. Further, George Lakoff and others who are working to understand our category proclivities and formations have identified a variety of kinesthetic image schemas (in-out, center-periphery, up-down, and so on), basic-level concepts (i.e., concepts relating to basic colors and emotions and to things, such as plants, animals, body parts, artifacts), and metaphoric operations based on our experiences that are common across cultures.[27]

Admittedly, there can be no argument for a universal human essence that would guarantee agreement among all fully rational human beings, but, as one philosopher has noted,

there is the closest thing to this that we can get, once we have given up on essences
and absolutes: Human beings share a basic biological makeup, they share the same
cognitive mechanisms, and they share certain general physical, interpersonal, and cultural needs that are the bases for universally shared purposes, interests, and projects
that show themselves in every culture we have encountered.[28]

Further, according to Alvin Goldman, "the general lines of [imaginative]
construction [of new patterns and structures] may be largely species-specific;
this would account for the commonality of the concepts we generate, the
predicates we project, the possibilities we envisage."[29] Moreover, Owen
Flanagan has reported that there is some evidence that the child, "if given
social interaction, may be innately disposed to develop a theory of mind, a
theory of its own mind and those of others, a theory primed by evolution
to frame the self and others as single integrated intentional systems."[30] Let
me bring this entirely too sketchy account of universals to a close by noting
something about their epistemic importance, focusing only on partitioning
principles. As Goldman has said,

where innate partitioning principles are *shared and relatively small in number the
prospects for successful communication are greatly enhanced*. Such communication has
immeasurable epistemic benefits: innumerable truths and truth-acquiring methods
can be learned from others via language. Thus, the mere sharing of highly constrained
partitioning operations—whatever they may be—is a great epistemic boon.[31]

From the preceding discussion we can arrive at a kind of humanism that
makes cultural critique and cultural reform possible. We cannot criticize or
evaluate other cultures or our own from some position outside culture, but
we can share understandings and conceptions of what Aristotle called human
flourishing and adjust our own and criticize those of others in the light of
such evolving standards, adopting what we admire and censuring what we
deplore. Our criticism can be offered only from within our tradition or
culture, to be sure, but from a basis of shared "intercultural meanings" we
can organize and mount "intercultural criticism." As one cultural critic
notes, "In every society some human beings are regarded as more than mere
objects, and that seems to me to be a basis from which one might begin to
argue 'from inside' against patriarchy and other forms of oppression and
enslavement"[32] Intercultural meanings and values are important precisely
because they make possible intercultural criticism. In giving up absolutes
and relativism, we gain access to the sorts of communication and discussion
that are, for Kwasi Wiredu and the rest of us, conditions of human community. The possibility of critiquing one culture from within another on
the basis of intercultural standards (and in the absence of a foundationalist
human nature or a fixed human essence) is given forceful expression by a
moral philosopher in the following terms:

As in the case of natural science there are no general timeless standards. [But] it is in the ability of one particular moral-philosophy-articulating-the-claims-of-a-particular-morality to identify and transcend the limitations of its rival or rivals, limitations which can be—although they may not in fact have been—identified by the rational standards to which the protagonists of the rival morality are committed by their allegiance to it, that the rational superiority of that particular moral philosophy and that particular morality emerge.[33]

In the end, then, it seems that because we are content-involved creatures and because content is inseparable from thought and thought from intentionality and, hence, agency, we cannot escape humanism; to have a thought or a world to talk about or be aware of, we must of necessity participate in systems of rationality, determining by our evolving standards which ones are good and right and true ones for us. Those who would deny the enduring value and significance of humanism, as we have construed it, must inevitably implicate themselves it seems in pragmatic inconsistency. In their denial they establish not only the falsity of their views but also the truth of those they reject or deny.

Notes

INTRODUCTION

1. Thomas Nagel, "Go with the Flow: Richard Rorty's Magic Formula for Disposing of Philosophical Problems," *Times Literary Supplement* (28 August 1998): 3.

2. Anthony Easthope, "Theories, Not Theory," *Times Literary Supplement* (13 March 1998): 8–9. For a joyfully exuberant account of the many-sects-one-faith character of current theory, see Perry Meisel, "Let a Hundred Isms Blossom," in which we find: "literary study in America has never been in better shape. Enriched by a variety of European methodologies since the early 70's, it has grown into a vast, synthetic enterprise characterized by powerful continuities rather than by disjunctions. Feminism, deconstruction, 'reader-response,' 'New Historicism,' 'postcolonialism'—all share similar ends and similar ways of getting there in a momentous collaboration," *New York Times Book Review* (28 May 2000): 27.

3. R. S. Crane makes the case for this system of relativity of statement to questions and of questions to frameworks in several essays. See, for example, "The Multiplicity of Critical Languages," in *The Languages of Criticism and the Structure of Poetry* (Toronto: University of Toronto Press, 1953), 26.

4. See my *Paradigms Regained: Pluralism and the Practice of Criticism* (Philadelphia: University of Pennsylvania Press, 1991), and my *Reason and the Nature of Texts* (Philadelphia: University of Pennsylvania Press, 1996).

5. William P. Alston, *A Realist Conception of Truth* (Ithaca, NY: Cornell University Press, 1996), 173.

6. Barbara Herrnstein Smith, *Belief and Resistance: Dynamics of Contemporary Intellectual Controversy* (Cambridge, MA: Harvard University Press, 1997), 61–62.

7. To any critic who might be inclined to say that the list of current orthodoxies is hopelessly outdated and does not represent the state of thinking in theory, I can

say (1) that every evidence—journal articles, recent books on literary theory (both advertised and published), conference papers, department meetings, cocktail-party conversations, and so on—testifies otherwise, and (2) that for convenient access to a genuinely representative account of the current state of theory the reader should consult Michael Chaouli's essay, "A Vast Unravelling," in the "Commentary" section of the *Times Literary Supplement* (26 February 1999): 14–15, in which virtually all the items of the "Current Orthodoxies" list find direct or implied defense. Responding to this spirited defense of the new order in theory, Raymond Tallis perhaps captures the sentiments of many when he notes how easily and comfortably "the rhetoric of subversive criticism [subversive, that is, of both common sense and hard-won knowledge about mind, reality, language, meaning, and so on] can sit side by side with the most uncritical and childlike acceptance of colonic material of a taurine provenance." For Tallis's remarks, see *Times Literary Supplement* (12 March 1999): 17.

8. The concept of the "meme" as a social analogue to the biological gene was first put into circulation by the biologist Richard Dawkins in *The Selfish Gene* (Oxford: Oxford University Press, 1976).

9. I borrow this example from John Greenwood; see his "Reasons to Believe," in *The Future of Folk Psychology: Intentionality and Cognitive Science*, ed. John D. Greenwood (Cambridge: Cambridge University Press, 1991), 72.

10. Colin McGinn, *Ethics, Evil, and Fiction* (Oxford: Clarendon Press, 1997), 45.

CHAPTER ONE

1. The complete list of "Current Orthodoxies" is appended to the introduction.

2. Although particular *reference* is necessary to these modes of criticism, *it*, like meaning, is relativized to culture, class, power, or some other social or political category. Moreover, even though these critics do insist on relating signs to extratextual persons and things, they are still deeply indebted to a post-Saussurean view of the workings of language. The close ties between deconstruction and new historicism (and cultural materialism) will be examined in chapter five.

3. In "Epistle I" of Alexander Pope's *An Essay on Man*, lines 194–96 read

Why has not Man a microscopic eye?
For this plain reason, Man is not a Fly.

4. William P. Alston, *A Realist Conception of Truth* (Ithaca, NY: Cornell University Press, 1996), 174–75; my emphases.

5. John Searle, *The Construction of Social Reality* (New York: The Free Press, 1995), 166. Emphasis in original.

6. Michael Devitt, *Coming to Our Senses: A Naturalistic Program for Semantic Localism* (Cambridge: Cambridge University Press, 1996), 103.

7. See Devitt, *Coming to Our Senses*, 102.

8. Homosexuality as a *social* (as distinct from a strictly *sexual*) marker is certainly created in particular social circumstances, is socially constructed. It exists as one half of a binary, as a category that has a specific social significance as the negative partner to the positive heterosexuality. In short, in this formation the term has social force and social consequences. Of course, some socially laden terms have less force and

less baneful personal consequences than others; for example, such terms as "sibling rivalry," "balance of power," and "brinkmanship" leave fewer scars on the body politic and the body personal than "homosexual" does. Nevertheless, for the current discussion it should be clear that whatever the meanings and values attached to terms at particular times, in the interests of whatever peculiar political forces or power structures, the *applicability* of the terms, once they have been assigned their particular meaning and reference ranges, is fixed for all speakers. I shall return to the issue of socially constructed meanings in chapter five, when I discuss new historicism.

9. Lynne Rudder Baker, *Explaining Attitudes: A Practical Approach to the Mind* (Cambridge: Cambridge University Press, 1995), 229.

10. A somewhat fuller discussion of this point—of the relations among "reality," truth, and mind-dependence—can be found in chapter two.

11. Akeel Bilgrami, *Belief and Meaning* (Oxford: Blackwell, 1992), 134.

CHAPTER TWO

1. Of course, if the units of syntax are meaningless apart from intentionality, they are also relation-less apart from syntax, which is itself something imposed by agents on structure-less materiality. In other words, both meaning and syntax are functions of intentionality. Syntactic *units* have neither meaning nor syntactic value in the absence of our impositions.

2. Donald Davidson, "The Myth of the Subjective," in *Relativism: Interpretation and Confrontation*, ed. Michael Krausz (Notre Dame, IN: University of Notre Dame Press, 1989), 166. My emphases.

3. Throughout this section, I am indebted to Fred Dretske's *Naturalizing the Mind* (Cambridge, MA: MIT Press, 1995); see especially his discussion of these matters on pages 115–16, 139–40.

4. I discuss additional "human universals" in chapter ten.

5. John Searle, *The Construction of Social Reality* (New York: The Free Press, 1995), 6–7.

6. I here give abbreviated expression to Davidson's complex view, as presented in Simon Evnine's useful summary in *Donald Davidson* (Stanford, CA: Stanford University Press, 1991), 41. For Davidson's more elaborated exposition of the rationality of action, including speech and writing, see his "Actions, Reasons, and Causes," reprinted in Donald Davidson, *Essays on Actions and Events* (Oxford: Clarendon Press, 1980), 3–19.

7. Dretske, *Naturalizing the Mind*, 152.

8. Michael Dummett, *Origins of Analytic Philosophy* (Cambridge, MA: Harvard University Press, 1994), 187–88.

9. Dretske, *Naturalizing the Mind*, 152.

10. William Child, *Causality, Interpretation, and the Mind* (Oxford: Clarendon Press, 1994), 137; my emphasis. Child is here giving summary expression to Davidson's position.

11. Colin McGinn, *Minds and Bodies: Philosophers and Their Ideas* (New York: Oxford University Press, 1997), 130.

12. As I have argued earlier, sensation and experience do not play an epistemological role, but, rather, a crucially important causal role.

13. Donald Davidson, "Knowing One's Own Mind," in *The Twin Earth Chronicles*, ed. Andrew Pessin and Sanford Goldberg (Armonk, NY: M. E. Sharpe, 1996), 339–40.

14. Akeel Bilgrami, *Belief and Meaning* (Oxford: Blackwell, 1992), 14.

15. We can plainly see this in the various reactions of our friends to our impending divorce or of our colleagues to the acceptance of our book manuscript by a distinguished press.

16. Frederick Schmitt, *Truth: A Primer* (Boulder, CO: Westview Press, 1995), 148, 149. For a severe attack against the correspondence view of truth and a ringing endorsement of constructivist truth, see Barbara Herrnstein Smith, "Netting Truth," *PMLA* 115 (2000): 1089–95.

17. Lynne Rudder Baker, *Explaining Attitudes: A Practical Approach to the Mind* (Cambridge: Cambridge University Press, 1995), 73–74.

18. Baker, *Explaining Attitudes*, 77.

19. Baker, *Explaining Attitudes*, 80.

20. The ideas expressed here derive from Searle, *The Construction of Social Reality*, 153.

21. William P. Alston, *A Realist Conception of Truth* (Ithaca, NY: Cornell University Press, 1996), 173; my emphases.

22. Raymond Tallis, *In Defense of Realism* (London: Edward Arnold, 1988), 29.

23. Searle, *The Construction of Social Reality*, 156–57; my emphasis.

24. Searle, *The Construction of Social Reality*, 155.

25. Searle, *The Construction of Social Reality*, 187.

26. Searle, *The Construction of Social Reality*, 187. Also relevant here is Hilary Putnam's view that most objects are not "causally dependent on language users." Putnam goes on to observe that "There would have been stars even if language users had not evolved. . . . There would have been a world, all right, but there would not have been any *truths* about the world." See *Reading Putnam*, ed. Peter Clark and Bob Hale (Oxford: Blackwell, 1994), 265.

27. Dretske, *Naturalizing the Mind*, xiii.

28. Searle, *The Construction of Social Reality*, 190.

CHAPTER THREE

1. This language is quoted from (3.a.) of the list of "Current Orthodoxies."

2. This language is taken from (5.a.) of the list of "Current Orthodoxies."

3. Hilary Putnam, *Reason, Truth, and History* (Cambridge: Cambridge University Press, 1981), 123.

4. Alexander Pope, *Essay on Criticism*, lines 9–11.

5. Barbara Herrnstein Smith, *Belief and Resistance: Dynamics of Contemporary Intellectual Controversy* (Cambridge, MA: Harvard University Press, 1997), 77–78; my emphases.

6. Smith, *Belief and Resistance*, 78–79.

7. Smith, *Belief and Resistance*, 79; Smith's emphases and brackets throughout.

8. David Hume, *A Treatise of Human Nature*, ed. L. A. Selby-Bigge and P. H. Nidditch (Oxford: Clarendon Press, 1978), 186.

9. Smith, *Belief and Resistance*, 80; my emphases.

10. Samuel Johnson, *The History of Rasselas, Prince of Abyssinia*, in *The Yale Edition of the Works of Samuel Johnson*, vol. 16, ed. Gwin J. Kolb (New Haven, CT: Yale University Press, 1990), 172.

11. This summary account is taken from William P. Alston, *The Reliability of Sense Perception* (Ithaca, NY: Cornell University Press, 1993), 53. For one of Wittgenstein's arguments, see *Philosophical Investigations*, trans. G.E.M. Anscombe (Oxford: Blackwell, 1953), #258–70.

12. As noted earlier, these topics are foregrounded in chapter four.

13. Hilary Putnam, *Words and Life*, ed. James Conant (Cambridge, MA: Harvard University Press, 1994), 247.

14. Akeel Bilgrami, *Belief and Meaning* (Oxford: Blackwell, 1992), 104, 101.

15. Simon Evnine, *Donald Davidson* (Stanford, CA: Stanford University Press, 1991), 179.

16. James Harris, *Against Relativism: A Philosophical Defense of Method* (La Salle, IL: Open Court, 1992), 149.

17. Thomas Nagel, *The Last Word* (New York: Oxford University Press, 1997), 37–38.

CHAPTER FOUR

1. Michael Devitt, *Realism and Truth*, 2nd ed. (Oxford: Blackwell, 1991), 193.

2. I am here putting my own unauthorized spin on what I take to be implicit in John Searle's following remarks: "To say something and mean it is to impose the conditions of satisfaction of the belief onto the utterance. Since the utterance is itself the condition of satisfaction of the intention to make it, the essence of meaning is the intentional imposition of conditions of satisfaction onto conditions of satisfaction." Searle goes on to mention lies. The remarks quoted here are taken from "Response," in *John Searle and His Critics*, ed. Ernest Lepore and Robert Van Gulick (Oxford: Blackwell, 1991), 86.

3. Michael Devitt, *Coming to Our Senses: A Naturalistic Program for Semantic Localism* (Cambridge: Cambridge University Press, 1996), 246, 138.

4. Colin McGinn, *Problems in Philosophy: The Limits of Inquiry* (Oxford: Blackwell, 1993), 65.

5. Donald Davidson, "Knowing One's Own Mind," in *The Twin Earth Chronicles*, ed. Andrew Pessin and Sanford Goldberg (Armonk, NY: M. E. Sharpe, 1996), 339–40.

6. Thomas Nagel, *The Last Word* (New York: Oxford University Press, 1997), 44–45.

7. Donald Davidson, "Locating Literary Language," in *Literary Theory After Davidson*, ed. Reed Way Dasenbrock (University Park, PA: The Pennsylvania State University Press, 1993), 298.

8. Mark Greenberg, "What Connects Thought and Action?" *Times Literary Supplement* (23 June 1995): 8.

9. Donald Davidson, "Rational Animals," *Dialecta* 36 (1982): 317–27. The passage is quoted here from John Heil, *The Nature of True Minds* (Cambridge: Cambridge University Press, 1992), 194.

10. John Searle, *The Construction of Social Reality* (New York: The Free Press, 1995), 18–19.

11. Hilary Putnam, *Realism with a Human Face*, ed. James Conant (Cambridge, MA: Harvard University Press, 1990), 115.

12. Putnam, *Realism with a Human Face*, 115.

13. Davidson, "Knowing One's Own Mind," 339.

14. Michael Dummett, *Origins of Analytic Philosophy* (Cambridge, MA: Harvard University Press, 1994), 158.

15. John Heil, *The Nature of True Minds* (Cambridge: Cambridge University Press, 1992), 212.

CHAPTER FIVE

1. For example, Richard Rorty has this to say about truth: the view "that 'true sentences work because they correspond to the way things are' is no more illuminating than 'it is right because it fulfills the Moral Law.' Both remarks . . . are empty metaphysical compliments—harmless as rhetorical pats on the back to the successful inquirer or agent, but troublesome if taken seriously and 'clarified' philosophically." Rorty, *Consequences of Pragmatism (Essays: 1972–1980)* (Minneapolis: University of Minnesota Press, 1982), xvii. For my discussion of correspondence and truth, see chapters one and two. For a trenchant analysis of Rorty's views on "objective truth," see Susan Haack, *Manifesto of a Passionate Moderate* (Chicago: University of Chicago Press, 1998); see especially the first two chapters.

2. As the argument progresses, I shall show how our newly emergent social and cultural criticism, which occasionally highlights the role of authors and is regularly interested in assigning blame (and, hence, in at least temporarily stable meanings), has its roots in the linguistic and philosophic assumptions of deconstruction.

3. Julia Kristeva, *Desire in Language: A Semiotic Approach to Literature and Art*, ed. Leon S. Roudiez, trans. Thomas Gora, Alice Jardine, and Leon S. Roudiez (New York: Columbia University Press, 1980), 66.

4. Vincent B. Leitch, *Deconstructive Criticism: An Advanced Introduction* (New York: Columbia University Press, 1983), 3.

5. J. Hillis Miller, *Topographies* (Stanford, CA: Stanford University Press, 1995), 292.

6. Michel Foucault, *The Order of Things: An Archaeology of the Human Sciences* (New York: Vintage, 1973), 342–43. Roland Barthes's most celebrated pronouncement on the death of the author as institution is to be found, not surprisingly, in "The Death of the Author," which can be conveniently located in *Image-Music-Text*, trans. Stephen Heath (New York: Hill and Wang, 1978).

7. Jacques Derrida, *Positions* (Chicago: University of Chicago Press, 1981), 26.

8. France is expressing his faith in Cordelia; see *King Lear* I. i. 222–23.

9. It is important to remember that a *similarity* (as distinct from an *identity*) relation is a relation of difference. For example, "sleet" is similar to "sleep" in that it is like "sleep" in all respects but one (i.e., where one has "t" the other has "p"), but the trace of "sleep" in "sleet" makes all the difference. Similarity relations are differential relations in this system.

10. Hilary Putnam, *Realism with a Human Face*, ed. James Conant (Cambridge, MA: Harvard University Press, 1990), 114.

11. If any reader doubts this, I urge her to make some strong claims in support

of agency, truth, and correspondence at the next cocktail party or scholarly conference she attends and then to record the astonished reactions of her associates.

12. Louis Montrose, "The Elizabethan Subject and the Spenserian Text," in *Literary Theory/Renaissance Texts*, ed. Patricia Parker and David Quint (Baltimore: Johns Hopkins University Press, 1986), 305.

13. Tyler Burge, "Individualism and the Mental," in *The Twin Earth Chronicles*, ed. Andrew Pessin and Sanford Goldberg (Armonk, NY: M. E. Sharpe, 1996), 125. Burge goes on to observe that these "Philosophical discussions of social factors have tended to be obscure, evocative, metaphorical, or platitudinous, or to be bent on establishing some large thesis about the course of history and the destiny of man. There remains much room for sharp delineation [in these discussions]."

14. Stephen Greenblatt, "Culture," in *Critical Terms for Literary Study*, ed. Frank Lentricchia and Thomas McLaughlin (Chicago: University of Chicago Press, 1990), 230.

15. Both of these passages are taken from Greenblatt, "Culture," 231.

16. Jean E. Howard, *The Stage and Social Struggle in Early Modern England* (London: Routledge, 1994), 14.

17. Howard, *The Stage*, 12.

18. For a detailed discussion of this aspect of historicist/ideological criticism, see chapter four, "Ideology, Textual Practice, and Bakhtin," of my *Reason and the Nature of Texts* (Philadelphia: University of Pennsylvania Press, 1996).

19. Stephen Greenblatt, *Shakespearean Negotiations: The Circulation of Social Energy in Renaissance England* (Berkeley: University of California Press, 1988).

20. Donald Pizer, "Bad Critical Writing," *Philosophy and Literature* 22 (1998): 70–71.

21. Greenblatt, "Culture," 230.

22. In an earlier work I outline what I take to be the inherent weaknesses of ideology-based criticism by focusing on Bakhtin's "ideologemes," units of discourse embedded in, for example, literary works that express or exhibit, in Bakhtin's terms, "a particular way of viewing the world, one that strives for social significance." Clearly, Bakhtin's "ideologemes" are blood relations to Greenblatt's circulating units of social energy and kissing cousins to Dawkins's "memes." For my discussion, see chapter four, "Ideology, Textual Practice, and Bakhtin," of *Reason and the Nature of Texts* (Philadelphia: University of Pennsylvania Press, 1996).

23. Richard Dawkins, *The Selfish Gene* (Oxford: Oxford University Press, 1976), 206. For a more fully elaborated, book-length treatment of memes, now elevated to a science—"memetics, the study of how ideas and beliefs spread" (as the blurb says)—see Aaron Lynch, *Thought Contagion: How Belief Spreads Through Society: The New Science of Memes* (New York: Basic Books, 1996). And for a study of memetics in principle and practice, see Susan Blackmore, *The Meme Machine* (Oxford: Oxford University Press, 1999).

24. Daniel C. Dennett, *Consciousness Explained* (Boston: Little, Brown and Co., 1991), 202. For Dennett's extended treatment of these matters, see chapter seven, "The Evolution of Consciousness."

25. John Searle, *The Mystery of Consciousness* (New York: A New York Review Book, 1997), 105.

26. Dennett, *Consciousness Explained*, 203.

27. Greenblatt, "Culture," 230.

28. Pizer, "Bad Critical Writing," 71.

29. Pizer, "Bad Critical Writing," 71.

30. The phrases "resolved into" and "deduced from" are taken from R. S. Crane's discussion of two levels of causation, the preconstructional and the constructional. For this discussion, see his "Critical and Historical Principles of Literary History," in *The Idea of the Humanities and Other Essays Critical and Historical*, vol. 2 (Chicago: University of Chicago Press, 1967), 45–146.

31. Louis Montrose, *The Purpose of Playing: Shakespeare and the Cultural Politics of the Elizabethan Theatre* (Chicago: University of Chicago Press, 1996), 13.

32. Marie-Laure Ryan, "Truth Without Scare Quotes: Post-Sokalian Genre Theory," *New Literary History* 29 (1998): 816.

33. Ryan, "Truth Without Scare Quotes," 815–16.

34. Hilary Putnam, *Words and Life*, ed. James Conant (Cambridge, MA: Harvard University Press, 1994), 308.

35. Donald Davidson, "Locating Literary Language," in *Literary Theory After Davidson*, ed. Reed Way Dasenbrock (University Park, PA: The Pennsylvania State University Press, 1993), 298.

36. Donald Davidson, "Knowing One's Own Mind," in *The Twin Earth Chronicles*, ed. Andrew Pessin and Sanford Goldberg (Armonk, NY: M. E. Sharpe, 1996), 339.

37. Michael Dummett, *The Seas of Language* (Oxford: Clarendon Press, 1993), 104.

38. Dummett, *Seas of Language*, 104–05.

39. Samuel Johnson. *A Journey to the Western Islands of Scotland*, ed. Mary Lascelles. *The Yale Edition of the Works of Samuel Johnson*, vol. 10 (New Haven: Yale University Press, 1971), 40.

40. This discussion of the role of background assumptions and belief networks in the determination of specific content has been influenced by many sources, especially John Searle's "Literary Theory and Its Discontents," in which we find the following: "Speech acts . . . cannot be fully determined by the explicit semantic content of a sentence or even by the speaker's intentional content in the utterance of the sentence, because *all meaning and understanding goes on within a network of intentionality and against a background of capacities that are not themselves part of the content that is meant or understood, but which is essential for the functioning of the content.* . . . To put the point generally, both literal meaning and speaker meaning only determine a set of conditions of satisfaction . . . given a set of Background capacities." To illustrate the point, he gives a homely example: "Suppose I say, 'Give me a hamburger, medium rare, with ketchup and mustard, no relish.' That utterance, we may suppose, is intended almost entirely literally. I have said more or less exactly what I meant. But now suppose they bring me the hamburger encased in a solid block of concrete." Searle then goes on to show how the request could be misunderstood in an indefinite number of ways in the absence of certain background capacities and a network of other beliefs. For this essay, see *The Emperor reDressed: Critiquing Critical Theory*, ed. Dwight Eddins (Tuscaloosa: The University of Alabama Press, 1995). The quoted passages are on pages 169–70. For similar views, see Mark Greenberg, "What Connects Thought and Action?" *Times Literary Supplement* (23 June 1995): 7; and Eddy Zemach, "On Meaning and Reality," in *Relativism: Interpretation and Confronta-*

tion, ed. Michael Krausz (Notre Dame, IN: University of Notre Dame Press, 1989), 51–79.

41. John Searle, *The Construction of Social Reality* (New York: The Free Press, 1995), 123.

42. Searle, *Construction of Social Reality*, 123.

43. For Olson's full discussion, see the introduction to his *Longinus, On the Sublime and Sir Joshua Reynolds, Discourses on Art* (Chicago: Packard and Co., 1945).

CHAPTER SIX

1. In *Rambler* 2, Johnson writes: "what is known is rejected, because it is not sufficiently considered, that men more frequently require to be reminded than informed." See Samuel Johnson, *The Rambler*, ed. W. J. Bate and Albrecht B. Strauss. *The Yale Edition of the Works of Samuel Johnson*, vol. 3 (New Haven, CT: Yale University Press, 1969), 14.

2. Hilary Putnam, *Words and Life*, ed. James Conant (Cambridge, MA: Harvard University Press, 1994), 309.

3. Raymond Tallis, *In Defense of Realism* (London: Edward Arnold, 1988), 29.

4. John Searle, *The Construction of Social Reality* (New York: The Free Press, 1995), 214.

5. Those readers interested in making a start on the vast literature dealing with the relations of facts and fictions, fictional facts and factual fictions, and so on might look into the following relatively recent works, most of which are taken from the philosophical literature rather than that of literary theory: D. W. Winnicott, *Playing and Reality* (Harmondsworth, England: Penguin, 1971); Jerrold Levinson, "Truth in Fiction," in *Philosophical Papers*, vol. 1 (New York: Oxford University Press, 1983), 261–80; Thomas G. Pavel, *Fictional Worlds* (Cambridge, MA: Harvard University Press, 1986); David Novitz, *Knowledge, Fiction, and Imagination* (Philadelphia: Temple University Press, 1987); Gregory Currie, *The Nature of Fiction* (Cambridge: Cambridge University Press, 1990); Kendall Walton, *Mimesis as Make-Believe: On the Foundations of the Representational Arts* (Cambridge, MA: Harvard University Press, 1990); R.M.J. Dammann, "Emotion and Fiction," *British Journal of Aesthetics* 32 (1992): 13–20; Alex Byrne, "Truth in Fiction: The Story Continued," *Australasian Journal of Philosophy* 71 (1993): 23–35; Peter Lamarque and Stein Haugom Olsen, *Truth, Fiction, and Literature: A Philosophical Perspective* (Oxford: Clarendon Press, 1994), and Robert Stecker, *Artworks: Definition, Meaning, Value* (University Park, PA: The Pennsylvania State University Press, 1996).

6. This notion of our subsidiary awareness of another intelligence I borrow from Ralph Rader, though my appropriation of the concept is adapted to my local purposes. For Rader's use of the concept in his definition of the novel, see "The Emergence of the Novel in England: Genre in History vs. History of Genre," *Narrative* 1 (1993): 69–93.

7. Searle, *Construction of Social Reality*, 154.

8. Owen Flanagan, *Self Expressions: Mind, Morals, and the Meaning of Life* (New York: Oxford University Press, 1996), 67.

9. Flanagan, *Self Expressions*, 69–70.

10. Flanagan, *Self Expressions*, 66.

11. Searle, *Construction of Social Reality*, 7.

12. Hilary Putnam, *Pragmatism: An Open Question* (Oxford: Blackwell, 1995), 11–12.

13. Donald Davidson, "Locating Literary Language," in *Literary Theory After Davidson*, ed. Reed Way Dasenbrock (University Park, PA: The Pennsylvania State University Press, 1993), 304.

14. All the material quoted is from Johnson's "Preface," in *Johnson on Shakespeare*, ed. Arthur Sherbo, *The Yale Edition of the Works of Samuel Johnson*, vol. 7 (New Haven, CT: Yale University Press, 1968), 78.

15. For Olson's full discussion, the reader should consult chapter five, "Emotion, Fiction, and Belief," of his *Tragedy and the Theory of Drama* (Detroit: Wayne State University Press, 1961), 127–47.

16. Bijoy H. Boruah, *Fiction and Emotion: A Study in Aesthetics and the Philosophy of Mind* (Oxford: Clarendon Press, 1988), 22.

17. Boruah, *Fiction and Emotion*, 122; my emphases.

18. Boruah, *Fiction and Emotion*, 122.

19. Boruah, *Fiction and Emotion*, 41. A similar point is made by Peter Lamarque in "How Can We Fear and Pity Fictions?," *British Journal of Aesthetics* 21 (1981): 291–304. For a useful discussion of the rational basis of emotions, see Martha C. Nussbaum, *Poetic Justice: The Literary Imagination and Public Life* (Boston: Beacon Press, 1995), 53–55. The reader interested in pursuing the issue of emotion in relation to fiction, rationality, and belief would find the following works helpful and informative, I think: Ronald de Sousa, *The Rationality of Emotion* (Cambridge, MA: MIT Press, 1987); Robert M. Gordon, *The Structure of Emotions: Investigations in Cognitive Philosophy* (Cambridge: Cambridge University Press, 1987), and the essays collected in *Emotion and the Arts*, ed. Mette Hjort and Sue Laver (New York: Oxford University Press, 1997).

20. Elder Olson expresses and argues for a similar view in chapter six, "Dramatic Effect and Dramatic Form," of *Tragedy and the Theory of Drama* (Detroit: Wayne State University Press, 1961).

21. For a more extended discussion of a text's "internal and external goods" or values, see the last chapter of this book and chapter eight, "Teaching Critical Principles in Introductory Literature Courses," of my *Reason and the Nature of Texts* (Philadelphia: University of Pennsylvania Press, 1996), 149–62.

CHAPTER SEVEN

1. For an illuminating brief discussion of such performatives, see John Searle, *Mind, Language, and Society: Philosophy in the Real World* (New York: Basic Books, 1998), 114–15. Of course, the category of "performatives" derives from J. L. Austin. For a full-scale examination of the distinction between "constative" and "performative" utterances, see his *How to Do Things with Words*, ed. J. O. Urmson (Cambridge, MA: Harvard University Press, 1962).

2. Thomas Nagel, *The Last Word* (New York: Oxford University Press, 1997), 90.

3. For a useful discussion of problems inherent in the incommensurability thesis, see James F. Harris, *Against Relativism: A Philosophical Defense of Method* (La Salle,

IL: Open Court, 1992), especially pages 79–93. I am indebted here to pages 84–85.

4. Akeel Bilgrami, *Belief and Meaning* (Oxford: Blackwell, 1992), 124.

5. Michael Devitt and Kim Sterelny, *Language and Reality: An Introduction to the Philosophy of Language* (Cambridge, MA: MIT Press, 1987), 180. For another illuminating discussion of the view that reference, not meaning, is the crucial notion for theory comparison, see Israel Scheffler, *Science and Subjectivity*, 2nd ed. (Indianapolis: Hackett, 1982); see especially Chapter Three, "Meaning and Objectivity," pages 45–66.

6. John D. Greenwood, "Reasons to Believe," in *The Future of Folk Psychology: Intentionality and Cognitive Science*, ed. John D. Greenwood (Cambridge: Cambridge University Press, 1991), 72. Hilary Putnam supplies his own striking illustration of essentially the same point, using as his test case the wave and particle theory of light; see his *Mind, Language, and Reality* (Cambridge: Cambridge University Press, 1975), 24–25.

7. Michael Devitt, *Realism and Truth*, 2nd ed. (Oxford: Blackwell, 1991), 193. Simon Evnine gives cogently condensed expression to Davidson's similar view that "actions are events which are intentional under some description, the description under which they are rationalized by the contents of the mental states which are the reasons for them." See Evnine, *Donald Davidson* (Stanford, CA: Stanford University Press, 1991), 41. For Davidson's extended discussion of the point, see his "Actions, Reasons, and Causes," which is reprinted in *Essays on Actions and Events* (Oxford: Clarendon Press, 1980), 3–19.

8. Christopher Cherniak, *Minimal Rationality* (Cambridge, MA: MIT Press, 1986), 3.

9. Of course, reports of the demise or disappearance of the author are greatly exaggerated, if we can judge by the apparently ineradicable and insatiable appetite for biographies of authors or by the number of new editions of works by authors of greater and lesser reputation or by the number of articles and books either focusing on the achievements of single authors or, more generally, coming to the defense of authors as the source of artistic effects. I'm sure every reader can supply many titles under each of these headings. As examples of the last two efforts, I note, by way of illustration only, Helen Vendler, *The Art of Shakespeare's Sonnets* (Cambridge, MA: Harvard University Press, 1997), and Denis Donoghue, *The Practice of Reading* (New Haven, CT: Yale University Press, 1998). Also, it is interesting to note that in his introduction to a *PMLA* special topics section titled "In Pursuit of Ethics," Lawrence Buell observes that recent inquiry in criticism and theory "tends to favor recuperation of authorial agency in the production of texts, without [Buell is quick to note] ceasing to acknowledge that texts are also in some sense socially constructed." See *PMLA* 114 (1999): 12.

10. For some helpful comments on the limitations of inductive logic, see Hilary Putnam, *Renewing Philosophy* (Cambridge, MA: Harvard University Press, 1992), 8–14.

11. Paisley Livingston, *Literature and Rationality: Ideas of Agency in Theory and Fiction* (Cambridge: Cambridge University Press, 1991), 17. The phrase within quotation marks at the end of this passage is taken from Wlad Godzich, "Where the Action Is," in Thomas G. Pavel, *The Poetics of Plot: The Case of English Renaissance*

Drama (Minneapolis: University of Minnesota Press, 1985), vii–xxii. On the attack against the Enlightenment and humanism, I shall have more to say in the last chapter.

12. Gayle Greene, "The Myth of Neutrality, Again," in *Shakespeare Left and Right*, ed. Ivo Kamps (New York: Routledge, 1991), 24–25; my emphases. I should note that Greene's essay is in large measure a response to Richard Levin's "Feminist Thematics and Shakespearean Tragedy," *PMLA* 103 (1988): 125–38. Greene is responding particularly to Levin's concluding statement calling upon feminists and all other interested critics to give their "support to a scientific study of the complex factors in human development, which would investigate the similarities as well as the differences between men and women, based on evidence that compelled the assent of all rational people, regardless of their gender or ideology" (136). Interestingly, Greene and twenty-three other co-signers submitted a letter to the editor of *PMLA* angrily registering their disagreement with and disapproval of Levin's essay, taking exception to, among other things, his concluding peace offering, with its appeal to all "rational people" and informing him, irrelevantly, of that of which, they were sure, he was "unaware," namely, that "what passes for 'rationality' in a particular historical moment is likely to look irrational from the perspective of another, that affirmations of shared attributes often mask oppression based on unexplored assumptions of hierarchical difference, that many dreadful thoughts and brutal deeds have compelled the assent of people fully convinced of their own rationality and the irrationality of a cultural other. The view that 'science' and 'rationality' can comprehend 'complex factors in human development' without the messy intrusions of 'gender and ideology' is an Enlightenment dream, long since turned to nightmare" (*PMLA* 104 [1989]: 78).

13. I have taken the Kolodny remarks from Gayle Greene's "The Myth of Neutrality, Again," 25. To examine these remarks in their original context, see Annette Kolodny, "A Map for Rereading: or, Gender and the Interpretation of Literary Facts," *New Literary History* 11 (1981): 451–67.

14. Brian Vickers, "Derrida and the *TLS*," *Times Literary Supplement* (12 February 1999): 12.

15. The following is but a very brief—almost criminally truncated—list of some writers supplying philosophically deep challenges to prevailing views or devastating critiques of influential arguments (full bibliographical particulars can be found in the bibliography): Raymond Tallis, Paisley Livingston, M. H. Abrams, Frederick Crews, James Phelan, Ralph Rader, Richard Levin, Wendell Harris, John Ellis, John Searle, Colin McGinn, J. Claude Evans, Reed Way Dasenbrock, Walter Davis, Umberto Eco, Harold Bloom, David Bromwich, Michael Fischer, Martha Nussbaum, John Holloway, Annette Barnes, and many others.

16. The preceding note contains a convenient roster of critics who have contributed to the project of exposing the limitations of, among other things, the linguistic presuppositions of many theorists. Here I would call special attention to Raymond Tallis's *Not Saussure: A Critique of Post-Saussurean Literary Theory*, 2nd ed. (New York: St. Martin's Press, 1995).

17. Throughout the book, the prose is riddled with these pusillanimous, escape-hatch "perhapses." Indeed, our current theorists characteristically never enter a room without first checking out exit opportunities, never call a spade a spade without also acknowledging that it might also be a hoe and/or an entrenching tool.

18. I shall briefly discuss in the last chapter some of the ways in which what we

talk about (the content of our thought and expression) is determined by our biological and cognitive endowment, noting, among other things, the large epistemic benefits that we reap from this shared endowment. Here, I would simply observe that our ability to share concepts depends upon our common biological endowment.

19. All the quoted passages are from Barbara Herrnstein Smith, *Belief and Resistance: Dynamics of Contemporary Intellectual Controversy* (Cambridge, MA: Harvard University Press, 1997), 61–62. Smith makes essentially the same case in her earlier *Contingencies of Value: Alternative Perspectives for Critical Theory* (Cambridge, MA: Harvard University Press, 1988); see especially chapter seven, "Matters of Consequence."

20. Fish's conception of interpretive communities can be conveniently found in the second part of *Is There a Text in This Class?: The Authority of Interpretive Communities* (Cambridge, MA: Harvard University Press, 1980). A later elaboration of this conception of the constraints imposed on readers by interpretive communities is his "Anti-Professionalism," *New Literary History* 17 (1985): 89–108.

21. In "Locating Literary Language," Donald Davidson writes, "We would not have a language, or the thoughts that depend on language (which comprise all beliefs, desires, hopes, expectations, intentions and other attitudes having propositional content), if there were not others who understood us and whom we understood; and such mutual understanding requires a world shared both causally and conceptually. Intersubjective interaction with the world is a necessary condition of our possession of the concepts of truth and objectivity; that is why I reject as unintelligible most forms of skepticism and of conceptual relativism." For this passage, see *Literary Theory After Davidson*, ed. Reed Way Dasenbrock (University Park, PA: The Pennsylvania State University Press, 1993), 303.

22. These examples I borrow from Samuel Johnson's apologue, *Rasselas*, which was published in 1759.

23. Colin McGinn, *Problems in Philosophy* (Oxford: Blackwell, 1993), 65.

CHAPTER EIGHT

1. In keeping with the broad purposes of this book to focus on large conceptual issues, to emphasize alternatives to the principles and doctrines of the current orthodoxies, and to avoid detailed confrontations with this or that particular argument, I have neglected in this section to discuss the work of specific critics who give the reader-response and reception theories their most forceful articulation. Those readers whose interests run more to such theories than to unimpeachable arguments demonstrating the dependence of stable meanings on the intentional states of authors should consult, for reception theory, Hans Robert Jauss's "Literary History as a Challenge to Literary Theory" and, for reader-response theory, Stanley Fish's "Literature in the Reader: Affective Stylistics." Both pieces appear in *New Literary History* 2 (1970–71). Readers might also profitably consult the collection *Reader-Response: From Formalism to Post-Structuralism*, ed. Jane P. Tompkins (Baltimore: Johns Hopkins University Press, 1980). For a psychological approach to response theory, see David Bleich, *Subjective Criticism* (Baltimore: Johns Hopkins University Press, 1978), and for this criticism in its "interpretive community" mode, see Stanley Fish, *Is There a Text in This Class?: The Authority of Interpretive Communities* (Cambridge, MA: Harvard University Press, 1980).

2. Donald Davidson, "Locating Literary Language," in *Literary Theory After Davidson*, ed. Reed Way Dasenbrock (University Park, PA: The Pennsylvania State University Press, 1993), 298.

3. Hilary Putnam, *Realism with a Human Face*, ed. James Conant (Cambridge, MA: Harvard University Press, 1990), 115.

4. The quoted material is taken from John Searle, *The Construction of Social Reality* (New York: The Free Press, 1995), 75.

5. Putnam, *Realism with a Human Face*, 114.

6. Donald Davidson, "Knowing One's Own Mind," in *The Twin Earth Chronicles*, ed. Andrew Pessin and Sanford Goldberg (Armonk, NY: M. E. Sharpe, 1996), 339.

7. Barthes's essay is conveniently available in his collection of essays *Image-Music-Text*, trans. Stephen Heath (New York: Hill and Wang, 1978); Foucault's in his collection of essays *Language, Counter-Memory, Practice: Selected Essays and Interviews*, trans. Donald F. Bouchard and Sherry Simon, ed. Donald F. Bouchard (Ithaca, NY: Cornell University Press, 1977).

8. For access to what is arguably the definitive analysis of the transformation of the conception of the poet from maker or craftsman to divine analogue and of the roles played by Shaftesbury, Collins, Coleridge, Schlegel, and a host of others in this history, the reader should consult M. H. Abrams, *The Mirror and the Lamp: Romantic Theory and the Critical Tradition* (New York: W. W. Norton, 1958); see especially pages 114–24, 167–77, and 280–85. Another deeply informed and informative study of poetic genius is James Engell's *The Creative Imagination* (Cambridge, MA: Harvard University Press, 1981).

9. Michael Dummett, *Origins of Analytic Philosophy* (Cambridge, MA: Harvard University Press, 1994), 158.

10. Hilary Putnam, *Words and Life*, ed. James Conant (Cambridge, MA: Harvard University Press, 1994), 446.

11. The comment about inconsistencies is made by Imlac in the eighth chapter of Samuel Johnson's *Rasselas*, "The History of Imlac."

CHAPTER NINE

1. Hilary Putnam, "Comments and Replies," in *Reading Putnam*, eds. Peter Clark and Bob Hale (Oxford: Blackwell, 1994), 265.

2. In giving his book the title *The Construction of Social Reality*, John Searle clearly positions himself in opposition to (or at least in dialogue with) those enrolled in the "social construction of reality" school of thought.

3. I here play variations on lines 99–102 of Canto One of Alexander Pope's *The Rape of the Lock*. The original lines, describing the fickleness of young women like Belinda, read: "With varying vanities, from every part, / They [the sylphs] shift the moving Toyshop of their [the young belles', the coquettes'] heart; / Where wigs with wigs, with sword-knots sword-knots strive, / Beaux banish beaux, and coaches coaches drive."

4. Bertrand Russell, *The Problems of Philosophy* (Oxford: Oxford University Press, 1912), 42–43. My immediate source for this passage is Colin McGinn, *Ethics, Evil, and Fiction* (Oxford: Clarendon Press, 1997), 41–42. Throughout this section I am indebted to McGinn's discussion of the a priori nature of our ethical knowledge.

5. As with all the major topics discussed in this book, the literature on parallels between the acquisition of linguistic and of moral principles is extensive. For purely illustrative purposes—to suggest something of the diversity of the writers making the comparison—I would cite John Rawls, *A Theory of Justice* (Cambridge, MA: Harvard University Press, 1971), especially pages 46–47; and Steven Pinker, *How the Mind Works* (New York: W. W. Norton, 1997), especially chapters five and seven.

6. Noam Chomsky, *Language and the Problems of Knowledge: The Managua Lectures* (Cambridge, MA: MIT Press, 1988), 152–53. My immediate source for this passage is Colin McGinn, *Ethics, Evil, and Fiction* (Oxford: Clarendon Press, 1997), 45.

7. McGinn, *Ethics, Evil, and Fiction*, 45.

8. Thomas Nagel, *The Last Word* (New York: Oxford University Press, 1997), 21.

9. McGinn, *Ethics, Evil, and Fiction*, 49.

10. Catherine Z. Elgin, "The Relativity of Fact and the Objectivity of Value," in *Relativism: Interpretation and Confrontation*, ed. Michael Krausz (Notre Dame, IN: University of Notre Dame Press, 1989), 88.

11. Crispin Wright, *Truth and Objectivity* (Cambridge, MA: Harvard University Press, 1992), 45.

12. Kenneth Burke, "Poetics in Particular, Language in General," in *Language as Symbolic Action: Essays on Life, Literature, and Method* (Berkeley: University of California Press, 1966), 33.

13. Alasdair MacIntyre, *After Virtue: A Study in Moral Theory* (Notre Dame, IN: University of Notre Dame Press, 1981), 188.

14. Fred Dretske, *Naturalizing the Mind* (Cambridge, MA: MIT Press, 1995), 43.

15. Herbert F. Tucker, "From the Editors," *New Literary History* 30 (1999): 1.

16. Elder Olson, *On Value Judgments in the Arts* (Chicago: University of Chicago Press, 1976), 309.

CHAPTER TEN

1. For examples of Richard Levin's consideration of this scapegoat function of humanism, the reader should consult the following two essays: "Bashing the Bourgeois Subject," *Textual Practice* 3 (1989): 76–86, and "Son of Bashing the Bourgeois Subject," *Textual Practice* 6 (1992): 264–70.

2. Geoffrey Galt Harpham, "So . . . What *Is* Enlightenment? An Inquisition into Modernity," *Critical Inquiry* 20 (1994): 524–56.

3. On the topic of David Hume and the truths of Christianity, James Boswell records Johnson as saying on Thursday, 21 July 1763: "Hume, and other sceptical innovators, are vain men, and will gratify themselves at any expence. Truth will not afford sufficient food to their vanity; so they have betaken themselves to errour. Truth, Sir, is a cow which will yield such people no more milk, and so they are gone to milk the bull." *Life of Johnson*, Oxford Standard Authors (London: Oxford University Press, 1960), 314.

4. Of course, I here give expression, in a slightly paraphrased form, to Marx's view in *The German Ideology*.

5. Michel Foucault, *The Order of Things: An Archaeology of the Human Sciences* (New York: Vintage, 1973), 342–43.

6. Joan Wallach Scott, *Gender and the Politics of History* (New York: Columbia University Press, 1988), 4.

7. For John Rawls, see *A Theory of Justice* (Cambridge, MA: Harvard University Press, 1971); and for Isaiah Berlin, see, for example, *Four Essays on Liberty* (London: Oxford University Press, 1969).

8. Hilary Putnam, *Reason, Truth, and History* (Cambridge: Cambridge University Press, 1981), 50.

9. F.C.S. Schiller, *Studies in Humanism* (London: Macmillan, 1919), 12.

10. Hilary Putnam, *Realism with a Human Face*, ed. James Conant (Cambridge, MA: Harvard University Press, 1990), 29.

11. Ruth Anna Putnam, "Michael Walzer: Objectivity and Social Meaning," in *The Quality of Life*, ed. Martha Nussbaum and Amartya Sen (Oxford: Clarendon Press, 1993), 184.

12. We can easily call to mind the sorts of justifications that rulers have supplied to the ruled, slaveowners to slaves, husbands to wives, men to women, deans to departmental chairs over the course of history. For this representation of Dewey's position, I am indebted to Hilary Putnam's "Pragmatism and Moral Objectivity," in *Words and Life*, ed. James Conant (Cambridge, MA: Harvard University Press, 1994), 160–61.

13. Putnam, *Words and Life*, 297.

14. Putnam, *Words and Life*, 301.

15. I here give in loose paraphrase a point made by Putnam on several occasions; see, for example, his *Renewing Philosophy* (Cambridge, MA: Harvard University Press, 1992), 177.

16. For a more extensive discussion of relativism—and skepticism—as the verso of metaphysical realism, the reader should consult Hilary Putnam's "The Question of Objectivity," in *Words and Life*, 295–312.

17. I have here simply illustrated and expanded on the sameness/difference relations that Michael Devitt examines in *Realism and Truth*, 2nd ed. (Oxford: Blackwell, 1991); see especially pages 277–78.

18. Devitt, *Realism and Truth*, 277.

19. Michael Dummett, *The Seas of Language* (Oxford: Clarendon Press, 1993), 104–05.

20. The numerical example is Goodman's, but the point, of course, applies to any relational system. For Goodman's discussion, see "Just the Facts, Ma'am!," in *Relativism: Interpretation and Confrontation*, ed. Michael Krausz (Notre Dame, IN: University of Notre Dame Press, 1989), 80–85.

21. Crispin Wright, *Truth and Objectivity* (Cambridge, MA: Harvard University Press, 1992), 45.

22. Wright, *Truth and Objectivity*, 45.

23. I have taken Winter's view from Mark Johnson's *Moral Imagination: Implications of Cognitive Science for Ethics* (Chicago: University of Chicago Press, 1993), 240. For Winter's full discussion, see his "*Bull Durham* and the Uses of Theory," *Stanford Law Review* 42 (1990): 639–93.

24. Dummett, *Seas of Language*, 452.

25. Susan Hurley, "Martha Nussbaum: Non-Relative Virtues: An Aristotelian Ap-

proach," in *The Quality of Life*, ed. Martha Nussbaum and Amartya Sen (Oxford: Clarendon Press, 1993), 271.

26. Kwasi Wiredu, *Philosophy and an African Culture* (Cambridge: Cambridge University Press, 1980), 220–21.

27. Among many other works, see, for example, George Lakoff, *Women, Fire, and Dangerous Things: What Categories Reveal about the Mind* (Chicago: University of Chicago Press, 1987), especially pages 5–153; Donald E. Brown, *Human Universals* (Philadelphia: Temple University Press, 1991); and George Lakoff and Mark Johnson, *Philosophy in the Flesh: The Embodied Mind and Its Challenge to Western Thought* (New York: Basic Books, 1999).

28. Mark Johnson, *Moral Imagination: Implications of Cognitive Science for Ethics* (Chicago: University of Chicago Press, 1993), 237.

29. Alvin I. Goldman, *Epistemology and Cognition* (Cambridge, MA: Harvard University Press, 1986), 140.

30. Owen Flanagan, *Self Expressions: Mind, Morals, and the Meaning of Life* (New York: Oxford University Press, 1996), 70.

31. Goldman, *Epistemology and Cognition*, 247.

32. Ruth Anna Putnam, "Michael Walzer: Objectivity and Social Meaning," in *The Quality of Life*, ed. Martha Nussbaum and Amartya Sen (Oxford: Clarendon Press, 1993), 183.

33. Alasdair MacIntyre, *After Virtue: A Study in Moral Theory* (Notre Dame, IN: University of Notre Dame Press, 1981), 268–69.

Bibliography

Abrams, M. H. *The Mirror and the Lamp: Romantic Theory and the Critical Tradition*. New York: Norton, 1958.

———. *Natural Supernaturalism: Tradition and Revolution in Romantic Literature*. New York: Norton, 1971.

———. *Doing Things with Texts: Essays in Criticism and Critical Theory*. New York: Norton, 1989.

———. "What Is a Humanistic Criticism?" In *The Emperor reDressed: Critiquing Critical Theory*, ed. Dwight Eddins, 13–44. Tuscaloosa: University of Alabama Press, 1995.

Alston, William P. *The Reliability of Sense Perception*. Ithaca, N.Y.: Cornell University Press, 1993.

———. *A Realist Conception of Truth*. Ithaca, NY: Cornell University Press, 1996.

Anscombe, G.E.M. *Intention*. Oxford: Blackwell, 1957.

Audi, Robert. *Action, Intention, and Reason*. Ithaca, NY: Cornell University Press, 1993.

———. *The Architecture of Reason: The Structure and Substance of Rationality*. New York: Oxford University Press, 2001.

Austin, J. L. *How to Do Things with Words*, ed. J. O. Urmson. Cambridge, MA: Harvard University Press, 1962.

Avramides, Anita. *Meaning and Mind: An Examination of a Gricean Account of Language*. Cambridge, MA: MIT Press, 1989.

Baier, Annette C. *The Commons of the Mind*. La Salle, IL: Open Court, 1997.

Baker, G. P., and P.M.S. Hacker. *Wittgenstein: Rules, Grammar, and Necessity*. Oxford: Blackwell, 1985.

Baker, Lynne Rudder. *Explaining Attitudes: A Practical Approach to the Mind*. Cambridge: Cambridge University Press, 1995.

Bakhtin, M. M. *The Dialogic Imagination: Four Essays*, trans. Caryl Emerson and
    Michael Holquist, ed. Michael Holquist. Austin: University of Texas Press,
    1981.
Barnes, Annette. *On Interpretation: A Critical Analysis*. Oxford: Blackwell, 1988.
Barthes, Roland. *Image-Music-Text*, trans. Stephen Heath. New York: Hill and
    Wang, 1978.
Battersby, James L. *Paradigms Regained: Pluralism and the Practice of Criticism*.
    Philadelphia: University of Pennsylvania Press, 1991.
————. *Reason and the Nature of Texts*. Philadelphia: University of Pennsylvania
    Press, 1996.
Berger, Peter L., and Thomas Luckmann. *The Social Construction of Reality: A Trea-
    tise in the Sociology of Knowledge*. Garden City, NY: Anchor-Doubleday, 1967.
Berlin, Isaiah. *Four Essays on Liberty*. London: Oxford University Press, 1969.
Bernstein, Richard J. *Beyond Objectivism and Relativism: Science, Hermeneutics, and
    Praxis*. Philadelphia: University of Pennsylvania Press, 1983.
Bilgrami, Akeel. *Belief and Meaning*. Oxford: Blackwell, 1992.
Blackburn, Simon. *Essays in Quasi-Realism*. Oxford: Oxford University Press, 1993.
Blackmore, Susan. *The Meme Machine*. Oxford: Oxford University Press, 1999.
Bleich, David. *Subjective Criticism*. Baltimore: Johns Hopkins University Press, 1978.
Bloom, Harold. *The Western Canon: The Books and School of the Ages*. New York:
    Harcourt Brace and Co., 1994.
Boghossian, Paul A. "What Is Social Construction." *Times Literary Supplement* (23
    February 2001): 6–8.
Boolos, George, ed. *Meaning and Method: Essays in Honour of Hilary Putnam*. Cam-
    bridge: Cambridge University Press, 1990.
Booth, Wayne C. *Critical Understanding: The Powers and Limits of Pluralism*. Chi-
    cago: University of Chicago Press, 1979.
Borradori, Giovanna. *The American Philosopher*. Chicago: University of Chicago
    Press, 1994.
Boruah, Bijoy H. *Fiction and Emotion: A Study in Aesthetics and the Philosophy of
    Mind*. Oxford: Clarendon Press, 1988.
Boswell, James. *Life of Johnson*. Oxford Standard Authors. London: Oxford Univer-
    sity Press, 1960.
Bratman, Michael E. *Intentions, Plans, and Practical Reason*. Cambridge, MA: Har-
    vard University Press, 1987.
Bromwich, David. *Politics by Other Means: Higher Education and Group Thinking*.
    New Haven, CT: Yale University Press, 1992.
Brown, Donald E. *Human Universals*. Philadelphia: Temple University Press, 1991.
Bruner, Jerome S. *Actual Minds, Possible Worlds*. Cambridge, MA: Harvard Univer-
    sity Press, 1986.
Buell, Lawrence. "In Pursuit of Ethics." *PMLA* 114 (1999): 7–19.
Burge, Tyler. "Individualism and the Mental." In *The Twin Earth Chronicles*, ed.
    Andrew Pessin and Sanford Goldberg, 125–141. Armonk, NY: M. E. Sharpe,
    1996.
Burke, Kenneth. *Language as Symbolic Action: Essays on Life, Literature, and Method*.
    Berkeley: University of California Press, 1966.
Butler, Christopher. *Interpretation, Deconstruction, and Ideology: An Introduction to
    Some Current Issues in Literary Theory*. Oxford: Clarendon Press, 1984.

Byrne, Alex. "Truth in Fiction: The Story Continued." *Australasian Journal of Philosophy* 71 (1993): 23–35.

Carruthers, Peter. *Introducing Persons: Theories and Arguments in the Philosophy of Mind.* London: Croon Helm, 1986.

———. *Language, Thought, and Consciousness: An Essay in Philosophical Psychology.* Cambridge: Cambridge University Press, 1996.

Chang, Ruth, ed. *Incommensurability, Incomparability, and Practical Reason.* Cambridge, MA: Harvard University Press, 1997.

Chaouli, Michael. "A Vast Unravelling." *Times Literary Supplement* (26 February 1999): 14–15.

Cherniak, Christopher. *Minimal Rationality.* Cambridge, MA: MIT Press, 1986.

Child, William. *Causality, Interpretation, and the Mind.* Oxford: Clarendon Press, 1994.

Chomsky, Noam. *Language and the Problems of Knowledge: The Managua Lectures.* Cambridge, MA: MIT Press, 1988.

Churchland, Paul M. *Scientific Realism and the Plasticity of Mind.* Cambridge: Cambridge University Press, 1979.

———. *The Engine of Reason, the Seat of the Soul: A Philosophical Journey into the Brain.* Cambridge, MA: MIT Press, 1995.

Clark, Peter, and Bob Hale, ed. *Reading Putnam.* Oxford: Blackwell, 1994.

Crane, R. S. *Critics and Criticism: Ancient and Modern.* Chicago: University of Chicago Press, 1952.

———. *The Languages of Criticism and the Structure of Poetry.* Toronto: University of Toronto Press, 1953.

———. *The Idea of the Humanities and Other Essays Critical and Historical.* 2 vols. Chicago: University of Chicago Press, 1967.

———. *Critical and Historical Principles of Literary History.* Chicago: University of Chicago Press, 1971.

Crews, Frederick. *Skeptical Engagements.* New York: Oxford University Press, 1986.

———. *The Critics Bear It Away: American Fiction and the Academy.* New York: Random House, 1992.

Culler, Jonathan. *On Deconstruction: Theory and Criticism after Structuralism.* Ithaca, NY: Cornell University Press, 1982.

Cummins, Robert. *Meaning and Mental Representation.* Cambridge, MA: MIT Press, 1989.

———. *Representations, Targets, and Attitudes.* Cambridge, MA: MIT Press, 1996.

Currie, Gregory. *The Nature of Fiction.* Cambridge: Cambridge University Press, 1990.

Dammann, R.M.J. "Emotion and Fiction." *British Journal of Aesthetics* 32 (1992): 13–20.

Dasenbrock, Reed Way, ed. *Redrawing the Lines: Analytic Philosophy, Deconstruction, and Literary Theory.* Minneapolis: University of Minnesota Press, 1989.

———, ed. *Literary Theory after Davidson.* University Park, PA: The Pennsylvania State University Press, 1993.

———. *Truth and Consequences: Intentions, Conventions, and the New Thematics.* University Park, PA: The Pennsylvania State University Press, 2001.

Davidson, Donald. "On the Very Idea of a Conceptual Scheme." *Proceedings and Addresses of the American Philosophical Association* 47 (1974): 5–20.

————. *Essays on Actions and Events.* Oxford: Clarendon Press, 1980.

————. "Rational Animals." *Dialecta* 36 (1982): 317–27.

————. *Inquiries into Truth and Interpretation.* Oxford: Clarendon Press, 1984.

————. "Radical Interpretaion." In *Inquiries into Truth and Interpretation*, 125–39. Oxford: Clarendon Press, 1984.

————. "Thought and Talk." In *Inquiries into Truth and Interpretation*, 155–70. Oxford: Clarendon Press, 1984. Originally in *Mind and Languae*, ed. Samuel Guttenplan. Oxford: Oxford University Press, 1975.

————. "A Coherence Theory of Truth and Knowledge." Reprinted in *Truth and Interpretation: Perspectives on the Philosophy of Donald Davidson*, ed. Ernest Lepore, 307–19. Oxford: Blackwell, 1986.

————. "The Myth of the Subjective." In *Relativism: Interpretation and Confrontation*, ed. Michael Krausz, 159–72. Notre Dame, IN: University of Notre Dame Press, 1989.

————. "Locating Literary Language." In *Literary Theory After Davidson*, ed. Reed Way Dasenbrock, 295–308. University Park, PA: The Pennsylvania State University Press, 1993.

————. "Knowing One's Own Mind." In *The Twin Earth Chronicles*, ed. Andrew Pessin and Sanford Goldberg, 323–41. Armonk, NY: M. E. Sharpe, 1996.

Davis, Walter A. *The Act of Interpretation: A Critique of Literary Reason.* Chicago: University of Chicago Press, 1978.

————. "The Fisher King: *Wille zur Macht* in Baltimore." *Critical Inquiry* 10 (1984): 668–94.

————. *Inwardness and Existence: Subjectivity in/and Hegel, Heidegger, Marx, and Freud.* Madison: University of Wisconsin Press, 1989.

Dawkins, Richard. *The Selfish Gene.* Oxford: Oxford University Press, 1976.

de Man, Paul. "Dialogue and Dialogism." *Poetics Today* 4 (1983): 99–107.

————. *The Resistance to Theory.* Manchester, England: Manchester University Press, 1986.

Dennett, Daniel C. *Consciousness Explained.* Boston: Little, Brown, and Co., 1991.

————. *Darwin's Dangerous Idea: Evolution and the Meanings of Life.* New York: Simon and Schuster, 1995.

————. *Kinds of Minds: Toward an Understanding of Consciousness.* New York: Basic Books, 1996.

Derrida, Jacques. *Of Grammatology*, trans. Gayatri Chakravorty Spivak. Baltimore: Johns Hopkins University Press, 1976.

————. *Writing and Difference*, trans. Alan Bass. Chicago: University of Chicago Press, 1978.

————. *Positions.* Chicago: University of Chicago Press, 1981.

de Sousa, Ronald. *The Rationality of Emotion.* Cambridge, MA: MIT Press, 1987.

Devitt, Michael. *Realism and Truth*, 2nd ed. Oxford: Blackwell, 1991.

————. *Coming to Our Senses: A Naturalistic Program for Semantic Localism.* Cambridge: Cambridge University Press, 1996.

Devitt, Michael, and Kim Sterelny. *Language and Reality: An Introduction to the Philosophy of Language.* Cambridge, MA: MIT Press, 1987.

Diamond, Cora, and Jenny Teichman, ed. *Intention and Intentionality: Essays in Honour of G.E.M. Anscombe.* Brighton, England: The Harvester Press, 1979.

Donoghue, Denis. *The Practice of Reading.* New Haven, CT: Yale University Press, 1998.

Dretske, Fred. *Explaining Behavior: Reasons in a World of Causes.* Cambridge, MA: MIT Press, 1988.

———. *Naturalizing the Mind.* Cambridge, MA: MIT Press, 1995.

Dummett, Michael. *Truth and Other Enigmas.* Cambridge, MA: Harvard University Press, 1978.

———. *The Seas of Language.* Oxford: Clarendon Press, 1993.

———. *Origins of Analytic Philosophy.* Cambridge, MA: Harvard University Press, 1994.

Easthope, Anthony. "Theories, Not Theory." *Times Literary Supplement* (13 March 1998): 8–9.

Ebbs, Gary. *Rule-Following and Realism.* Cambridge, MA: Harvard University Press, 1997.

Eco, Umberto. *The Limits of Interpretation.* Bloomington: Indiana University Press, 1990.

Eddins, Dwight, ed. *The Emperor reDressed: Critiquing Critical Theory.* Tuscaloosa: University of Alabama Press, 1995.

Elgin, Catherine Z. "The Relativity of Fact and the Objectivity of Value." In *Relativism: Interpretation and Confrontation,* ed. Michael Krausz, 86–98. Notre Dame, IN: University of Notre Dame Press, 1989.

———. *Considered Judgment.* Princeton: Princeton University Press, 1996.

———. *Between the Absolute and the Arbitrary.* Ithaca, NY: Cornell University Press, 1997.

Elgin, Catherine Z., and Nelson Goodman. *Reconceptions in Philosophy and Other Arts and Sciences.* Indianapolis: Hackett, 1988.

Ellis, John M. "What Does Deconstruction Contribute to a Theory of Criticism?" *New Literary History* 19 (1988): 259–79.

———. *Against Deconstruction.* Princeton: Princeton University Press, 1989.

———. *Literature Lost: Social Agendas and the Corruption of the Humanities.* New Haven, CT: Yale University Press, 1997.

Engell, James. *The Creative Imagination.* Cambridge, MA: Harvard University Press, 1981.

Evans, J. Claude. *Strategies of Deconstruction: Derrida and the Myth of the Voice.* Minneapolis: University of Minnesota Press, 1991.

Evnine, Simon. *Donald Davidson.* Stanford, CA: Stanford University Press, 1991.

Farrell, Frank B. *Subjectivity, Realism, and Postmodernism: The Recovery of the World in Recent Philosophy.* Cambridge: Cambridge University Press, 1994.

Fischer, Michael. *Does Deconstruction Make Any Difference?: Poststructuralism and the Defense of Poetry in Modern Criticism.* Bloomington: Indiana University Press, 1985.

Fish, Stanley. "Literature in the Reader: Affective Stylistics." *New Literary History* 2 (1970): 1262.

———. "Normal Circumstances, Literal Language, Direct Speech Acts, the Ordinary, the Everyday, the Obvious, What Goes Without Saying, and Other Special Cases." *Critical Inquiry* 4 (1978): 625–44.

———. *Is There a Text in This Class? The Authority of Interpretive Communities.* Cambridge, MA: Harvard University Press, 1980.

———. "Anti-Professionalism." *New Literary History* 17 (1985): 89–108.

———. *Political Correctness: Literary Studies and Political Change.* Oxford: Clarendon Press, 1995.

Flanagan, Owen. *Self Expressions: Mind, Morals, and the Meaning of Life.* New York: Oxford University Press, 1996.

Foucault, Michel. *The Order of Things: An Archaeology of the Human Sciences.* New York: Vintage, 1973.

———. *The Archaeology of Knowledge and the Discourse on Language,* trans. A. M. Sheridan Smith. New York: Harper, 1976.

———. *Language, Counter-Memory, Practice: Selected Essays and Interviews,* ed. Donald F. Bouchard, trans. Donald F. Bouchard and Sherry Simon. Ithaca, NY: Cornell University Press, 1977.

Freadman, Richard, and Seumas Miller. *Re-thinking Theory: A Critique of Contemporary Literary Theory and an Alternative Account.* Cambridge: Cambridge University Press, 1992.

Gallagher, Catherine. "Re-covering the Social in Recent Literary Theory." *Diacritics* 12 (1982): 40–48.

Geertz, Clifford. *The Interpretation of Cultures.* New York: Basic Books, 1973.

Goldman, Alvin I. *Epistemology and Cognition.* Cambridge, MA: Harvard University Press, 1986.

———. *Philosophical Applications of Cognitive Science.* Boulder, CO: Westview Press, 1993.

Gombrich, E. H. " 'They Were All Human Beings—So Much is Plain': Reflections on Cultural Relativism in the Humanities." *Critical Inquiry* 13 (1987): 686–99.

Gombrich, E. H., Julian Hochberg, and Max Black. *Art, Perception, and Reality.* Baltimore: Johns Hopkins University Press, 1972.

Goodman, Nelson. *Languages of Art: An Approach to a Theory of Symbols.* Indianapolis: Hackett, 1976.

———. *Ways of Worldmaking.* Indianapolis: Hackett, 1978.

———. "Notes on a Well-made World." *Partisan Review* 51 (1984): 276–88.

———. *Of Mind and Other Matters.* Cambridge, MA: Harvard University Press, 1984.

———. "Just the Facts, Ma'am!" In *Relativism: Interpretation and Confrontation,* ed. Michael Krausz, 80–85. Notre Dame, IN: University of Notre Dame Press, 1989.

Goodman, Nelson, and Catherine Z. Elgin. *Reconceptions in Philosophy and Other Arts and Sciences.* Indianapolis: Hackett, 1988.

Gordon, Robert M. *The Structure of Emotions: Investigations in Cognitive Philosophy.* Cambridge: Cambridge University Press, 1987.

Greenberg, Mark. "What Connects Thought and Action?" *Times Literary Supplement* (23 June 1995): 7–8.

Greenblatt, Stephen. *Renaissance Self-Fashioning.* Chicago: University of Chicago Press, 1980.

———. *Shakespearean Negotiations: The Circulation of Social Energy in Renaissance England.* Berkeley: University of California Press, 1988.

———. "Culture." In *Critical Terms for Literary Study*, eds. Frank Lentricchia and Thomas McLaughlin, 225–32. Chicago: University of Chicago Press, 1990.

Greene, Gayle. "The Myth of Neutrality, Again." In *Shakespeare Left and Right*, ed. Ivo Kamps, 23–30. New York: Routledge, 1991.

Greenwood, John D., ed. *The Future of Folk Psychology: Intentionality and Cognitive Science*. Cambridge: Cambridge University Press, 1991.

Grice, Paul. *Studies in the Way of Words*. Cambridge, MA: Harvard University Press, 1989.

Haack, Susan. *Evidence and Inquiry: Towards Reconstruction in Epistemology*. Oxford: Blackwell, 1993.

———. *Manifesto of a Passionate Moderate*. Chicago: University of Chicago Press, 1998.

Hacking, Ian. "Are You a Social Constructionist?" *Lingua Franca* (May/June, 1999): 65–72.

Harpham, Geoffrey Galt. "So . . . What *Is* Enlightenment? An Inquisition into Modernity." *Critical Inquiry* 20 (1994): 524–56.

Harris, James F. *Against Relativism: A Philosophical Defense of Method*. La Salle, IL: Open Court, 1992.

Harris, Wendell V. *Interpretive Acts: In Search of Meaning*. Oxford: Clarendon Press, 1988.

———. *Literary Meaning: Reclaiming the Study of Literature*. New York: New York University Press, 1996.

———. "Poststructural Theorizing and Hollow Dialectic." *Philosophy and Literature* 24 (2000): 424–34.

Hartman, Geoffrey H. *Saving the Text: Literature/Derrida/Philosophy*. Baltimore: Johns Hopkins University Press, 1981.

Heil, John. *The Nature of True Minds*. Cambridge: Cambridge University Press, 1992.

Hintikka, Jaakko. *Knowledge and Belief*. Ithaca, NY: Cornell University Press, 1962.

———. *The Intentions of Intentionality and Other New Models for Modalities*. Dordrecht, Netherlands: Reidel, 1975.

Hirsch, E. D., Jr. *Validity in Interpretation*. New Haven, CT: Yale University Press, 1967.

———. "The Politics of Theories of Interpretation." *Critical Inquiry* 9 (1982): 235–47.

———. "Transhistorical Intentions and the Persistence of Allegory." *New Literary History* 25 (1994): 549–67.

Hjort, Mette, and Sue Laver, eds. *Emotion and the Arts*. New York: Oxford University Press, 1997.

Hollis, Martin, and Steven Lukes, eds. *Rationality and Relativism*. Cambridge, MA: MIT Press, 1982.

Holloway, John. *The Slumber of Apollo: Reflections on Recent Art, Literature, Language, and the Individual Consciousness*. Cambridge: Cambridge University Press, 1983.

Hornsby, Jennifer. *Simple Mindedness: In Defense of Naive Naturalism in the Philosophy of Mind*. Cambridge, MA: Harvard University Press, 1997.

Horwich, Paul. *Meaning*. Oxford: Clarendon Press, 1998.

Howard, Jean E. "The New Historicism in Renaissance Studies." *English Literary Renaissance* 16 (1986): 13–43.

———. *The Stage and Social Struggle in Early Modern England.* London: Routledge, 1994.

Hume, David. *A Treatise of Human Nature,* ed. L. A. Selby-Bigge and P. H. Nidditch. Oxford: Clarendon Press, 1978.

Hurley, Susan. "Martha Nussbaum: Non-Relative Virtues: An Aristotelian Approach." In *The Quality of Life,* ed. Martha C. Nussbaum and Amartya Sen, 270–76. Oxford: Clarendon Press, 1993.

———. *Consciousness in Action.* Cambridge, MA: Harvard University Press, 1998.

Jackendoff, Ray. *Patterns in the Mind: Language and Human Nature.* New York: Basic Books, 1994.

Jameson, Fredric. *The Political Unconscious: Narrative as a Socially Symbolic Act.* Ithaca, NY: Cornell University Press, 1981.

Jauss, Hans Robert. "Literary History as a Challenge to Literary Theory." *New Literary History* 2 (1970): 7–37.

Johnson, Mark. *The Body in the Mind: The Bodily Basis of Meaning, Imagination, and Reason.* Chicago: University of Chicago Press. 1987.

———. *Moral Imagination: Implications of Cognitive Science for Ethics.* Chicago: University of Chicago Press, 1993.

Johnson, Samuel. *Johnson on Shakespeare. The Yale Edition of the Works of Samuel Johnson,* vols. 7–8, ed. Arthur Sherbo. New Haven, CT: Yale University Press, 1968.

———. *The Rambler. The Yale Edition of the Works of Samuel Johnson,* vols. 3–5, ed. W. J. Bate and Albrecht B. Strauss. New Haven, CT: Yale University Press, 1969.

———. *A Journey to the Western Islands of Scotland. The Yale Edition of the Works of Samuel Johnson,* vol. 10, ed. Mary Lascelles. New Haven, CT: Yale University Press, 1971.

———. *Rasselas and Other Tales. The Yale Edition of the Works of Samuel Johnson,* vol. 16, ed. Gwin J. Kolb. New Haven, CT: Yale University Press, 1990.

Johnson-Laird, Philip N. "How Is Meaning Mentally Represented?" In *Meaning and Mental Representation,* ed. Umberto Eco, Marco Santambrogio, and Patrizia Violi, 99–118. Bloomington: Indiana University Press, 1988.

Juhl, P. D. *Interpretation: An Essay in the Philosophy of Literary Criticism.* Princeton, NJ: Princeton University Press, 1980.

Kerrigan, William W. "The Case for Bardolatry: Harold Bloom Rescues Shakespeare from the Critics." *Lingua Franca* (November 1998): 29–37.

Kiser, Lisa J. *Telling Classical Tales.* Ithaca, NY: Cornell University Press, 1983.

———. *Truth and Textuality.* Hanover, NH: University Press of New England, 1991.

Kolodny, Annette. "A Map for Rereading: or, Gender and the Interpretation of Literary Facts." *New Literary History* 11 (1981): 451–67.

Krausz, Michael, ed. *Relativism: Interpretation and Confrontation.* Notre Dame, IN: University of Notre Dame Press, 1989.

Kripke, Saul A. *Wittgenstein on Rules and Private Language.* Oxford: Blackwell, 1982.

Kristeva, Julia. *Desire in Language: A Semiotic Approach to Literature and Art,* ed.

Leon S. Roudiez, trans. Thomas Gora, Alice Jardine, and Leon S. Roudiez. New York: Columbia University Press, 1980.

Lakoff, George. *Women, Fire, and Dangerous Things: What Categories Reveal about the Mind*. Chicago: University of Chicago Press, 1987.

Lakoff, George, and Mark Johnson. *Metaphors We Live By*. Chicago: University of Chicago Press, 1980.

———. *Philosophy in the Flesh: The Embodied Mind and Its Challenge to Western Thought*. New York: Basic Books, 1999.

Lamarque, Peter. "How Can We Fear and Pity Fictions?" *British Journal of Aesthetics* 21 (1981): 291–304.

Lamarque, Peter, and Stein Haugom Olsen. *Truth, Fiction, and Literature: A Philosophical Perspective*. Oxford: Clarendon Press, 1994.

Leitch, Vincent B. *Deconstructive Criticism: An Advanced Introduction*. New York: Columbia University Press, 1983.

Lepore, Ernest, ed. *Truth and Interpretation: Perspectives on the Philosophy of Donald Davidson*. Oxford: Blackwell, 1986.

Levin, Richard. "Feminist Thematics and Shakespearean Tragedy." *PMLA* 103 (1988): 125–38.

———. "Bashing the Bourgeois Subject." *Textual Practice* 3 (1989): 76–86.

———. "Son of Bashing the Bourgeois Subject." *Textual Practice* 6 (1992): 264–70.

Levinson, Jerrold. "Truth in Fiction." In *Philosophical Papers*, vol. 1, 261–80. New York: Oxford University Press, 1983.

Livingston, Paisley. *Literature and Rationality: Ideas of Agency in Theory and Fiction*. Cambridge: Cambridge University Press, 1991.

Lloyd, Dan. *Simple Minds*. Cambridge, MA: MIT Press, 1989.

Lucas, John. "Absence into Presence: Changes in Literary Criticism." *Times Literary Supplement* (14 November 1986): 1280.

Luntley, Michael. *Language, Logic, and Experience*. La Salle, IL: Open Court, 1988.

Lynch, Aaron. *Thought Contagion: How Belief Spreads Through Society: The New Science of Memes*. New York: Basic Books, 1996.

Lyons, William. *Approaches to Intentionality*. Oxford: Clarendon Press, 1995.

MacIntyre, Alasdair. *After Virtue: A Study in Moral Theory*. Notre Dame, IN: University of Notre Dame Press, 1981.

Marx, Karl, and Frederick Engels. Trans. S. Ryazanskaya. London: Lawrence and Wishart, 1965.

McCormick, Peter J. *Fictions, Philosophies, and the Problem of Poetics*. Ithaca, NY: Cornell University Press, 1988.

McDowell, John. *Mind and World*. Cambridge, MA: Harvard University Press, 1994.

———. *Mind, Value, and Reality*. Cambridge, MA: Harvard University Press, 1998.

———. *Meaning, Knowledge, and Reality*. Cambridge, MA: Harvard University Press, 1998.

McGinn, Colin. *Mental Content*. Oxford: Blackwell, 1989.

———. *Problems in Philosophy: The Limits of Inquiry*. Oxford: Blackwell, 1993.

———. *Ethics, Evil, and Fiction*. Oxford: Clarendon Press, 1997.

———. *Minds and Bodies: Philosophers and Their Ideas*. New York: Oxford University Press, 1997.

————. *The Mysterious Flame: Conscious Minds in a Material World.* New York: Basic Books, 1999.

————. *Knowledge and Reality: Selected Essays.* Oxford: Clarendon Press, 1999.

————. *Logical Properties: Identity, Existence, Predication, Necessity, Truth.* Oxford: Clarendon Press, 2000.

Meisel, Perry. "Let a Hundred Isms Blossom." *The New York Times Book Review* (28 May 2000): 27.

Merrill, G. H., "The Model-Theoretic Argument Against Realism." *Philosophy of Science* 47 (1980): 69–81.

Miller, J. Hillis. "The Critic as Host." *Critical Inquiry* 3 (1974): 439–47.

————. *Topographies.* Stanford, CA: Stanford University Press, 1995.

Millikan, Ruth Garrett. *Language, Thought, and Other Biological Categories: New Foundations for Realism.* Cambridge, MA: MIT Press, 1984.

Montrose, Louis. "The Elizabethan Subject and the Spenserian Text." In *Literary Theory/Renaissance Texts,* ed. Patricia Parker and David Quint, 303–40. Baltimore: Johns Hopkins University Press, 1986.

————. *The Purpose of Playing: Shakespeare and the Cultural Politics of the Elizabethan Theatre.* Chicago: University of Chicago Press, 1996.

Nagel, Thomas. *Other Minds: Critical Essays, 1969–1994.* New York: Oxford University Press, 1995.

————. *The Last Word.* New York: Oxford University Press, 1997.

————. "Go with the Flow: Richard Rorty's Magic Formula for Disposing of Philosophical Problems." *Times Literary Supplement* (28 August 1998): 3.

Newton-de Molina, David, ed. *On Literary Intention.* Edinburgh: Edinburgh University Press, 1976.

Norris, Christopher. *Contest of Faculties: Philosophy and Theory after Deconstruction.* New York: Methuen, 1985.

Novitz, David. *Knowledge, Fiction, and Imagination.* Philadelphia: Temple University Press, 1987.

Nussbaum, Martha C. *Poetic Justice: The Literary Imagination and Public Life.* Boston: Beacon Press, 1995.

————. *Cultivating Humanity: A Classical Defense of Reform in Liberal Education.* Cambridge, MA: Harvard University Press, 1997.

Olson, Elder. *Longinus, On the Sublime and Sir Joshua Reynolds, Discourses on Art.* Chicago: Packard and Co., 1945.

————. *Tragedy and the Theory of Drama.* Detroit: Wayne State University Press, 1961.

————. "The Dialectical Foundations of Critical Pluralism." *Texas Quarterly* 9 (1966): 202–30.

————. *On Value Judgments in the Arts and Other Essays.* Chicago: University of Chicago Press, 1976.

Palmer, F. R. *Semantics.* 2nd ed. Cambridge: Cambridge University Press, 1981.

Papineau, David. *Reality and Representation.* Oxford: Blackwell, 1987.

Pavel, Thomas G. *The Poetics of Plot: The Case of English Renaissance Drama.* Minneapolis: University of Minnesota Press, 1985.

————. *Fictional Worlds.* Cambridge, MA: Harvard University Press, 1986.

Pessin, Andrew, and Sanford Goldberg, eds. *The Twin Earth Chronicles: Twenty Years of Reflection on Hilary Putnam's "The Meaning of 'Meaning.'"* Armonk, NY: M. E. Sharpe, 1996.

Phelan, James. *Reading People, Reading Plots: Character, Progression, and the Interpretation of Narrative.* Chicago: University of Chicago Press, 1989.

————. *Narrative as Rhetoric: Technique, Audiences, Ethics, Ideology.* Columbus: Ohio State University Press, 1996.

Pinker, Steven. *How the Mind Works.* New York: Norton, 1997.

Pizer, Donald. "Bad Critical Writing." *Philosophy and Literature* 22 (1998): 69–82.

Polanyi, Michael, and Harry Prosch. *Meaning.* Chicago: University of Chicago Press, 1975.

Pope, Alexander. *An Essay on Man.* The Twickenham Edition of the Poems of Alexander Pope, vol. 3, ed. Maynard Mack. London: Methuen, 1950.

————. *Pastoral Poetry and An Essay on Criticism.* The Twickenham Edition of the Poems of Alexander Pope, vol. 1, ed. E. Audra and Aubrey Williams. London: Methuen, 1961.

Popper, Karl R. *Objective Knowledge: An Evolutionary Approach.* Rev. ed. Oxford: Clarendon Press, 1979.

Putnam, Hilary. *Mind, Language, and Reality.* Cambridge: Cambridge University Press, 1975.

————. *Meaning and the Moral Sciences.* London: Routledge and Kegan Paul, 1978.

————. *Reason, Truth, and History.* Cambridge: Cambridge University Press, 1981.

————. *Realism and Reason.* Cambridge: Cambridge University Press, 1983.

————. "The Craving for Objectivity." *New Literary History* 15 (1984): 229–39.

————. "A Comparison of Something with Something Else." *New Literary History* 17 (1985): 61–79.

————. *The Many Faces of Realism.* La Salle, IL: Open Court, 1987.

————. *Representation and Reality.* Cambridge, MA: MIT Press, 1988.

————. *Realism with a Human Face*, ed. James Conant. Cambridge, MA: Harvard University Press, 1990.

————. *Renewing Philosophy.* Cambridge, MA: Harvard University Press, 1992.

————. *Words and Life*, ed. James Conant. Cambridge, MA: Harvard University Press, 1994.

————. "Comments and Replies." In *Reading Putnam*, ed. Peter Clark and Bob Hale. Oxford: Blackwell, 1994.

————. *Pragmatism: An Open Question.* Oxford: Blackwell, 1995.

Putnam, Ruth Anna. "Poets, Scientists, and Critics." *New Literary History* 17 (1985): 17–21.

————. "Michael Walzer: Objectivity and Social Meaning." In *The Quality of Life*, ed. Martha C. Nussbaum and Amartya Sen, 178–84. Oxford: Clarendon Press, 1993.

Quine, Willard Van Orman. *Word and Object.* Cambridge, MA: MIT Press, 1960.

————. *Ontological Relativity and Other Essays.* New York: Columbia University Press, 1969.

————. "On the Reasons for Indeterminacy of Translation." *Journal of Philosophy* 67 (1970): 178–83.

————. "Worlds Away." *Journal of Philosophy* 73 (1976): 859–63.

————. *Theories and Things.* Cambridge, MA: Harvard University Press, 1981.

————. *Pursuit of Truth.* Cambridge, MA: Harvard University Press, 1990.

Rader, Ralph. "The Concept of Genre and Eighteenth-Century Studies." In *New Approaches to Eighteenth-Century Literature*, ed. Philip Harth, 79–115. New York: Columbia University Press, 1974.

———. "Fact, Theory, and Literary Explanation." *Critical Inquiry* 1 (1974): 245–72.

———. "The Emergence of the Novel in England: Genre in History vs. History of Genre." *Narrative* 1 (1993): 69–93.

Ramberg, Bjørn. *Donald Davidson's Philosophy of Language: An Introduction*. Oxford: Blackwell, 1989.

Rawls, John. *A Theory of Justice*. Cambridge, MA: Harvard University Press, 1971.

Rorty, Richard. *Philosophy and the Mirror of Nature*. Princeton: Princeton University Press, 1979.

———. *Consequences of Pragmatism*. Minneapolis: University of Minnesota Press, 1982.

———. "Texts and Lumps." *New Literary History* 17 (1985): 1–16.

———. *Objectivity, Relativism, and Truth*. Cambridge: Cambridge University Press, 1991.

———. *Truth and Progress*. Cambridge: Cambridge University Press, 1998.

Russell, Bertrand. *The Problems of Philosophy*. Oxford: Oxford University Press, 1912.

Ryan, Marie-Laure. "Truth Without Scare Quotes: Post-Sokalian Genre Theory." *New Literary History* 29 (1998): 811–30.

Sacks, Mark. *The World We Found: The Limits of Ontological Talk*. London: Duckworth, 1989.

Salmon, Nathan. "How Not to Derive Essentialism from the Theory of Reference." *Journal of Philosophy* 76 (1979): 703–74.

Schauber, Ellen, and Ellen Spolsky. *The Bounds of Interpretation: Linguistic Theory and Literary Text*. Stanford, CA: Stanford University Press, 1986.

Scheffler, Israel. *Science and Subjectivity*. 2nd ed. Indianapolis: Hackett, 1982.

Schiffer, Stephen. *Remnants of Meaning*. Cambridge, MA: MIT Press, 1987.

Schiller, F.C.S. *Studies in Humanism*. London: Macmillan, 1919.

Schmitt, Frederick F. *Truth: A Primer*. Boulder, CO: Westview Press, 1995.

Scott, Joan Wallach. *Gender and the Politics of History*. New York: Columbia University Press, 1988.

Searle, John. *Intentionality: An Essay in the Philosophy of Mind*. Cambridge: Cambridge University Press, 1983.

———. "The World Turned Upside Down." Review of *On Deconstruction: Theory and Criticism after Structuralism*, by Jonathan Culler, *New York Review of Books* (27 October 1983): 74–79.

———. *Minds, Brains, and Science*. Cambridge, MA: Harvard University Press, 1984.

———. *John Searle and His Critics*, ed. Ernest Lepore and Robert Van Gulick. Oxford: Blackwell, 1991.

———. *The Rediscovery of Mind*. Cambridge, MA: MIT Press, 1992.

———. "Literary Theory and Its Discontents." In *The Emperor reDressed: Critiquing Critical Theory*, ed. Dwight Eddins, 166–98. Tuscaloosa: University of Alabama Press, 1995.

———. *The Construction of Social Reality*. New York: The Free Press, 1995.

———. *The Mystery of Consciousness*. New York: A New York Review Book, 1997.

———. *Mind, Language, and Society: Philosophy in the Real World*. New York: Basic Books, 1998.

Sen, Amartya. *Development as Freedom*. New York: Anchor Books, 2000.

Shusterman, Richard. "Analytic Aesthetics, Literary Theory, and Deconstruction." *The Monist* 69 (1986): 22–38.

———. "Organic Unity: Analysis and Deconstruction." In *Redrawing the Lines: Analytic Philosophy, Deconstruction, and Literary Theory*, ed. Reed Way Dasenbrock, 93–115. Minneapolis: University of Minnesota Press, 1989.

Smith, Barbara Herrnstein. *Contingencies of Value: Alternative Perspectives for Critical Theory*. Cambridge, MA: Harvard University Press, 1988.

———. *Belief and Resistance: Dynamics of Contemporary Intellectual Controversy*. Cambridge, MA: Harvard University Press, 1997.

———. "Netting Truth." *PMLA* 115 (2000): 1089–95.

Spivak, Gayatri Chakravorty. "Translator's Preface." In *Of Grammatology*, by Jacques Derrida, trans. Gayatri Chakravorty Spivak. Baltimore: Johns Hopkins University Press, 1976.

Staten, Henry. "The Secret Name of Cats: Deconstruction, Intentional Meaning, and the New Theory of Reference." In *Redrawing the Lines: Analytic Philosophy, Deconstruction, and Literary Theory*, ed. Reed Way Dasenbrock, 27–48. Minneapolis: University of Minnesota Press, 1989.

Stecker, Robert. *Artworks: Definition, Meaning, Value*. University Park, PA: The Pennsylvania State University Press, 1996.

Stich, Stephen. *Deconstructing the Mind*. New York: Oxford University Press, 1996.

Stout, Jeffrey. "The Relativity of Interpretation." *The Monist* 69 (1986): 103–18.

Strawson, Galen. *Mental Reality*. Cambridge, MA: MIT Press, 1984.

Tallis, Raymond. *In Defense of Realism*. London: Edward Arnold, 1988.

———. *Not Saussure: A Critique of Post-Saussurean Literary Theory*. 2nd ed. New York: St. Martin's Press, 1995.

Todorov, Tzvetan. *Mikhail Bakhtin: The Dialogical Principle*, trans. Wlad Godzich. Minneapolis: University of Minnesota Press, 1984.

Tompkins, Jane P., ed. *Reader-Response: From Formalism to Post-Structuralism*. Baltimore: Johns Hopkins University Press, 1980.

Tucker, Herbert F. "From the Editors." *New Literary History* 30 (1999): 1–3.

Vendler, Helen. *The Art of Shakespeare's Sonnets*. Cambridge, MA: Harvard University Press, 1997.

Vickers, Brian. "Derrida and the *TLS*." *Times Literary Supplement* (12 February 1999): 12.

Walton, Kendall. *Mimesis as Make-Believe: On the Foundations of the Representational Arts*. Cambridge, MA: Harvard University Press, 1990.

Watson, Walter. *The Architectonics of Meaning: Foundations of the New Pluralism*. Albany, NY: SUNY Press, 1985.

Weightman, John. "On Not Understanding Michel Foucault." *American Scholar* 58 (1989): 383–406.

Wheeler, Samuel C., III. "Wittgenstein as Conservative Deconstructor." *New Literary History* 19 (1988): 239–58.

———. "Metaphor According to Davidson and de Man." In *Redrawing the Lines: Analytic Philosophy, Deconstruction, and Literary Theory*, ed. Reed Way Dasenbrock, 116–39. Minneapolis: University of Minnesota Press, 1989.

White, Hayden. *Metahistory: The Historical Imagination in Nineteenth-Century Europe*. Baltimore: Johns Hopkins University Press, 1973.

Whiteside, Anna, and Michael Issacharoff, eds. *On Referring in Literature*. Bloomington: Indiana University Press, 1987.

Williams, Bernard. *Ethics and the Limits of Philosophy*. Cambridge, MA: Harvard University Press, 1985.

Winnicott, D. W. *Playing and Reality*. Harmondsworth England: Penguin, 1971.

Winter, Steven. "*Bull Durham* and the Uses of Theory." *Stanford Law Review* 42 (1990): 639–93.

Wiredu, Kwasi. *Philosophy and an African Culture*. Cambridge: Cambridge University Press, 1980.

Wittgenstein, Ludwig. *Philosophical Investigations*, trans. G.E.M. Anscombe. Oxford: Blackwell, 1953.

———. *The Blue and Brown Books*. Oxford: Blackwell, 1958.

———. *Remarks on Colour*. Berkeley: University of California Press, 1987.

Wright, Crispin. *Realism, Meaning, and Truth*. Oxford: Blackwell, 1987.

———. *Truth and Objectivity*. Cambridge, MA: Harvard University Press, 1992.

Zemach, Eddy M. "On Meaning and Reality." In *Relativism: Interpretation and Confrontation*, ed. Michael Krausz, 51–79. Notre Dame, IN: University of Notre Dame Press, 1989.

Index

About the Author

JAMES L. BATTERSBY is Professor Emeritus of English at Ohio State University and has previously taught at the University of California, Berkeley. He has published extensively on 18th-century literature and criticism, the works of Samuel Johnson, and modern critical theory. His most recent books include *Paradigms Regained: Pluralism and the Practice of Criticism* (1991) and *Reason and the Nature of Texts* (1996).